China–India Economics

A review of the existing literature on the China–India comparative theme conveys the distinct impression that the literature largely projects China and India as intrinsically competitive entities. While much has been written on where and why China and India are contesting, particularly from a political sense, very little attention has been devoted to mutual collaboration, whether existing or potential. Such possibilities are at their greatest in economics, which will dominate the future China–India relationship.

This book explores Sino-Indian ties from a comparative economic perspective and argues that it is erroneous to visualise the ties either from exclusively competitive or collaborative perspectives. The future relationship between the two countries will be characterised simultaneously by two 'C's, competition and collaboration, which are both linked to common challenges facing them. Arguing that while competition in the economic sphere is inevitable, given their size and aspirations, the book contends that negative externalities from competition will encourage both countries to collaborate and expand the scope of such collaboration. The book's refreshing angle makes it a must-read for those interested in Sino-Indian relationship.

Amitendu Palit is an economist specialising in comparative economic studies, international trade and investment, political economy and public policies. His current research interests are China–India comparative economic analysis, political economy of trade and economic frameworks, economic reforms, public policies and the intersection of politics and economics. He worked for several ministries in India, particularly the Ministry of Finance, where he spent a decade. He has several academic publications to his credit. His first book (co-authored) on *Special Economic Zones in India: Myths and Realities* was published in 2008. A columnist for India's *Financial Express*, Dr Palit writes for *China Daily*, *Wall Street Journal*, *Business Times* and several other leading global publications. He features regularly on Channel News Asia, CNBC, Doordarshan (India), Bloomberg and other television channels. He is married to Dr Parama Sinha Palit and is currently based in Singapore as Head (Partnership and Programme) and Visiting Senior Research Fellow at the Institute of South Asian Studies in the National University of Singapore (NUS).

Routledge studies in the modern world economy

1 **Interest Rates and Budget Deficits**
A study of the advanced economies
Kanhaya L. Gupta and Bakhtiar Moazzami

2 **World Trade after the Uruguay Round**
Prospects and policy options for the twenty-first century
Edited by Harald Sander and András Inotai

3 **The Flow Analysis of Labour Markets**
Edited by Ronald Schettkat

4 **Inflation and Unemployment**
Contributions to a new macroeconomic approach
Edited by Alvaro Cencini and Mauro Baranzini

5 **Macroeconomic Dimensions of Public Finance**
Essays in honour of Vito Tanzi
Edited by Mario I. Blejer and Teresa M. Ter-Minassian

6 **Fiscal Policy and Economic Reforms**
Essays in honour of Vito Tanzi
Edited by Mario I. Blejer and Teresa M. Ter-Minassian

7 **Competition Policy in the Global Economy**
Modalities for co-operation
Edited by Leonard Waverman, William S. Comanor and Akira Goto

8 **Working in the Macro Economy**
A study of the US labor market
Martin F.J. Prachowny

9 **How Does Privatization Work?**
Edited by Anthony Bennett

10 **The Economics and Politics of International Trade**
Freedom and trade: volume II
Edited by Gary Cook

11 **The Legal and Moral Aspects of International Trade**
Freedom and trade: volume III
Edited by Asif Qureshi, Hillel Steiner and Geraint Parry

12 **Capital Markets and Corporate Governance in Japan, Germany and the United States**
Organizational response to market inefficiencies
Helmut M. Dietl

13 **Competition and Trade Policies**
Coherence or conflict
Edited by Einar Hope

14 **Rice**
The primary commodity
A.J.H. Latham

15 **Trade, Theory and Econometrics**
Essays in honour of John S. Chipman
Edited by James C. Moore, Raymond Riezman and James R. Melvin

16 **Who benefits from Privatisation?**
Edited by Moazzem Hossain and Justin Malbon

17 **Towards a Fair Global Labour Market**
Avoiding the new slave trade
Ozay Mehmet, Errol Mendes and Robert Sinding

18 **Models of Futures Markets**
Edited by Barry Goss

19 **Venture Capital Investment**
An agency analysis of UK practice
Gavin C. Reid

20 **Macroeconomic Forecasting**
A sociological appraisal
Robert Evans

21 **Multimedia and Regional Economic Restructuring**
Edited by Hans-Joachim Braczyk, Gerhard Fuchs and Hans-Georg Wolf

22 **The New Industrial Geography**
Regions, regulation and institutions
Edited by Trevor J. Barnes and Meric S. Gertler

23 **The Employment Impact of Innovation**
Evidence and policy
Edited by Marco Vivarelli and Mario Pianta

24 **International Health Care Reform**
A legal, economic and political analysis
Colleen Flood

25 **Competition Policy Analysis**
Edited by Einar Hope

26 **Culture and Enterprise**
The development, representation and morality of business
Don Lavoie and Emily Chamlee-Wright

27 **Global Financial Crises and Reforms**
Cases and caveats
B.N. Ghosh

28 **Geography of Production and Economic Integration**
Miroslav N. Jovanović

29 **Technology, Trade and Growth in OECD Countries**
Does specialisation matter?
Valentina Meliciani

30 **Post-Industrial Labour Markets**
Profiles of North America and Scandinavia
Edited by Thomas P. Boje and Bengt Furaker

31 **Capital Flows without Crisis**
Reconciling capital mobility and economic stability
Edited by Dipak Dasgupta, Marc Uzan and Dominic Wilson

32 **International Trade and National Welfare**
Murray C. Kemp

33 **Global Trading Systems at Crossroads**
A post-Seattle perspective
Dilip K. Das

34 **The Economics and Management of Technological Diversification**
Edited by John Cantwell, Alfonso Gambardella and Ove Granstrand

35 **Before and Beyond EMU**
Historical lessons and future prospects
Edited by Patrick Crowley

36 **Fiscal Decentralization**
Ehtisham Ahmad and Vito Tanzi

37 **Regionalisation of Globalised Innovation**
Locations for advanced industrial development and disparities in participation
Edited by Ulrich Hilpert

38 **Gold and the Modern World Economy**
Edited by MoonJoong Tcha

39 **Global Economic Institutions**
Willem Molle

40 **Global Governance and Financial Crises**
Edited by Meghnad Desai and Yahia Said

41 **Linking Local and Global Economies**
The ties that bind
Edited by Carlo Pietrobelli and Arni Sverrisson

42 **Tax Systems and Tax Reforms in Europe**
Edited by Luigi Bernardi and Paola Profeta

43 **Trade Liberalization and APEC**
Edited by Jiro Okamoto

44 **Fiscal Deficits in the Pacific Region**
Edited by Akira Kohsaka

45 **Financial Globalization and the Emerging Market Economies**
Dilip K. Das

46 **International Labor Mobility**
Unemployment and increasing returns to scale
Bharati Basu

47 **Good Governance in the Era of Global Neoliberalism**
Conflict and depolitization in Latin America, Eastern Europe, Asia and Africa
Edited by Jolle Demmers, Alex E. Fernández Jilberto and Barbara Hogenboom

48 **The International Trade System**
Alice Landau

49 **International Perspectives on Temporary Work and Workers**
Edited by John Burgess and Julia Connell

50 **Working Time and Workers' Preferences in Industrialized Countries**
Finding the balance
Edited by Jon C. Messenger

51 **Tax Systems and Tax Reforms in New EU Members**
Edited by Luigi Bernardi, Mark Chandler and Luca Gandullia

52 **Globalization and the Nation State**
The impact of the IMF and the World Bank
Edited by Gustav Ranis, James Vreeland and Stephen Kosak

53 **Macroeconomic Policies and Poverty Reduction**
Edited by Ashoka Mody and Catherine Pattillo

54 **Regional Monetary Policy**
Carlos J. Rodríguez-Fuentez

55 **Trade and Migration in the Modern World**
Carl Mosk

56 **Globalisation and the Labour Market**
Trade, technology and less-skilled workers in Europe and the United States
Edited by Robert Anderton, Paul Brenton and John Whalley

57 **Financial Crises**
Socio-economic causes and institutional context
Brenda Spotton Visano

58 **Globalization and Self Determination**
Is the nation-state under siege?
Edited by David R. Cameron, Gustav Ranis and Annalisa Zinn

59 **Developing Countries and the Doha Development Round of the WTO**
Edited by Pitou van Dijck and Gerrit Faber

60 **Immigrant Enterprise in Europe and the USA**
Prodromos Panayiotopoulos

61 **Solving the Riddle of Globalization and Development**
Edited by Manuel Agosín, David Bloom, George Chapelier and Jagdish Saigal

62 **Foreign Direct Investment and the World Economy**
Ashoka Mody

63 **The World Economy**
A global analysis
Horst Siebert

64 **Production Organizations in Japanese Economic Development**
Edited by Tetsuji Okazaki

65 **The Economics of Language**
International analyses
Edited by Barry R. Chiswick and Paul W. Miller

66 **Street Entrepreneurs**
People, place and politics in local and global perspective
Edited by John Cross and Alfonso Morales

67 **Global Challenges and Local Responses**
The East Asian experience
Edited by Jang-Sup Shin

68 **Globalization and Regional Integration**
The origins, development and impact of the single European aviation market
Alan Dobson

69 **Russia Moves into the Global Economy: Breaking Out**
John M. Letiche

70 **The European Economy in an American Mirror**
Barry Eichengreen, Michael Landesmann and Dieter Stiefel

71 **Working Time Around the World**
Trends in working hours, laws, and policies in a global comparative perspective
Jon C. Messenger, Sangheon Lee and Deidre McCann

72 **International Water Treaties**
Negotiation and cooperation along transboundary rivers
Shlomi Dinar

73 **Economic Integration in the Americas**
Edited by Joseph A. McKinney and H. Stephen Gardner

74 **Expanding Frontiers of Global Trade Rules**
The political economy dynamics of the international trading system
Nitya Nanda

75 **The Macroeconomics of Global Imbalances**
European and Asian perspectives
Edited by Marc Uzan

76 **China and Asia**
Economic and financial interactions
Edited by Yin-Wong Cheung and Kar-Yiu Wong

77 **Regional Inequality in China**
Trends, explanations and policy responses
Edited by Shenggen Fan, Ravi Kanbur and Xiaobo Zhang

78 **Governing Rapid Growth in China**
Equity and institutions
Edited by Ravi Kanbur and Xiaobo Zhang

79 **The Indonesian Labour Market**
Shafiq Dhanani, Iyanatul Islam and Anis Chowdhury

80 **Cost-Benefit Analysis in Multi-level Government in Europe and the USA**
The case of EU cohesion policy and of US federal investment policies
Alessandro Ferrara

81 **The Economic Geography of Air Transportation**
Space, time, and the freedom of the sky
John Bowen

82 **Cartelization, Antitrust and Globalization in the US and Europe**
Mark LeClair

83 **The Political Economy of Integration**
Jeffrey Cason

84 **Critical Issues in Air Transport Economics and Business**
Rosario Macario and Eddy Van de Voorde

85 **Financial Liberalisation and Economic Performance**
Luiz Fernando de Paula

86 **A General Theory of Institutional Change**
Shiping Tang

87 **The Dynamics of Asian Financial Integration**
Edited by Michael Devereux, Philip Lane, Park Cyn-young and Wei Shang-jin

88 **Innovative Fiscal Policy and Economic Development in Transition Economies**
Aleksandr Gevorkyan

89 **Foreign Direct Investments in Asia**
Edited by Chalongphob Sussangkarn, Yung Chul Park and Sung Jin Kang

90 **Time Zones, Communications Networks, and International Trade**
Toru Kikuchi

91 **Miraculous Growth and Stagnation in Post-War Japan**
Edited by Koichi Hamada, Keijiro Otsuka, Gustav Ranis and Ken Togo

92 **Multilateralism and Regionalism in Global Economic Governance**
Trade, investment and finance
Edited by Junji Nakagawa

93 **Economic Growth and Income Inequality in China, India and Singapore**
Trends and policy implications
Pundarik Mukhopadhaya, G. Shantakumar and Bhanoji Rao

94 **Foreign Direct Investment in China**
Spillover Effects on Domestic Enterprises
Deng Ziliang

95 **Enterprise Forms and Economic Efficiency:**
Capitalist, cooperative and government firms
Kazuhiko Mikami

96 **Diversity and Transformations of Asian Capitalism**
Edited by Robert Boyer, Hiroyasu Uemura and Akinori Isogai

97 **Knowledge Transfer in the Automobile Industry**
Global–local production networks
Dessy Irawati

98 **Exchange Rates and Foreign Direct Investment in Emerging Asia**
Selected issues and policy options
Ramkishen S. Rajan

99 **Singapore, the Energy Economy**
From the first refinery to the end of cheap oil, 1960–2010
Ng Weng Hoong

100 **China–India Economics**
Challenges, competition and collaboration
Amitendu Palit

China–India Economics

Challenges, competition and collaboration

Amitendu Palit

Routledge
Taylor & Francis Group
LONDON AND NEW YORK

First published 2012
by Routledge
2 Park Square, Milton Park, Abingdon, Oxon OX14 4RN

Simultaneously published in the USA and Canada
by Routledge
711 Third Avenue, New York, NY 10017

Routledge is an imprint of the Taylor & Francis Group, an informa business

British Library Cataloguing in Publication Data
A catalogue record for this book is available from the British Library

Library of Congress Cataloging in Publication Data
A catalog record for this book has been requested

ISBN: 978-0-415-59831-6 (hbk)
ISBN: 978-0-415-82456-9 (pbk)
ISBN: 978-0-203-70580-3 (ebk)

Typeset in Times
by Wearset Ltd, Boldon, Tyne and Wear

For Parama

Contents

Figures and tables

Figures

Tables

Acknowledgements

This book is not exactly a labour of love. It is more an experience of growing with the idea of how China and India, the Asian behemoths, are reacting and responding to each other's economic growth and progress. It has been a fascinating journey in the world of Sino-Indian economic relations made memorable by numerous meetings and interactions with several people. I owe deep gratitude to all and apologise for my inability to pen down all the names.

I benefited a lot from the different meetings and interviews that I had in China in September 2010 during my fieldwork for the book. I specially thank Professor Yao Yang, Acting Director, China Centre for Economic Research (CCER), Peking University; Professor Zhang Li Yan, Tianjin University of Finance and Economics; Professor Zhang Guihong, Executive Director, Centre for UN Studies, Fudan University; Professor Jiandong Ju, Department of Economics, School of Economics and Management, Tsinghua University; Dr Anuradha Bhattacharjee, Visiting Research Scholar, Tianjin University of Finance and Economics; K. Nagaraj Naidu, First Secretary (Economic and Commercial), Embassy of India, Beijing; E.B. Rajesh, Chief Representative, Confederation of Indian Industry (CII), Shanghai; Peter Tsai, Country Manager, International Flavors and Fragrances Inc. (IFF), Shanghai; Dr Hong Ma, Assistant Professor, Department of Economics, School of Economics and Management, Tsinghua University; Harpreet Singh Puri, Business Consultant, Beijing; and Andrew Peaple, Columnist, *The Wall Street Journal*. In course of my visits to different universities in China, I have met several young researchers and scholars and have had fruitful and enlightening discussions. I take this opportunity to express my sincere thanks to all of them.

While planning and conceptualising the book, I profited considerably from discussions with Professor Prasenjit Duara, Director, Asia Research Institute (ARI), National University of Singapore (NUS) and Mr Girija Pande, Chairman of the Asia-Pacific region for Tata Consultancy Services (TCS). My extensive conversations with Professor Zheng Yong Nian, Director, East Asia Institute (EAI) of the NUS and good friends Dr Zhao Hong and Dr Tong Yueting, Sarah, both senior research fellows at the EAI, have helped in gathering several valuable insights.

The book has been written during my fellowship at the Institute of South Asian Studies (ISAS) in the National University of Singapore (NUS). I wish to thank Ambassador Gopinath Pillai, Chairman ISAS, for his continuous patronage. I am indebted to Professor Tan Tai Yong, Director ISAS, for his keen interest in my work, constant encouragement and facilitation of the research that went into the writing of this book. Dr S. Narayan, Head of Research at ISAS, has been strongly encouraging. I wish to specially thank all my research and administrative colleagues at ISAS for their active interest in the book and for being supportive of the effort all through. Very special thanks also go to Yongling Lam, Editor, Taylor & Francis, for being most cooperative throughout the writing of this book. At a personal level, I thank my parents Dibyendu and Kalyani Palit, and my parent in-laws Dr P. C. Sinha and Sanghamitra Sinha, for their unebbing encouragement during my writing.

I could not have written this book had my wife Parama not prodded and pushed me along, particularly during the times when frustrations over missed deadlines loomed large. She ensured that I stayed firmly on course and put up with all my quirks and long hours at work with amazing patience. The book is more her effort than mine. All errors and shortcomings, however, are entirely mine.

1 China–India economics

Contour and context

The economic relationship between China and India was too small to notice even a decade ago. With bilateral trade at around US$2 billion and hardly any investments either way, neither country could have visualised the other as a major economic partner in the years to come. A decade later, however, there are distinct signs of the economic relationship maturing into one of the most robust commercial associations of modern times. This is not only because of the astounding rate of growth in bilateral trade, which has shot up to US$60 billion within less than a decade. It is also because of the increasingly larger roles that Chinese and Indian entrepreneurs and businesses are beginning to play in each other's economies through a variety of industrial ventures and innovative initiatives. As two of the world's fastest-growing emerging market economies, both are exciting prospects for each other. Together, they also symbolise the emergence of an economically resurgent Asia.

While the economic ties were small at the beginning of the current century, they were practically non-existent when the Indian Prime Minister Rajiv Gandhi visited China a little more than a couple of decades ago, in December 1988, at the invitation of the Chinese Premier Li Peng. The visit was intended to break the ice between the two countries, which had had an acrimonious relationship for more than two decades. Economics or trade barely found mention in the joint Press Communiqué issued by the two countries on the occasion except for the establishment of a Joint Economic Group (JEG).[1] This was in marked contrast to the communiqué issued during Premier Wen Jiabao's visit to India in December 2010, 22 years after Rajiv Gandhi's visit. The statement, on this occasion, was conspicuous in its emphasis on economic cooperation and the progress achieved in bilateral trade and investment ties. Not only did it spell out various directions of future economic engagement such as setting a trade target of US$100 billion to be achieved by 2015, and cooperation in infrastructure, environment, finance and information technology, the statement also institutionalised a strategic economic dialogue between the two countries to 'enhance macroeconomic cooperation, to promote exchanges and interactions and join hands to address issues and challenges appearing in the economic development and enhance economic cooperation'.[2] Economics clearly dominated the agenda, leaving little doubt about the views of both countries on the important role it was playing and was expected to play in the relationship between the Asian giants.

As most are aware, economics is one of the relatively bright spots in a bilateral relationship that is still shrouded by mistrust and unease. Paradoxically, economic engagement between China and India has been increasing and expanding despite the two countries failing to move forward on various other grounds. The boundary dispute involving claims over territories in the Himalayas has been the biggest stumbling block in the improvement of relations.[3] Little progress has been made on resolving the dispute though both countries have been discussing the issue at periodic intervals. Tibet has been another contentious aspect of bilateral ties. With both countries taking tiny steps (e.g. concluding a border trade protocol for resuming land trade through the Nathula Pass between Sikkim and Tibet in 2003, or signing an agreement for exchange and cooperation in defence in 2006) for maintaining cordiality and increasing bonhomie without actually addressing the flashpoints, the relationship has remained edgy despite improving substantially on some fronts.

Why has economics flourished despite tacky ties, to emerge as the strongest hope in mending fences between two estranged neighbours? The answer probably lies in the hunger of economic agents on both sides to respond to benefits accruable from well-defined comparative advantages in production and consumption. Trade has grown on expected lines, with exports from both countries bridging domestic supply gaps in the other, which mostly arise from structural and occasionally policy-driven distortions. Such growth has been facilitated by both countries figuring in the global trade club of nations administered by the World Trade Organisation (WTO). Clearly, both countries have been alert to and aware of the opportunities created by globalisation and have acted rationally by responding to them, notwithstanding the physical location of such opportunities in a neighbour with strained ties. The instincts driving trade and investment between the two countries have been further energised by the rapid economic growth experienced by both in recent years. High growth – and the imperatives for maintaining such growth – has created a virtuous and mutually reinforcing process where both countries have been trading goods and services across borders in a sustained and aggressive fashion, paying little heed to the discord these borders continue to create. In this respect, economics has been the most powerful tool forcing the two countries to review their relationship in a larger and positive domain compared with the narrow circumspect prism of dispute-based distrust.

History is supportive of economics playing the lead role in Sino-Indian ties, as commerce was the binding factor between the two countries for centuries. Sino-Indian commercial engagement flourished for centuries, with the 'Silk route' – connecting Europe and the Mediterranean to East and Southeast Asia through the Gulf, Central Asia and India – being the conduit for movement of goods. The route served not only as passage for goods, but also as the key channel for travel of Buddhist monks back and forth between India and China. While these commercial and cultural exchanges are documented from the first century onwards, the two countries were probably trading even earlier, given the references to Chinese silk in *Arthashastra*, written in fourth century BC.[4] With

India and China being by far the largest economies in the world until the early nineteenth century and the maturing of the industrial revolution in Europe, and Asia being the most economically prosperous continent, there is little surprise in their trading vigorously with each other in a variety of products, particularly silk and spices. The trade links were slowly lost as both countries went into economic decline from the nineteenth century and lost the reins of world commerce. The latest round of economic globalisation, which picked up from the 1980s and gathered momentum following the end of the Cold War, has drawn the two countries back into an increasingly dense web of commercial exchanges. In between, of course, there was a brief history of armed exchanges and diplomatic friction lasting for almost three decades from the early 1960s. Coming at a time when both countries, with their large populations traumatised by decades of economic marginalisation and strains of war, were grappling with the political and economic challenges of adjusting to an ideologically divided world after the Second World War, the conflict of the 1960s drove a deep psychological wedge between them. Insecurities with respect to each other increased at an alarming rate, some of which prevail even today. India nurses these insecurities to a greater degree, as it was at the receiving end of the 1962 conflict and continues to suffer the burden of the historical baggage.

Given the 'trust deficit' characterising the relationship (trust deficit is discussed further later in this chapter), economic engagement between China and India cannot overlook the ominous, even if theoretical, possibility of such engagement in the future being disrupted by strained political ties. Chapter 6 examines this possibility by looking at the bilateral relations of China and India with other countries that provide contextual similarities to the Sino-Indian relationship. What is critical in this context is the degree of comfort (or lack of it) with which both countries approach their co-existence. As neighbours with a recent history of hostilities, and a much longer history of shared peace, both countries need to approach their future ties giving due weight to the contrasting realities: they are strong economic partners but weak political allies.

It is also important to view the economics between China and India from a larger global perspective. The interface between the world's most populous and fastest-growing economies cannot be bottled up within a bilateral domain; it has wider ramifications for the rest of the world as well. There are several spheres where Sino-Indian economics will create ripples. These include world markets for energy, natural resources, raw materials, labour and technology. Both countries will function in these markets as competitors as well as collaborators, depending upon how they perceive their roles in these markets vis-à-vis the challenges they face. Indeed, the future contours of China–India economics – as the later chapters explore in greater detail – will revolve round the dynamics involving three 'C's: common *challenges* to development, and the *competition* and *collaboration* for managing these challenges.

That both China and India are developing, and are yet among the largest and fastest-growing economies of the world, gives birth to a unique set of dynamics governing their bilateral economics. Both countries have to overcome multiple challenges of managing high growth with effective development as they prepare to take up the reins of the world economic order in the years and decades to come. These challenges, often similar and discussed in Chapter 2, will give rise to two divergent arms in their interface: competition and collaboration. Whether the latter will co-exist in the China–India economics as an intrinsic feature of their broader bilateral relationship in the years to come, or whether one will overcome the other, will depend upon how the two countries accept and adjust their economic and political relationships. The process will be influenced by a set of economic, social and institutional features that determine the context of the relationship. The rest of the chapter discusses these features with a focus on their likely influences on bilateral economic ties. The features are obviously not exhaustive and there could be many more equally critical factors determining the pace and quality of economic engagement. However, the factors discussed are certainly among the most critical and would go a long way in determining the quality of bilateral economic outcomes in the medium and long terms.

Large populous economies with multiple domestic issues and concerns

'Large' is an unavoidable adjective with respect to both China and India. The two countries are among the largest in the world in terms of land areas and populations. With land areas of 9,326,410 sq km and 2,987,000 sq km respectively, mainland China and India are the second and seventh largest countries in the world, and the largest and third largest respectively in Asia. In terms of number of people, they are the world's largest and second largest countries respectively, with populations of 1.34 billion and 1.20 billion. From a comparative perspective, India, in spite of being one of the largest countries in Asia and the world, has a land size that is only a little more than one-third of China's. While in area terms China is much bigger than India, the population gap between the two is narrowing. According to the latest population censuses in both countries, India is catching up fast with China, with its population expected to be as much as or more than China's by 2030. India's comparatively higher rate of population growth despite a relatively smaller geographical area implies a more dense distribution of population than China's: almost 400 people every square kilometre in India compared with fewer than 150 people every square kilometre in China.

Being large for China and India is not limited to their geographical areas and number of people. Their 'size' is evident in several other aspects of their economies and economic transactions with the rest of the world. They are among the world's leading primary energy consumers and are projected to account for more than 50 per cent of the growth in global energy use in the next couple of decades. They are among the world's largest oil consumers as well as importers of crude oil. They also figure among the world's top producers and consumers of coal. This is hardly surprising given that both countries are among the world's largest electricity consumers. China and India are now ranked the world's first and third largest emitters of atmospheric carbon dioxide too.[5] Energy consumption and carbon emission trends in the two countries are unlikely to change in the foreseeable future as both countries are expected to grow rapidly as the world's major automobile markets. High energy consumption and the concomitant effect on the environment arising from higher use of cars are also inevitable impacts of urbanisation. The sizes of urban populations in the two countries are among the largest in the world, though as shares of total populations urban communities in China and India are less than those of many developed countries and emerging markets. India is the world's largest dairy market but ironically has per capita milk consumption lower than the global average owing to its large population. China, despite not being a traditional milk-drinking country, now has one of the world's largest dairy markets. Between them, the two countries produce almost 60 per cent of the world's vegetables, 35 per cent and 12 per cent of the world's sheep and goat meat and cattle meat, and 55 per cent of the world's tea.[6] They have the world's largest labour forces – 780 million and 478.3 million respectively – which are five and three times, respectively, the American labour force of 154.9 million.[7]

Large endowments of factors of production determining economic output – land, natural resources and labour – entail for both countries a variety of issues in nurturing, managing and productively exploiting the factors. The issues are not limited to complexities arising from physical management of these factors but also stem from impact of such management on livelihoods. For both countries, it is imperative to take note of concerns of multiple communities and stakeholders, who could perhaps be individually small from a macro-perspective, given the large sizes of the two economies, but are nonetheless significant in determining political stability, social harmony and economic balance. It is impossible for either country to overlook the concerns of different producers while developing external exchange and transaction relations. This probably explains why, despite having large economic sizes (as measured by both nominal GDP at current market prices and purchasing power parity (PPP)), they retain economic structures with several imperfections that hardly reflect well-functioning markets. The persistence of high tariff walls in India and diverse non-tariff barriers (NTBs) in China underline the efforts of both countries to address domestic concerns by ensuring that specific producers do not suffer injuries to their livelihoods due to rush of imports. Both countries, given their large domestic economies and multiple interest groups, and the significant roles they play in supply and demand of global resources and commodities, have to be mindful of the numerous producer and stakeholder concerns they need to manage. On certain occasions, these concerns become common and encourage both to work together for influencing global policy actions. The Doha Development Agenda (DDA) of the WTO and climate change negotiations are perfect examples.

From a bilateral perspective, multiple stakeholder interests influence the pattern of Sino-India economic relations and will continue to do so in future. Only large countries with diverse specialisations and producer interests display the kind of contrasting reactions to different aspects of bilateral commercial engagement with each other as do China and India. Thus, while chemical manufacturers in India agitate over loss of ground in the domestic market to Chinese imports and demand protective action through the imposition of anti-dumping duties, Indian telecom service providers eagerly look forward to imported mobile handsets and equipment from China for expanding networks. Similarly, while NIIT from India seamlessly expands IT learning and outreach programmes in China, pharmaceutical manufacturers from India encounter extensive problems in procuring import licences from China. Large size and diverse domestic interests will continue to produce conflicting responses to the China–India bilateral economics, depending on the respective perceptions producers and consumers from each country have about the other.

Developing economies assuming significant positions in the world economy

The world economic order in the new century is turning out to be different from what most had envisaged even a couple of decades ago. The last century, and a considerable part of the nineteenth century also, was marked by Western Europe and the USA's domination of the global world order. Maddison's (2007)[8] estimates of world GDP for several centuries show that in 1700 Asia (excluding Japan) accounted for 57.7 per cent of world output, with India and China accounting for 24.4 per cent and 22.3 per cent and Western Europe having a share of 21.8 per cent. By 1820, Asia held 56.4 per cent, with China and India having shares of 32.9 per cent and 16.0 per cent and Europe's share at 23.0 per cent. The decades thereafter witnessed a steady decline in Asia's economic clout accompanied by an increase in the economic influence of Europe and the US, with their shares in world GDP increasing to 33.0 per cent and 18.9 per cent by 1913, when Asia accounted for only 22.3 per cent and China and India's shares came down to 8.8 per cent and 7.5 per cent respectively. Asia, China and India became more insignificant players in the world economy by the middle of the last century, when in 1950 Maddison's estimates find them holding only 15.6 per cent, 4.6 per cent and 4.2 per cent of world GDP respectively. While by 1973 Asia's share had marginally improved to 16.4 per cent (primarily due to strong performances by the newly industrialising economies of Northeast and Southeast Asia, such as the Republic of Korea, Taiwan, Hong Kong and Singapore), China and India still held small shares of 4.6 per cent and 3.1 per cent in world output. Europe and the US accounted for around half of the global output almost throughout the last century.

The overt dominance of the two Western continents in the global economic order is showing distinct signs of ebbing in the current century, underlying a shift in the economic balance of power. According to the International Monetary Fund's (IMF) PPP GDP estimates for the year 2010, Europe and the US now account for less than 40 per cent of global output. China and India's combined share is now a little more than 19 per cent of world output, which is a significant increase from the lowly 7.7 per cent combined share they had in 1973.

While China, India and the Asian region's strong comeback in global economics after almost two centuries implies a decisive alteration in the locus of global growth and economic activity, which is expected to intensify after the latest financial crisis that has ravaged Western economies, China and India's emergence as fastest-growing major economies has created a somewhat unprecedented situation in global economy. Srinivasan (2006) argues their high growth and occupation of increasingly greater spaces in world production, as well as large consumption of raw materials and resources that is occasionally manifest in mutual competition, are viewed by most rich nations not only as the advent of two new markets with untapped business opportunities but also as threats to their own economic prosperities. China is the first developing economy to figure among the top ten economies of the world in several decades. India, another developing economy, is on the threshold of doing so.[9] They represent clear deviations from the popularly accepted notion that the world's largest economies are also developed countries. Both countries, notwithstanding their high trend rates of economic growth, are still much below the development levels achieved by the advanced economies. Both figure among 'medium' human development countries, with China ranking 89 in the world human development ranking of countries while India follows at a distance with a rank of 119 (UNDP 2010). While their economies are large and expanding at rapid rates, the gaps between growth and development are noticeable as they lag behind almost half the world in human development ratings. It would probably be embarrassing for both countries to note that people not only earn more on a per capita basis, but also live longer, and children too are expected to study longer in several countries of Latin America (e.g. Argentina, Brazil, Chile, Columbia, Peru, Uruguay), the Caribbean islands (e.g. Barbados, Jamaica, Trinidad and Tobago), the Middle East (e.g. Iran, Jordan, Kuwait, Qatar, Turkey, United Arab Emirates), Central Asia (Azerbaijan, Kazakhstan, Russia, Turkmenistan, Ukraine) and Southeast Asia (e.g. Brunei, Malaysia, Singapore). Income poverty is conspicuous in both countries, particularly in India, with 41.6 per cent of the population living below the income poverty line of PPP $1.25 per day, compared with 15.9 per cent in China (UNDP 2010, pp. 161–2). With their current populations, these proportions imply that more than 700 million people in the two countries combined are living below the poverty line. It is probably even more embarrassing to note that even in an internationally shunned state like Myanmar, only 19 per cent of the population does not have access to improved sanitation facilities, while the comparable proportions are 45 per cent for China and 69 per cent for India (UNDP 2010, pp. 169–70). Both countries are struggling to achieve best quality standards in food and unsafe drinking water continues to remain a problem in both countries.

The world faces a piquant situation where the two largest developing economies are steadily beginning to account for increasingly greater shares of global output. China and India lead a pack of developing country emerging market economies such as Brazil, Russia and South Africa that are expected to catch up with Europe and the US in the foreseeable future.[10] The increasingly dominant roles played by developing and emerging market economies in the global economy are expected to influence its dynamics in a manner not experienced before. Emerging market concerns are expected to figure more prominently in global discourses and global institutions (such as the Bretton Woods twins, IMF and the World Bank), and the WTO and G20 are likely to be represented and guided more powerfully by emerging market concerns. As discussed in Chapter 5, these changes are becoming evident, with quotas and voting powers in the IMF and World Bank reflecting the greater weight of emerging markets and the WTO and G20 becoming more accommodating towards emerging markets on global trade and financial issues. At the same time, it is also obvious that the growing dominance of emerging market economies, particularly those of China and India, who are not only emerging markets but also symbols of an Asian resurgence, will not take place unopposed. The criticism faced by both countries on their positions on global trade and climate issues, as well as the flak drawn by China on its rapidly enlarging economic aid, are clear examples. There may also be consternation over the fact that China, India and other emerging markets have begun striking markedly different postures on key strategic issues such as the North Atlantic Treaty Organisation's (NATO)'s aggressive moves into Libya.

How do the increasingly significant roles played in global economic affairs by the two largest developing country and emerging market economies – China and India – impact their bilateral economic ties? Two influences are worth noting. As developing countries in the global economic big league, China and India comprise a conspicuous minority; their core concerns are often different from those of the high-income members of the Organisation for Economic Cooperation and Development (OECD) and have traditionally received less attention in a global decision-making process dominated by the G7. But with their views on global economic subjects, particularly after the financial crisis, becoming almost indispensable, both countries sense the opportunity and substantive value in working together on common concerns and forcing international institutions to respond more favourably. Such common actions on subjects like climate change, for example, are expected to become more frequent as both countries maintain their rapid economic progress and become more influential in the world economy despite remaining developing countries. Indeed, as developing countries in the world's top economic hierarchy, China and India, along with other emerging markets, are well placed to reorient international institutions in a manner of their choice.

As developing countries, again, both China and India suffer from demand–supply imbalances in several critical spheres of their domestic economies. These imbalances, mostly reflected in gaps between high demand for commodities and resources generated by rapid industrialisation and growing populations vis-à-vis domestic supplies, are particularly noticeable in access to energy products and water resources. While similar gaps elsewhere, such as building urban infrastructure, controlling environmental degradation, expanding healthcare services and increasing education facilities, are common concerns stemming from inadequate development in both countries and drivers for potential collaborative efforts, supply deficiencies in energy and water influence the bilateral economic interface from a competitive aspect. Positive correlations between economic growth and energy consumption are evident in both countries, along with fairly high energy intensities for domestic economic activity (ADB 2008). Oil scarcity, defined by the IMF (2011) as reflecting shortage of supply with respect to a specified level of demand at prevailing prices and measured by higher prices paid for sourcing additional supplies, is afflicting both countries. Both are at those phases in their economic development trajectories where income elasticity of oil consumption is fairly high, resulting in large increases in oil consumption along with increase in GDP (Zhao 2009). While over time, the income elasticity in both might reduce as they become more oil-efficient by shifting to non-oil sources of energy, overall income elasticity of primary energy consumption is not expected to reduce in either in the medium term. The result of high economic growth and the concomitant demand for energy is a race for energy assets in various parts of the world. Though not manifest in a race per se, the declining availability of water for household and industrial consumptions is creating considerable tensions between the two neighbours, with both depending on glacial flows from the Himalayas and co-existing in the politically disharmonious geography of upper and lower riparian states. High growth and inadequate development, coupled with anxieties over the degree of each other's strategic leverages in regional and domestic markets, give rise to competitive and occasionally frictional interfaces. These, as Chapter 3 discusses, are not limited to rush for energy assets and spats over sharing of water resources, but are also evident in the rivalry for securing bilateral trade deals and actions inhibiting access to domestic markets for exports from each other.

Trust deficit

Centuries of robust cultural and commercial exchanges between the world's two ancient civilisations have been marred by an acrimonious history of around three decades during the second half of the previous century. Dispute over borders resulting from claims of both sides over what they believe their own sovereign territories led to a military conflict in 1962. China emerged victorious in the conflict, declaring a unilateral ceasefire and withdrawing its forces after pushing fairly deep into the Indian territory. The conflict left a deep scar on bilateral relations, leading to suspension of diplomatic ties. The latter resumed only in the late 1970s. Even after the restoration of diplomatic ties, the relationship remained distinctly lukewarm till Indian Prime Minister Rajiv Gandhi's visit to China in 1988.

The 1962 conflict and the subsequent thaw in bilateral relations between the two countries have been instrumental in engineering a 'trust deficit' between them, which has drawn strength from the contrasting alignments during the Cold War and strategic developments thereafter. India pursued a policy of 'non-alignment'[11] during the Cold War, though from the 1970s it developed relatively closer ties with the erstwhile socialist Soviet Union. The alignment was accompanied by distinct changes in India's economic policies as it allowed state monopolies to dominate almost all critical industrial activities and production and distribution of public goods. On the other hand, China, despite following communist ideology, and pursuing Soviet-style centralised economic development policies during the 1950s, developed serious ideological differences with the Soviet Union from the late 1950s. India's close proximity with the Soviet Union naturally did not go down well with China. In a similar vein, China's growing closeness with India's estranged western neighbour, Pakistan, with whom India had repeated military conflicts during the mid-1960s and early 1970s, served to develop further adverse perceptions regarding China in India. As China and the US came closer in an effort to control the Soviet Union and its allies, these perceptions worsened. Domestic developments within India, particularly the militant communist movement popularly known as the Naxalite movement[12] encouraging armed peasant revolution and drawing inspiration from Mao Zedong's political philosophies and actions, also served to convey the impression that China was keen on destabilising India. The Cold War years, therefore, saw the two countries having minimal exchanges and viewing each other's actions and intents with suspicion.

Despite the Cold War fading away into history, China and India find themselves edgy and uncomfortable in handling their relationship in a globalised world where the economic progress of both has resulted in their increasing strategic influence in world affairs. The unease probably stems from the not-too-distant past involving military skirmishes and the unresolved border dispute and political differences over Tibet. During the post-Cold War years, China has successfully posited itself as one of the world's fastest-growing and rapidly expanding economies. The economic gap between the two countries is still considerable, with China a fair distance ahead of India in most major economic indicators. Indeed, India's recognition as a major global economy is a much more recent phenomenon than China's. But with India's progress also becoming noticeable and its strategic clout slowly increasing, the two Asian neighbours have begun looking at each other with considerable care and caution. On one hand, they appreciate and recognise each other's economic strengths and value the bilateral economic partnership that is gaining strength every day. On the other hand, they are unable to overcome the trust deficit that continues to be augmented by strategic developments in each other's backyard. India's growing proximity with the US and Japan is eyed suspiciously by China, while India is anxious about China's deepening links with its neighbours in South Asia (e.g. Bangladesh, Nepal, Pakistan and Sri Lanka), with most of whom India has unstable relationships. As Pant (2010) points out, the two sides are locked in a classic security dilemma that results in each action taken by the other being viewed with suspicion.

The trust deficit is deepened by a lack of adequate knowledge about each other's systems, institutions, societies, habits and culture. Though commercial interface has led to an increase in people-to-people contact, it is still limited owing to problems of connectivity and occasional difficulties in obtaining travel permits. Air connections between Beijing and Delhi are still limited, with India's national carrier Air India yet to connect to Beijing. Curiously, Ethiopian Airlines, on its way from Addis Abbaba, is one of the most preferred airlines for commuting from Delhi to Beijing and back. Most passengers have to travel through regional hubs such as Bangkok or Singapore for travelling between the two cities, leading to greater delays and difficulties. Moreover, other than Beijing and Shanghai in China and Delhi and Mumbai in India, there is little connectivity between other cities of China and India. Limited connectivity is a hindrance to greater people-to-people contact. It is true that high-level state visits between the two countries, particularly at the government and political level, have increased sharply in recent times, creating avenues for greater interface. Nonetheless, both countries need to travel a long way before they achieve a fair degree of comfort in dealing with each other. Till then, the trust deficit will keep on manifesting in various spheres of the bilateral relationship, including economic. From the Indian side, the manifestation of the trust deficit includes examples such as putting Chinese imports of telecom equipment under security scanners and refusing long-term visas to Chinese workers. On China's part, there have been efforts to block multilateral loans in the Indian state of Arunachal Pradesh and also the issuing of 'non-normal' (stapled) visas to Indian visitors from the state of Jammu and Kashmir – both actions reflecting China's views towards parts of territories in these states as being disputed. The presence of enough hardliners and hawks on both sides – in security establishments, think-tanks and also sections of the media – keen on perpetuating the 'threat' that each implies for the other ensures that the trust deficit is unlikely to contract soon and will continue to hover in the backdrop of economic engagement.

Role of state in production

China and India have long histories of domestic productions being dominated by state actors. While management of output and organisation of production were entirely state prerogatives in China for almost three decades until after it became a republic, India had relatively greater participation of the private sector in production. This was because the 'command economy' was relatively more difficult to implement in letter and spirit in a democratic set-up, which also offered considerable space to private ambitions. However, over time India took measures that led to greater control and emergence of state monopolies in several vital areas of manufacturing and services such as heavy industry, insurance, banking and telecommunication. For both countries, therefore, reforms aiming at economic restructuring and liberalisation implied acting hard on the state-owned enterprises (SOEs).

Both countries have been trying to restructure their SOEs with the objective of making them more relevant and competitive in a globalised environment and consistent with the changes taking place elsewhere in their economies. China's reforms in this respect (*gaizhi*) have been deeper and more exhaustive than India's. After achieving marginal success in the 1980s for galvanising SOEs through means such as introducing performance contracts for enterprise managements, it took more drastic measures in the 1990s, including transfer of shares of enterprises to non-state stakeholders and large-scale lay-offs and retrenchment of the labour forces to restructure the SOEs. Ownership reforms were the most critical in this stage, along with labour reforms (Gupta and Palit 2010). While these reforms have arguably reduced direct state presence in production, with SOEs now holding about a third of total assets in industrial and service sectors,[13] it is worth noting that large SOEs still dominate several key activities in China, such as steel (Baoshan Steel), telecom (China Mobile), banking (Bank of China), civil aviation (Air China) and energy (China National Petroleum Corporation, China Petroleum and Chemical Corporation). The role of SOEs in the Chinese economy has received a new spurt following the large fiscal stimulus unleashed by the government in recent years as a corrective measure for addressing the adverse impact of the global financial crisis. In India's case, reforms for restructuring state enterprises have largely been confined to the offloading of minority government equity and have been less drastic than those in China, though there are examples of outright privatisation (e.g. Maruti Udyog, Modern Foods Industries). Nonetheless, enterprises owned by the central government account for a share of around 23 per cent of the country's GDP and also account for around 6 per cent of the organised sector employment.[14] India's state enterprises are dominant in banking (State Bank of India), insurance (Life Insurance Corporation of India), energy (Oil and Natural Gas Corporation, Indian Oil Corporation), steel (Steel Authority of India Limited), coal (Coal India Limited) and several other sectors.

The prevalence of SOEs in both countries and in a variety of sectors ensures that certain systems and practices associated with these enterprises continue to prevail in both economies, albeit less forcefully than before. The presence of these enterprises also underlines the critical role of government in both economies as consumers. The state owns all property in China, in both rural and urban areas. In India too, states hold large segments of municipal land, particularly in urban areas. In addition, other than the large size of state apparatuses and bureaucracies, governments remain major buyers of local manufactures in both countries and SOEs serve as the vehicles for absorption of local products. Elaborate government procurement systems favouring purchases from domestic manufacturers, particularly small enterprises in both countries, have invited criticism from multilateral trade and regulatory bodies on the grounds of such practices violating 'level playing field' conditions in trade and investment. Some estimates point to China's government procurement market being as large as US$500 billion (Lynch 2010). While the Indian procurement market would be smaller, organisations such as the Directorate General of Supplies and Disposal (DGS&D) act as mandated procurement agencies for the state and fix price lines for government purchases.

The important role played by SOEs in several segments of both economies – both as producers and as consumers – has some implications for Sino-Indian bilateral economic engagement. The first is recognition of the fact that, in several areas, enterprises from both countries will act on the basis of motives dictated by larger national and strategic interests as opposed to purely private instincts. Thus, while India's private electricity producers will have no qualms over importing Chinese project goods as long as they are competitive in price and quality relative to those available at home, similar imports meant for state enterprises in telecom and engineering, despite being competitive, might run into difficulties as the enterprises would be required to satisfy national security criteria. Similarly, Indian exports, like those from many other countries, will find it difficult to compete with local manufacturers in China on various occasions as the latter will be preferred by SOEs in purchase. They may, though, face better prospects in areas where SOEs are less dominant in purchase and where private firms judge purchases more by product-specific attributes rather than according to state directives. The second critical issue that the still significant roles of state and state enterprises in both countries imply is that economic actors from both sides must learn and respond to the rather unique ways of doing business with SOEs in both countries, which could be very different from the ways of doing business with private organisations. Dealing with SOEs amounts to dealing with state agencies, necessitating greater knowledge about these institutions – something which is not easy to obtain in either China or India. In both countries there are sectors with simultaneous presences of private and state enterprises. For the other-country players, therefore, entry and business strategies cannot be just sector-specific; they need to be enterprise-specific as well and are likely to be very different between enterprises.

Different systems, institutions and practices

It is probably not enough to distinguish China and India's political systems by categorising them as autocratic and democratic. It is common knowledge that China embraced communism after becoming a republic at the end of the Second World War and followed a planned socialist model of state-led development for almost three decades till Deng Xiaoping decided to inject the spirit of the market into the economy. Notwithstanding economic reforms, which helped in China's integration with the world economy and facilitated its growth as one of the world's largest trading nations and a major destination for foreign capital inflows among emerging market economies, China has refrained from adopting political reforms. It does not have a multi-party political system and is unlikely to do so in the near future, as was clearly indicated by Wu Bangguo, Chairman of the National People's Congress (NPC) Standing Committee, in his recent address during the presentation of the 12th Five Year Plan (Wong and Lye 2011). China has remained committed to one-party control and a socialist political system despite privatising many parts of its economy and introducing market mechanisms. India, on the other hand, is a thriving vibrant democracy. But again, for several years after independence, its economic policies were 'mixed', with central planning and the state being the key allocator of resources although the private sector was allowed to function in relatively 'non-essential' activities. The last couple of decades have changed much of this, with the Indian economy becoming increasingly outward-oriented and the state also vacating a considerable part of the space it held in production. Because of their own peculiar political economic systems – a socialist market economy in China and a mixed economy gradually converting to a market economy in India – the features of the laws, systems and institutions in the two economies are different and often incomprehensible to the other side.

Philosophical and historical influences have shaped the legal systems in both countries, giving each distinct features. While India's legal system essentially follows that of the British and came into force right after the adoption of its constitution in 1950, China's current civil law system grew in the 1980s, after the adoption of its current constitution in 1982. During subsequent years, Chinese laws have undergone changes due to efforts at making them consistent with economic modernisation and particularly for making them compatible with the principles of the WTO (Burke *et al.* 2006). One of the key differences between the legal systems in China and India is that while Indians can approach the Supreme Court for safeguarding constitutional rights, similar mechanisms do not exist in China, where socialist law is a regulator of political behaviour. While the existence of an independent judiciary in India makes the latter distinct from the legislature and executive, the judiciary in China does not enjoy similar independence and is subject to extra-judicial interferences (Burke *et al.* 2006).

The Chinese Communist Party (CCP) continues to function as the most dominant organisation in China, enjoying substantive powers for taking vital decisions on economic issues. The system is not so in India, where the parliamentary legislature, rather than the ruling party, decides on major issues. The implications of the different systems become evident on specific occasions, such as when Chinese energy SOEs successfully outbid their Indian counterparts in acquiring energy assets in third-country markets because they could increase bid prices immediately when the need arose, whereas Indian SOEs could not do so as they required time-consuming legislative approval. There are occasions in India when legislation introduced by the government in Parliament struggles to become law despite the numerical superiority of the ruling party in Parliament, since legislation is debated (there are instances when ruling party members of Parliament have held different views on legislation introduced by government) and ratified before becoming implementable – a process involving much more time than in China. Several pending pieces of legislation in the Indian Parliament provide examples of the lengthy and intensive nature of the process involved; such delays are hardly ever experienced in China, where the CCP, on urgent occasions, can cut through all layers in order to implement its plans. Indeed, this is where businesses following long-term prospects and policies in the two countries are often confused by differences in the speed at which policies are implemented in autocratic China and democratic India; despite being a socialist system, the former can expedite matters faster whereas India tends to get bogged down. The difference in speed is not always entirely on account of less and more efficient processes between the two countries: acquiring property, as will be explained in Chapter 2, requires almost the same time in Guwahati in India and Lanzhou in China, roughly two and a half months. In China the political system, and particularly the CCP, plays a much more decisive role in pushing policies, particularly economic policies, compared with India, both at macro- and micro-levels; this is evident from the large powers vested not only with the CCP but also with provincial governments and local administrations. In India political parties, including those in power, are on occasion handicapped in implementing policies, not only because they have to move through legislatures but also because of the powerful influence of civil society and the judiciary. A pertinent example is land acquisition, which has created widespread resentment in both countries. In India, civil society agitation, backed by political support, stopped the processes of acquisition (e.g. in West Bengal), blocked industries from using the chosen land and led to huge political unrest. In China, however, despite evidence of popular discontent including self-immolation over forcible acquisition of property, there has hardly been any turbulence. These differences impact bilateral economic interfaces when businesses of both sides respond to commercial opportunities: approaching local governments and identifying suitable local partners for the purpose are a must for Indian investors eyeing opportunities in mainland China; similarly, having local collaborators is essential for Chinese businesses keen on entering India.

An important similarity between the two economies, though manifesting itself in different forms, usually escapes notice in the discussion of their respective economic structures. Informal networks and associations play major roles in influencing growth and expansion of business in both countries. *Guanxi*, signifying networks and meaningful relationships that are often critical for obtaining favourable decisions and breakthroughs in expanding business, is widely prevalent in China. Indeed, informal settlement of deals and disputes through *guanxi*, as opposed to a formal legal system, is often the preferred mode of action for several stakeholders in China. In a set-up where provincial governments have sweeping says in business matters, *guanxi* connections are important determinants for take-off of projects and their commercial success.

Personalised networks of influence involving families, other business agents and also government functionaries are critical for business in India as well. While networks in India do not operate on exactly the same lines as *guanxi*, they are equally important for getting things done. Despite having an independent judiciary and a strong rule of law in other respects, multiple procedures and agencies have led to various complexities for carrying out business. These complexities can probably be overcome only through *jugaad*, which in Indian parlance refers to connections with influential people and agencies for doing the needful. It is probably a reflection on the quality of institutions in both countries, notwithstanding economic reforms, that make networks or connections vital for making progress. These interpersonal connections are also vital for local businesses in obtaining finance through informal means; informal finance continues to be a major source of credit in both countries primarily because of its easy availability and lack of enough formal credit instruments (Tsai 2005).

For those unfamiliar with these rules of the game, which include vast numbers of Chinese (about India) and Indians (about China), information asymmetry can be a vital stumbling block. The asymmetries do not arise simply from insufficient knowledge about *guanxi* or *jugaad*, which are distinct from *chaebol* in Korea and *keiretsu* in Japan in terms of the nuances of network dynamics, but also from inadequate knowledge about the cultures and systems that perpetuate these networks and make them effective. Indeed, the quality and success of the future economic and commercial interface between the two countries, as they sense and respond to emerging opportunities in each other's high-growth markets, will depend to a large extent upon how economic agents and firms understand the ways of 'doing' business in both countries by overcoming information asymmetries. India is rather more challenging in this respect since it provides marked contrasts in different spheres of its economy – a modern, efficiently regulated, well-functioning capital market accompanied by unregulated property markets with hardly any price-clearing mechanisms. China is probably more uniform in the nature of complexities (or their lack) across sectors.

Fortunately, businesses on both sides are showing signs of overcoming information asymmetries perpetuated by lack of knowledge about systems and practices, through patience, an eagerness to learn and appreciation of the complementing synergies. Chinese technicians living in the eastern Indian state of Jharkhand – one of India's mineral-rich but industrially backward states – are not only teaching Indian workers specialised welding skills at the Chandankyari steel plant but are also picking up Hindi phrases, chewing betelnut powder and visiting village barbers.[15] On the other hand, Indian software education service providers – Aptech and NIIT – are digging more and more deeply into the Chinese market on the basis of their own unique teaching skills and learning methods. It is interesting to note that Aptech preferred to function in China through an equal ownership joint venture with a local partner, despite having the option of setting up a wholly owned subsidiary, simply because it wanted to overcome extant information asymmetry by capitalising the knowledge of a local partner.[16] While Chinese construction workers are imparting new skills to their Indian counterparts, NIIT is playing a similar role in building skilled information and communication technology manpower in China. Even more remarkable are the hardly discussed corporate and institutional collaborations exploiting synergies in critical areas: China's Suntech Power collaborating with India's Sunborne Energy, for supplying solar panels, marking meaningful collaboration between economic agents of two energy-hungry countries desperate to access alternate non-fossil fuel energy sources,[17] as well as those taking place for patenting grassroots innovations for farming communities, which can make significant differences to the lives of millions of farmers in both countries.[18] These are examples lost in the pervasive hype over security concerns. Nonetheless, they underline a less-discussed aspect of bilateral engagement between the two countries: the ability to bond without being burdened by borders. Probably the most effective way of overcoming the trust deficit!

2 Common challenges and prospects for collaboration

Keen observers of China and India can hardly overlook the similarity of economic challenges facing both countries. As the world's largest developing countries, they need to keep growing fast for several years to ensure that their poor and low-income people have enough opportunities for improving living standards and quality of life. While high growth is a necessary condition for ameliorating poverty, it may not be sufficient unless distribution improves across income classes and categories, something both countries are aware of. What is becoming an increasing source of worry for both is the downside of the structural transformation following economic growth, along with the stresses of maintaining high growth.

This chapter discusses some of the structural consequences of economic expansion in both countries and the complex variety of challenges they create. As two of the world's most populous and rapidly urbanising countries, China and India are trying hard to efficiently manage their burgeoning cities by improving the access of city populations to affordable housing and better transport facilities. The task will become more onerous as urbanisation gathers momentum in the foreseeable future and modern industries draw work forces closer to their own locations. Land supplies in both countries are stretched to the limit, portending a gloomy outlook for affordable housing. At the same time, urbanisation and industrialisation add further pressure on energy uses in both countries, with neither of them unlikely to significantly reduce their reliance on fossil fuel in future, as they have to respond to the rising demand for energy. Air and water pollution, already alarming in both countries, will be aggravated through the rampant use of fossil fuels, as will carbon emissions. The lives of people in both countries will become more difficult owing to limitations that both countries face in curbing high natural resource and commodity prices.

As sufferers of similar ailments, China and India can benefit from each other's experiences in managing their difficulties. There are already areas where they have begun doing so. By drawing attention to some of the complex yet strikingly similar problems facing both countries in their development domains, this chapter underscores the prospective benefits that can materialise from closer cooperation in various areas. Indeed, these are the drivers of future economic collaboration between the two countries, since common challenges and the absence of easily available solutions make the imperatives for discussion and cooperation fundamental. However, while determinants and incentives of collaboration can be identified, there are roadblocks which might impede potential collaboration. The chapter deliberates on these issues also.

Demography

The complexity of the challenges faced by the world's two largest and fastest-growing economies has much to do with their people. As the world's most populous nations, both have to consistently strive for ensuring better qualities of lives for their residents. The large sizes of the populations, along with their diverse traits, make the objective more daunting.

At the beginning of the current decade, Chinese and Indian populations were estimated at 1.3 billion and 1.2 billion respectively.[1] With a combined population of 2.5 billion people, the two countries account for 37.2 per cent of the world's population. This is marginally less than the 37.8 per cent share in world population they had in the year 2000. One of the reasons for the decline in the share, which is forecast to decline further to 36.0 per cent by 2025 and to 34.3 per cent in 2040, is the reduction in the rate of growth of population in both countries. The reduction, however, is more for China than for India. The implementation of the one-child policy in China has led to a sharp moderation in population growth. The differences in growth rates are clear from the relative comparisons that show population growth in China at 3.6 per cent during the period 2000–5, compared with the rate of 8.4 per cent, more than double, in India during the same period. Over both the medium- and long-term time horizons, Chinese population growth is expected to slow down more rapidly than India's, with such growth expected to turn negative during the period 2030–5. India, however, will continue to experience positive growth in population and keep adding to its stock of people until at least the middle of the century.

The differing trend rates of growth in population for the two countries underscores a gradual change in the shares of the countries in world population over time (see Table 2.1). At the beginning of the century, in the year 2000, China and India accounted for 20.7 per cent and 17.1 per cent of the world population respectively. This gap is expected to steadily reduce, with both accounting for around 18.0 per cent of the world population by 2025 and India expected to move ahead of China in terms of number of people by 2030.[2]

An interesting point to note in the comparative sense is that China's rate of growth in population is already less than that of the world growth in population and will remain so in the coming decades (Table 2.2). India's population, however, is currently growing at a rate higher than that of world population and will match the rate of growth in the latter during the period 2025–30. Thereafter, India's rate of growth will be slower than the global growth in population. China's annual average rate of growth in population is expected to steadily decline from 0.7 per cent during 2000–5 to 0.1 per cent during 2025–30 before turning negative from the next decade. The rate of decline is expected to become

Table 2.1 China, India and world population projections

Year	*China's population (million)*	*India's population (million)*	*Combined population (million)*	*World population (million)*	*China's share in world population (%)*	*India's share in world population (%)*	*Combined share in world population (%)*
2000	1,266.9	1,042.6	2,309.5	6,115.4	20.7	17.1	37.8
2005	1,312.2	1,130.6	2,442.8	6,512.3	20.2	17.4	37.5
2010	1,354.1	1,214.5	2,568.6	6,908.7	19.6	17.6	37.2
2015	1,396.0	1,294.2	2,690.2	7,302.2	19.1	17.7	36.8
2020	1,431.1	1,367.2	2,798.3	7,674.8	18.7	17.8	36.5
2025	1,453.1	1,431.3	2,884.4	8,011.5	18.1	17.9	36.0
2030	1,462.5	1,484.6	2,947.1	8,308.9	17.6	17.9	35.5
2035	1,462.3	1,527.9	2,990.2	8,570.6	17.1	17.8	34.9
2040	1,455.0	1,564.7	3,019.7	8,801.2	16.5	17.8	34.3

Source: World Population Prospects: The 2008 Revision Populations Database; United Nations Population Division. See http://esa.un.org/unpp. The projections are from 2010 onward. All projected figures are based on the medium-variant growth scenario (see note). China and India's individual and combined shares in world population are the author's computations.

Note

The UN population projections have several variants. These include low, medium, high, constant fertility, instant-replacement fertility, constant mortality, no change and zero migration. All variants are based on different assumptions on future trend rates of fertility, mortality and international migration. The medium variant assumes medium fertility and normal rates for mortality and international migration. See http://esa.un.org/unpp/index.asp?panel=4 (accessed on 8 January 2011) for more details.

particularly sharp from 2020 onward with annual population growth reducing from 0.5 per cent during 2015–20 to 0.3 per cent during 2025–30 and further to 0.1 per cent during the second half of the decade. In contrast, India's population growth, despite declining, will do so at a slower rate that will result in the annual growth declining from 1.7 per cent in the first half of the first decade of the century (i.e. 2000–5) to 0.7 per cent during 2025–30.

Notwithstanding the differential rates of growth in population over the coming decades and the demographic outcomes which such differential growths might produce, China and India will remain the world's most populous countries. This commonality generates a number of similar development challenges for both countries, though nuanced aspects of some of these challenges might be specific to each country. The rest of the chapter discusses some of these challenges in detail and also looks at the collaborative prospects in addressing these concerns in certain aspects.

Urbanisation

For both China and India, managing urbanisation in an efficient manner has emerged as a critical challenge. The scope of the challenge is vast given that, between them, the two countries account for 37 per cent of the world's urban population (UNFPA 2007). Rapid economic growth and the greater role of manufacturing and services in the growth processes have resulted in sizeable migrations of rural population to urban areas. The outcome has been the proliferation of cities and the clustering of populations in some of the bigger cities. China reportedly had 669 cities in 2008 (Tang *et al.* 2010), with around 170 cities having a population of more than one million.[3] On a comparable scale, India was estimated to have 43 cities with populations of more than one million in 2010.[4] The number of cities, however, will be much more if urban agglomerations with

Table 2.2 China, India and world population growth

Period	*Population growth in China (%)*	*Population growth in India (%)*	*Population growth in world (%)*
2000–5	3.6	8.4	6.5
2005–10	3.2	7.4	6.1
2010–15	3.1	6.6	5.7
2015–20	2.5	5.6	5.1
2020–5	1.5	4.7	4.4
2025–30	0.6	3.7	3.7
2030–5	0.0*	2.9	3.2
2035–40	–0.5	2.4	2.7

Source: Author's computations based on figures reported in Table 2.1.

Note

* China's projected population growth for the period 2030–5 is negative at -0.01 per cent. However, rounding off shows a 0.0 per cent growth during the period.

populations of more than 100,000 are treated as cities, as they are by the Census of India.

With 47 per cent and 30 per cent of their populations respectively being urban, China and India might be considered less 'urban' than several of their emerging market counterparts such as Brazil, Mexico, Russia and South Africa. Urban populations in these countries are 87 per cent, 78 per cent, 73 per cent and 62 per cent respectively (UNFPA 2010). But percentages mask the sizes of urban populations in the two countries and the extent by which they dwarf similar populations elsewhere. The prevailing percentages indicate 636 million and 364 million urban people respectively in China and India. In contrast, Brazil's urban population of 170 million is roughly a quarter of China's, and less than half of India's urban population. South Africa's urban community (51 million) is less than a tenth of China's and India's, while Mexico's (86 million) and Russia's (102 million) urban populations are 14 per cent and 16 per cent of China's, and 24 per cent and 28 per cent of India's.[5] Urbanisation in China and India is of a scale that is hardly comparable with any other part of the world in terms of size and complexities, as discussed later.

Urban growth in China and India has been driven by migration from rural areas as well as a steady increase in the number of core urban residents. For China, migration has been the key determinant of a rising urban population since the 'one-child' policy has acted as a cap on increase in family sizes in urban areas. Migration from rural areas was not encouraged till the late 1970s, the time China embarked on aggressive industrialisation. Steady relaxation of the household registration (or *hukou*) system has allowed rural labour to migrate to cities, particularly the flourishing southeastern cities of Shanghai, Guangzhou and Suzhou. The sharp increase in migration from the mid-1980s that saw the number of rural migrant job-seekers increasing more than five-fold to 150 million in 2008 from 21.4 million in 1990 (Tang *et al.* 2010) has assured a largely inelastic supply of labour to China's coastal manufacturing hubs. With an annual migration flow of around 18 million per year (UNFPA 2007), China's urban population will continue to receive a strong impetus from rural areas.

India's urban growth, on the other hand, has prospered more from fertility than migration. Various studies point to natural increase in size of urban population as the main determinant of greater urbanisation in India. During the period 1961–2001, natural increase is found to have contributed 51–65 per cent of the increase in urban population (UNFPA 2007). Other studies (e.g. Pathak and Mehta 1995) point to a rapid rise in natural increase of urban population from 45 per cent during 1971–81 to around 59 per cent during 1981–91. India's natural increase-driven urban growth is structurally similar to that in most countries of Latin America, while the migration-driven urban growth in China is a deviation from usual patterns. However, while China can hope to stabilise the size of its urban population by reversing the flow of migration, India will have to contend with both migration to cities and natural increase in city populations, and therefore has a more complex challenge to overcome. Meanwhile, for the next couple of decades, at least until overall population growth declines substantively, both countries will be hard pressed to find solutions to the problems that rapid urbanisation has produced.

A typical problem facing both countries is growth in slums.[6] Outgrowth of slums is an inevitable consequence of housing and basic facilities in cities not being able to keep pace with increases in the number of urban residents. These settlements comprise the relatively low-income segments of cities (usually the lowest incomes) where households do not have access to quality drinking water and good sanitation, and also do not have secured tenures. China and India do not figure among developing countries having a high prevalence of slums. Between them, though, the two countries account for almost 37 per cent of the world's slums (UNFPA 2007). A common concern for both countries is the sharp increase in urban population that their cities are expected to experience in the medium term and the effect such an increase will have on the growth of slums. As research on urbanisation indicates, rapid urban growth without proper emphasis on development can lead to a high incidence of slums (Cheru 2005; Arimah 2010). The latter not only add to traffic congestion, difficulties in waste management and garbage disposal and law and order problems, in India they are also partly responsible for 'leakage' from formal electricity distribution networks as slum dwellers are often forced to obtain illegal electric meters and connections by paying bribes.

With urban growth rates of 2.6 per cent and 2.3 per cent respectively during the period 2005–10 (UNFPA 2010), China and India are not only urbanising faster than the world (1.9 per cent), but also faster than – or at least as fast as – Asia (2.3 per cent). The inevitable impact of such urbanisation is the burgeoning size of cities. China and India have some of the most populated urban agglomerations in the world.[7] These include: Delhi (second, 22.2 million), Mumbai (fourth, 20 million), Shanghai (seventh, 16.6 million), Kolkata (eighth, 15.6 million), Beijing (thirteenth, 12.4 million), Chongqing (twenty-third, 9.4 million), Shenzhen (twenty-sixth, 9.1 million), Guangzhou (twenty-eighth, 8.9 million), Tianjin (thirty-second, 7.9 million), Wuhan (thirty-third, 7.7 million), Chennai (thirty-fourth, 7.5 million), Bangalore (thirty-sixth, 7.2 million), Hyderabad (fortieth, 6.8 million), Ahmadabad (forty-seventh, 5.7 million) and Dongguan (fiftieth, 5.3 million).[8] These cities have displayed remarkably fast rates in growth of their populations, particularly during the last few decades. The population of Shenzhen, which was only 58,298 in 1980, increased to 875,000 in 1990, 6.1 million in 2000 and further to 9.0 million in 2010. The increase amounts to a phenomenal growth of 15,347 per cent, or a more than 15-fold expansion in population during 1980–2010. Dongguan in Guangdong province has also experienced an almost 40-fold increase in its population during 1980–2010 from 137,169 to 5.3 million. Among Indian cities, Delhi, Bangalore and Hyderabad have experienced 298.6 per cent, 156.6 per cent and 171.4 per cent growth in their respective populations during the period in question.[9] All the urban agglomerations in China and India mentioned above are expected to grow at rates varying from 11.8 per cent to 20.6 per cent during the period 2010–20, which translates to annual growth rates ranging from 1.2 per cent to 2.1 per cent

(Figure 2.1). These growth rates can well create situations that manifest themselves in the proliferation of slums and other civic difficulties.

The fast growth in urban agglomerations offers both countries no room for complacency, notwithstanding the fact that they have made reasonably good progress in improving the lives of slum dwellers. Latest estimates by the UN indicate that while China has been able to reduce the proportion of its urban population living in slums from 37.3 per cent in 2000 to 28.2 per cent in 2010, India has brought down the proportion from 41.5 per cent in 1990 to 28.1 per cent in 2010 (UN Habitat 2010). During the period 2000–10, China and India are reported to have improved conditions for 65.3 million and 59.7 million slum residents respectively – a commendable achievement among developing countries, with Indonesia and Brazil following with 21.2 million and 10.4 million improvements respectively (UN Habitat 2010).

The successes achieved by both countries reflect the adoption of certain common policies particularly improving the access of slum residents to low-cost affordable housing. China has offered fiscal incentives to developers for building cheap houses and has been able to offer more than 20 million low-cost houses to slum dwellers (UN Habitat 2010). India's efforts in this respect have focused on providing low-cost houses as well as security of tenure to dwellers. The Integrated Housing and Slum Development Programme (IHSDP) aims at slum development while the more recent Rajiv Awas Yojana (RAY), implemented in 2009, supports states trying to secure property rights for slum residents with the larger objective of building new infrastructure and civic amenities (Press Information Bureau 2011). The government of Delhi has allotted around 8,000 residential units under RAY.[10] Ambitious efforts to rede-

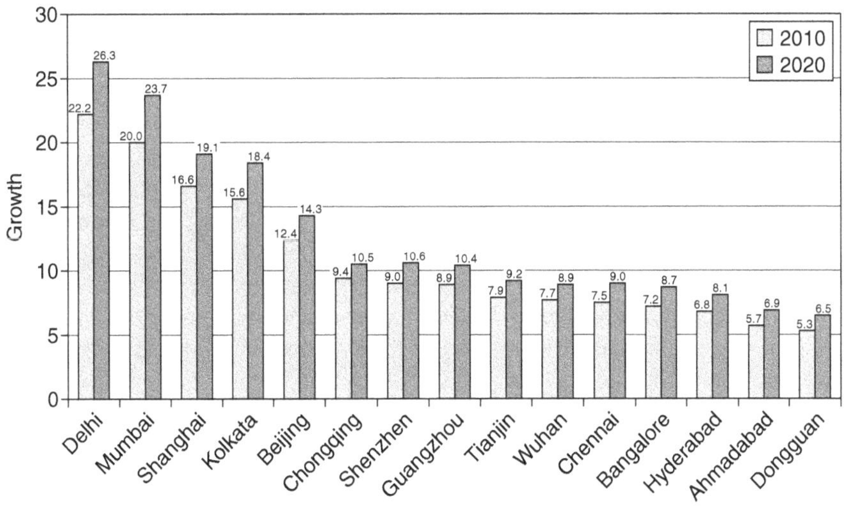

Figure 2.1 Projected population growth in major agglomerations (2010 and 2020) (source: www.geohive.com/earth/cy_aggmillion2.aspx).

velop Dharavi – a dense agglomeration in the heart of Mumbai occupying prime real estate space and often referred to as 'Asia's largest slum' – involve plans to provide residence to slum dwellers from profits garnered through the sale of high-end property (Savchuk *et al.* 2009). While efforts to reduce slum prevalence are laudable and are producing success, considerable inefficiencies, particularly in the use of urban land and generation of an affordable housing stock, have affected both China and India. Opaque land and real estate markets, discussed in detail later, will continue to remain problems for both countries in their efforts to provide low-cost housing to slum dwellers and other low-income groups.

Rapid urbanisation has also produced other challenges for civic facilities and infrastructure. Notable among these are transport problems. While non-motorised means of transport (e.g. walking and cycling) were traditionally most important for people in both countries, growth in consumer disposable incomes in urban areas has manifested itself through pronounced wealth effects in heavy purchases of passenger cars. Demand for cars has also been driven by circumstances, with public transport unable to emerge as a substitute for private transport in the larger Indian and Chinese cities, which are experiencing rapid growth in population. Inadequacies in public transport capacities have become glaring, with cities expanding boundaries to include new suburban stretches and more and more people moving to these new but remote areas owing to easier availability of residences. Geographical expansions of cities have not been accompanied by a commensurate increase in rapid public transport options like buses and metros, because of relatively low population densities in the new areas (Morris 2010). The result has been overt reliance on private transport for commuting between home and work, leading to higher demand for cars. As Pucher *et al.* (2007) point out, both countries suffer from weak transport infrastructures and have followed accommodating policies in car use. Increased car use, however, has resulted in greater road congestion, noise, air pollution and accidents.

Managing transportation in cities will increasingly become a bigger concern for civic authorities in both countries as China and India surge ahead as the world's biggest automobile markets. Rising per capita incomes in both countries following quick recoveries from the global financial crisis in 2008 saw car sales in China and India amounting to 13.8 million units and 1.9 million units respectively in 2010 (Nanda 2011). This is consistent with long-term trends in both countries that show positive correlations between increasing per capita incomes and car ownership. Statistics provided by the IMF on real per capita GDP (measured in purchasing power parity (PPP) terms) and motor vehicles per 1,000 people for the period 1971–2002[11] show a more than doubling of India's per capita income (US$1,029 to US$2,335) to be accompanied by an almost eight-fold increase (2.0 to 16.5 vehicles per 1,000 people) in motor vehicle ownership over the period. For China, the correlation is even more striking; an increase in income of seven and a half times (US$565.4 to US$4,278.9) producing an almost 27-fold increase in car ownership (0.6 to 16.0).

Despite this sharp increase in car sales, there remains considerable room for further sales as vehicle penetrations in both countries remain low. China has 40 cars per 1,000 people while India has only 14 per 1,000 people (Gomes 2011). Low penetrations combined with higher disposable incomes make both countries ideal markets for auto manufacturers. However, there are fairly serious implications of such growth. There are concerns that the costs of the auto boom fuelled by growth and urbanisation might be much more in the long run than the benefits obtained by car producers in the short run. Traffic congestion and air pollution are visible effects of such a boom. What is much less visible, though, is the demand for energy created by higher car sales, particularly gasoline, and the impact of such demand on two of the world's largest oil importers. For both countries, this entails a situation where higher propensity to consume induced by rising incomes and the steady substitution of inefficient public transport by private means creates win–win outcomes for consumers and producers of cars, but underscores grim downsides for imports and energy prospects in the long run. The problem is unusual and reflects the complex consequences of rapid growth, economic prosperity and swift urbanisation in large and populous emerging markets that are still more developing than developed.

Energy

For both China and India, high energy consumption has been not only a driver of economic growth but also a consequence of such growth. Greater supply of energy and its consumption by 'producers' (e.g. industry, particularly manufacturing, as well as modern services entailing heavy requirements of electricity, such as financial services) have led to fast growth of national output in both countries. High growth together with rise in incomes, in turn, has increased demand for modern appliances that run on electricity and oil. Urbanisation has contributed to the process by increasing demand for energy, both from new residential and commercial households and also from the larger number of people using cars. Given the growth and urbanisation trends in both countries, there is little possibility of demand for energy reducing. Research on the relationship between economic growth and energy consumption, irrespective of the nature of causality, has enough evidence to suggest that both reinforce each other. For India and China specifically, Paul and Bhattacharya (2004) and Qiang (2009) find empirical evidence for the causality. For the period 1980–2007, China's and India's GDPs are found to have grown at annual average rates of 9.9 per cent and 6.0 per cent respectively; the corresponding annual average growth rates in energy consumption are 5.5 per cent and 5.3 per cent for the two countries (ADB 2008). Thus the positive correlation between GDP growth and energy consumption is evident for both countries.

The issue of sustainability of energy consumption patterns in the two countries requires closer looks at their energy intensities and efficiencies achieved in energy use over time. Measured in terms of barrels of oil equivalent used for every US$1,000 of GDP, energy intensity of economic activity, which in simpler terms is the amount of energy required for obtaining an extra unit of economic output, was 5.1 for China and 3.7 for India in 2005 (ADB 2008). These intensities are fairly high among Asian countries. While the more mature relatively higher-income Asian economies like Japan (0.8), Korea (2.1) and Singapore (2.7) had lower intensities, Vietnam (4.1) was between China and India, and Indonesia (3.3), Malaysia (3.3) and Thailand (3.7) were either the same or a little less than India. At the same time, China's relatively higher energy intensity of economic activity is accompanied by a steady improvement in energy efficiency (Figure 2.2). Measured in terms of barrels of oil consumed every US$1 million of GDP, China is found to have been consuming less than India since the early 1990s. Both countries show a welcome tendency towards more efficient use of oil by deploying less and less of it in obtaining incremental growth. The reasons behind improving oil efficiencies are presumably shifts to less oil-intensive modes in both production and consumption, with emphasis on substitution of refined oil products like diesel by gas in transportation (particularly passenger cars) and also the emergence of dominant economic activities such as information technology and other services that use less oil.

As discussed in Chapter 3, the energy consumption patterns of both countries reflect the significant roles of oil and coal. Oil accounted for 18.6 per cent and 31.7 per cent of total energy consumed in China and India respectively in 2009. The corresponding shares of coal in the energy consumptions of the two countries in the same year were 70.6 per cent and 52.4 per cent respectively. As growth trajectories in both countries are expected to remain firmly upward, resulting in greater industrialisation, expansion of infrastructure capacities,

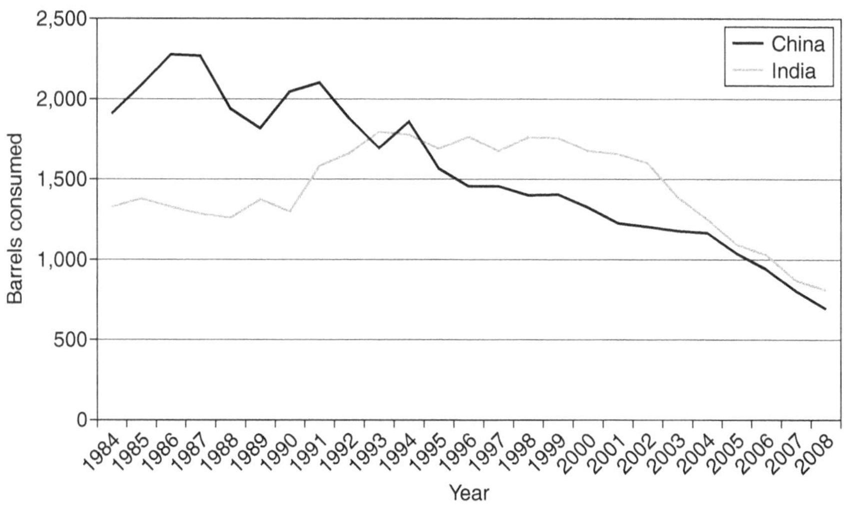

Figure 2.2 Energy efficiency in China and India (barrels consumed every US$1 million GDP) (source: *Oil Price Outlook*, FACTS Global Energy Group, August 2008; as made available in ADB 2008, p. 43).

urbanisation and more energy-intensive lifestyles, demand for oil and coal is not expected to abate in China and India given that their populations will keep growing till 2030 at currently projected rates (Table 2.2; India's population will keep growing even thereafter, while China's will decline). Notwithstanding efforts to shift to cleaner fuels, oil and coal will continue to dominate energy consumption in the foreseeable future.

China and India's access to energy resources is handicapped by their geographical co-ordinates. Chapter 3 discusses the global distribution of oil reserves that clearly puts China and India at a disadvantage, given that the Asia-Pacific region has much less oil than other parts of the world. Unavailability of adequate crude oil has forced both countries to import heavily, with the result that they are importing 51.8 per cent and 80.5 per cent of their total crude oil requirements. As two of the world's largest oil importers (China is the second largest oil importer while India is the fifth), they imported 4.3 million (China) and 2.2 million (India) barrels per day in 2009 (EIA 2010b). The volumes of imports will increase over time, making energy consumption in both countries significantly dependent on external oil supplies. These dependencies will also increase vulnerabilities to fluctuations in global oil prices.

There are two serious implications of sharp increases in crude oil prices. The first is inflated import bills and the second is a rise in domestic prices from 'pass-through' effects. Simulations of current account balances for the balance of payments (BOP) of China and India under different oil price scenarios show significant effects of a rise in crude oil prices (ADB 2008). An increase in crude oil prices from US$70 per barrel to US$150 per barrel is projected to reduce China's current account surplus by more than two percentage points of its GDP. For India, the current account deficit estimated over the same range of price rise is expected to increase by more than three percentage points of GDP. Whether crude oil prices will rise to such heights is, of course, a different matter. But the effect on current account balances brought on by an increase in imports, following an increase in oil prices, is undoubtedly substantive. A simple simulation based on crude oil imports of the two countries in 2009 (4,086,000 and 2,928,000 barrels daily for China and India respectively), assumed to have been purchased at an average price of US$98.4 per barrel (the average of 2009 spot prices for four varieties of crude oil – Dubai, Brent, Nigerian Forcados and West Texas Intermediate (WTI)), is seen to increase the oil import bills by around US$48 million for China and US$34 million for India if the same number of barrels are purchased at US$110 per barrel. The increases will be US$88 million and US$63 million respectively if the barrel price is pegged at US$120. Needless to say, the increases will be even more under scenarios where imports go up, leading to an increase in number of barrels purchased.

The Middle East and Africa are the two main sources of crude oil for China and India. The Dubai crude variety has fortunately been the cheaper among the different crudes, while Nigerian Forcados has been more expensive. But these differences in unit price do not mask the fact that both varieties have experienced sharp increases in the last decade (Figure 2.3). During the period 2000–8, the Dubai price increased from US$26.2 per barrel to US$94.3 per barrel. Nigerian Forcados increased from US$28.4 per barrel to US$101.4 per barrel over the same period. The year 2009 saw oil prices coming down sharply as economic activity contracted following the onset of the financial crisis. But the increase of almost two-and-a-half times in spot prices for both the Middle East and African varieties earlier in the decade is a trend that would be worrying both China and India. The concern would be that much more, given that the Middle East is a politically volatile region subject to supply disruptions and concomitant pressures on oil prices. The latest political uncertainties in Egypt and Libya that are threatening to spread deeper within the region are causes of anxieties for both in this respect. Similar concerns prevail for Africa as well.

While high crude prices will inflate imports and affect current account balances (particularly in India, which has a deficit current account), there will also be worries over their effect on domestic commodities. Crude oil price increases are not always 'passed on' to domestic consumers through corresponding increases in retail prices of refined petroleum products. State-owned downstream oil companies that buy imported crude for making refined products tend to avoid passing on the higher crude prices in order to reduce the burden on consumers. However, such efforts are not sustainable and refined product prices eventually have to increase. Higher refined petroleum product prices have a cascading effect in increasing prices of key services like transportation, leading to a spiralling in prices all across the domestic economy. As discussed later in the chapter, for China and India the rise in the prices of essential articles and services for consumption has become a serious issue. Global crude oil prices have played a major role in increasing domestic prices. Unfortunately, as both countries realise, this is an aspect of their economic management over which they have little control, due to their dependence on imported crude.

The helplessness of both countries is accentuated by the fact that their rapid growth has been a key driver of global oil prices. Higher demand for oil arising from high growth in China and India has been driving up global oil prices, and this demand is unlikely to reduce in future. Moreover, global supplies of crude oil are unlikely to respond in tune to the rising demand since the ability of the Organisation of Petroleum Exporting Countries (OPEC) to increase production volume appears to be lessening owing to a sharp reduction in the excess capacity of Saudi Arabia, the 'swing' state in the OPEC (Chithelen 2005). From a larger global perspective, there are concerns that capacity created at new projects may not immediately be able to compensate for lower output from existing oil fields and a supply crunch around the year 2015, leading to a sudden spurt in prices, cannot be ruled out (IEA 2007).

The demand–supply dynamic shows the two countries trapped in a rather ironical situation where their own rapid progress is creating difficulties for themselves. It is imperative for both to find solutions to the problem since it is not possible to restrain growth. Fortunately, they appear conscious of the urgency and the need to collaborate for achieving 'win–win' outcomes. During Chinese Premier Wen Jiabao's latest visit to India in December 2010, both sides

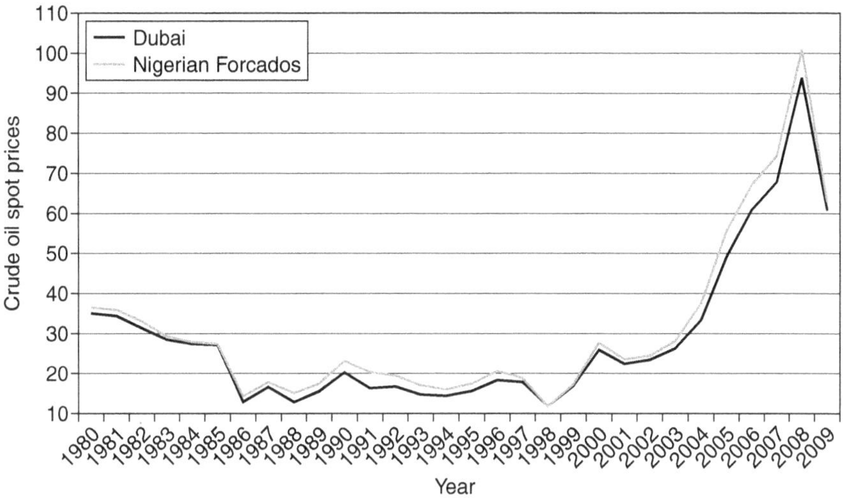

Figure 2.3 Crude oil spot prices (1980–2009) (source: BP 2010).

discussed the possibility of sharing information on respective crude import requirements (Prasad 2010). This will avoid the possibility of both entering the global oil market at the same time with large demands that would inevitably lead to flare-ups in prices. Such information-sharing and collaboration should also eventually lead to discussions on joint purchases of crude oil, which will avoid volatilities in oil prices.

Energy security concerns are justifiably high in China and India. These concerns have driven them to compete with each other, particularly in accessing third-country hydrocarbon resources. The nature and content of this competition in Africa, Southeast Asia and Central Asia is discussed in detail in Chapter 3. While the competition is perhaps inevitable, given the anxieties of both countries in securing oil and gas reserves for maintaining high growth and ensuring supply of energy to enlarging national populations, it has strong negative externalities. Prices of hydrocarbon assets being eyed by both countries will inevitably increase if both countries compete for them simultaneously. This is evident from the experience of both countries buying oilfields in Africa. A more efficient way of addressing energy security concerns without generating negative externalities is to jointly bid for third-country hydrocarbon resources. Again, fortunately this is a realisation that has gone down well with authorities in both countries, leading to several examples of Sino-Indian cooperation in bidding for hydrocarbon assets in third markets. The first such cooperation probably was in 2002 when India's Oil and Natural Gas Corporation (ONGC) picked up a stake in the China National Petroleum Corporation (CNPC)'s oilfield in Sudan (Mills 2009). Zhao (2009) points to the joint bid for acquiring equity in PetroCanada's oil operations in Syria, joint development of the Yadavaran oil field in Iran, and the formation of a joint venture company by CNPC and ONGC for buying a 50 per cent stake in Omimex de Colombia's assets in Columbia. The more significant collaboration examples are visible in Myanmar, which has also witnessed Sino-Indian rivalry in acquiring energy assets. ONGC Videsh Limited (OVL) has entered into an agreement with CNPC for lifting gas from Myanmar. GAIL (the Gas Authority of India Limited) and OVL also have stakes in a joint venture pipeline project fetching gas up to the China–Myanmar border; these are in addition to the tie-ups that these companies have with Chinese companies for oil and gas exploration in different parts of the world (Prasad 2010).

The reference scenarios of the International Energy Agency (IEA) point to coal being the main source of primary energy in both China and India over the next couple of decades. Coal is expected to account for 66 per cent of total primary energy in China in 2015 and is expected to marginally decline to a share of 63 per cent by 2030 (IEA 2007). For India, similar shares of coal in primary energy use are estimated at 43 per cent and 48 per cent in 2015 and 2030 respectively.[12] Coal will remain the main fuel in energy use owing to its role in electricity generation. Though its share is expected to decline in electricity generation in China from 89 per cent in 2005 to 88 per cent in 2015 and 84 per cent in 2030, and in India from 81 per cent to 77 per cent and 76 per cent over the same points in time, the rate of decline is perceptibly slow in both. Indeed, the projected increase of 73 per cent in global demand for coal during 2005–30 and the rise in share of coal in total energy demand during the period from 25 per cent to 28 per cent is primarily due to higher coal use by China and India.[13]

Both countries face similar supply constraints in coal that have forced them to rely on imports. Coal reserves and mines in China and India are located far away from the centres of industrial activity located on the coasts that have the highest demand for coal. China's largest coal reserves are in Shanxi, Shaanxi, Inner Mongolia, Henan, Xinjiang, Ningxia, Gansu, Qinghai and Hebei, all of which are located either in the north, west or northeast, making them fairly distant from the coastal industrial hubs in south and east China. Around 83 per cent of steam coal and 95 per cent of coking coal are mined in inland areas. These proportions are expected to increase to 90 per cent and 96 per cent respectively in 2030 (IEA 2007). Though rail infrastructure for transporting coal faster to the demand points is being upgraded, future carriage costs might increase as China taps into more and more remote reserves. Coastal areas, therefore, are likely to rely on imported coal, particularly steam coal, which is used extensively in electricity generation. In India's case, the distance of main mining spots from industrial hubs is an equally pressing supply constraint necessitating imports. India's major coalfields – Raniganj, Jharia, Bokaro, Singrauli and Talcher – are located in eastern and central parts of India, whereas its industrial hubs are largely in the south, west and north. As in China, coal supplies need to be transported by rail over long distances, adding to costs, which in India go up further for the end-users of the supplied coal on account of washing costs that have to be incurred for reducing high ash content. Unlike China, where the quality of coal is decidedly better and transport costs are the major factor driving imports, poor quality is an additional driver of coal imports in India, leading to increase in both steam and coking coal imports. Share of imports in total coal demand for India is expected to increase from 12 per cent in 2005 to 28 per cent in 2030 (IEA 2007).

Greater reliance on imports will increase the vulnerability of both countries to volatilities in international commodity prices. Though the exposure is unlikely to be as much as that in oil, given that demand for coal in both countries will continue to be largely price-inelastic, neither China nor India will be in a position to stop imports even if prices rise sharply. This adds another component to the 'imported' inflation that both will have to encounter in addition to the whims of crude prices. It might therefore be in the interests of both to consult each other on purchase of coal imports too, as they intend to for oil imports. As in crude oil, where imports for both are largely from same regions and source countries (e.g. the Middle East and Africa), China's and India's coal import sources are also largely similar: Australia, Russia, Indonesia and Vietnam. It should not be difficult to coordinate purchases in order to avoid escalation in prices brought on by each other's soaring appetites.

High prices

Inflation has always been a major concern for public policy in developing countries. In large populous countries like China and India, it is an even more important concern as they have large segments of economically marginal populations. High prices without commensurate rise in household incomes reduce purchasing powers in real terms, steadily eroding the command of households on their consumption baskets of essential articles. Inflation is a politically explosive phenomenon and can cause widespread unrest.

Comparative consumer price trends in China and India reveal India experiencing relatively higher price increases. Both countries, though, have witnessed spurts in prices from 2006 and particularly from 2007 onwards (Figure 2.4). This is consistent with similar trends in developing and emerging markets as a whole. Average inflation in China as measured by the change in annual consumer price index (CPI), despite increasing, has remained below the developing country average rate. During the last decade, the highest average increase recorded by the CPI in China has been around 6.0 per cent in 2008, when developing country and emerging market inflation was higher than 10.0 per cent (Figure 2.4). India's inflation rate was less than that in developing and emerging markets for most of the last decade. However, from 2008 its inflation has increased at a rapid rate and is now more than that in emerging markets. India has not only been experiencing double-digit inflation for the last couple of years, it is also unusual that while prices softened in emerging markets and in China in 2009, presumably on account of the depressive impact of the financial crisis, they hardly did so in India. This is probably an indication of the deep structural malaises in India affecting consumer prices, which remain powerful notwithstanding cyclical variations in economic activity.

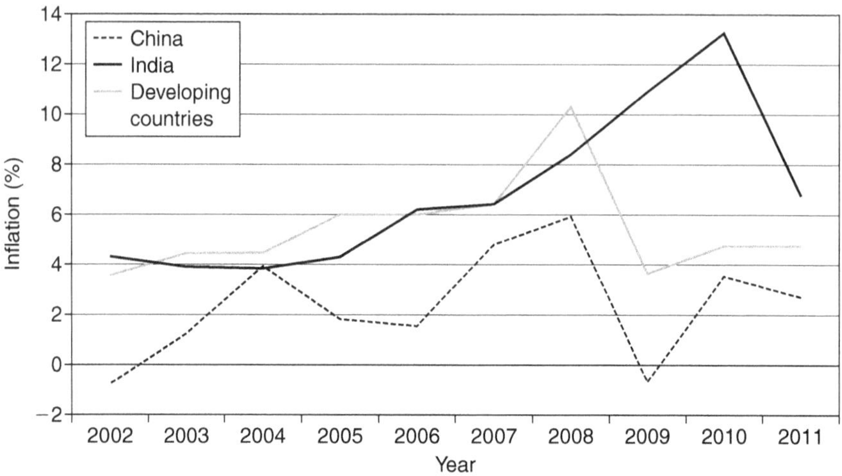

Figure 2.4 Inflation (%) in China, India and developing countries (2002–11) (source: IMF World Economic Outlook (WEO) Database; note: inflation rates depicted are annual average changes in Consumer Price Index (CPI). The rates of inflation for 2010 and 2011 are projected. Developing countries include 'Emerging and Developing Countries' as classified in the IMF WEO database).

Rise in global commodity prices along with excess demand and distribution inefficiencies (particularly in India) account for rising prices in both countries. China's and India's rapid growth during the last decade and their increasing demand for natural resources such as oil, metal and fertilisers have sharply increased international prices of these commodities. Addressing the implications of the recent crisis in the Arab world on energy prices, US President Barack Obama mentioned that, other than political uncertainty, energy prices are also influenced by faster growth in China and India and their large energy consumption.[14] The increases in global prices of natural resources influence domestic prices in China and India as higher costs of production lead to increases in consumer prices. This is in spite of both countries resorting to interventions and controls for protecting consumers from high prices. ADB's analysis of the rise in global rice prices resulting in corresponding increases in domestic prices (2008) shows such 'pass through' to be relatively less for oil in both China and India. For food prices, such as rice, India and China are noticed to have allowed some 'pass through' for incentivising producers, though they have hardly done so for wheat. Thus, while a rise in global commodity prices does explain a part of the rise in final consumer prices in both countries, there are other reasons behind such a rise. Empirical estimations by ADB (2008) indicate that consumer prices in China have been rising primarily on account of excess domestic demand rather than external price shocks. Demand is seen to account for 64 per cent of consumer price inflation in China, followed by 22 per cent by oil prices and

6 per cent by food prices. Similar analyses for India are unfortunately not available on the basis of consumer prices, but demand is expected to have played a vital role in price rises in India as well.

As discussed earlier, global crude oil prices are expected to continue to exert pressure on domestic prices in China and India because of their rapid growth and demand for energy. On the other hand, these nations are unlikely to avoid similar pressures from food articles as well, though probably not by a similar extent. With populations in both countries shifting towards greater consumption of non-cereal food items such as milk, fruits, soybeans and vegetables due to change in dietary habits induced by rising incomes and health consciousness, domestic production and supplies in both countries need to adjust to the changing trends. This will require time, during which both countries will rely on imports, which in turn will experience price increases due to higher demand from China and India. Research on drivers of commodity price rises in recent years shows the influence of the depreciating US dollar, diversion of agricultural commodities to biofuel production, and increasing speculation in commodity markets as other drivers of price rises (Abbot *et al.* 2009). These drivers are unlikely to disappear in the near future. For China and India, the impact of the growing linkage between global agricultural and energy markets arising from greater use of biofuels (e.g. ethanol and biodiesel) as substitutes for gasoline and diesel by several countries, leading to diversion of agricultural crops for biofuels, is an alarming trend. As large importers of soybean and vegetable oil respectively, China and India are victims of this trend as soybean supplies are declining owing to greater production of corn for biofuels, and the lower supplies increase the demand and price of other vegetable oils.

Demand-side pressures have been accentuating inflation in both countries. Estimation of 'output gaps'[15] by ADB (2008) for the period 2005–7 shows the gap to have increased sharply in both countries from around almost the same time – the second quarter of 2006 – implying that aggregate demand has exceeded utilisation rates of productive capacities in a way that was no longer non-inflationary and exerted pressure on domestic prices. These demand pressures on domestic prices have been reinforced by monetary policies. Since the middle of the last decade, both countries have been absorbing large chunks of capital inflows that have been driven by their booming economies and capital markets. In order to ensure that these inflows do not lead to appreciation of their exchange rates, both countries have been absorbing the inflows by releasing domestic currency. This has led to large infusions of cash in the domestic economy, fuelling propensities to consume and spend and leading to further pressure on prices. The volume of cash in both economies went up significantly after the outbreak of the financial crisis, when both adopted easy monetary policies. These have increased further following the recovery of the two economies and the corresponding increase in capital flows.

Managing inflation is a difficult problem for both countries. Raising interest rates and tightening monetary policies runs the risk of increasing costs of borrowing funds and discouraging investment. On the other hand, absorption of capital flows is also necessary given that both want to remain competitive in exchange rates and accumulate foreign exchange reserves. Managing capital flows without increasing liquidity and inflation is a major concern for both and a key area for consultation. They also have to tackle difficulties arising from rises in global commodity prices and occasional supply disruptions caused by seasonal fluctuations at home. As the Indian Prime Minister Dr Manmohan Singh explained at a meeting with Chief Secretaries of Indian states on 4 February 2011, in the absence of the ability to influence global commodity prices, domestic price stability depends crucially on managing prices of non-traded goods and services in face of rising consumption.[16]

The fallout of rising prices can also be a reduction in export competitiveness for both countries. Rising prices often force wage rates of workers to increase, even without a matching increase in productivity, in order to protect real incomes of workers. Cities in Guangdong province in China have been steadily increasing the minimum wages of workers because of inflation (Bradsher 2011b). Such increases, along with increases in material and other inputs, can result in China's exports becoming more expensive in world markets, leading to erosion in their competitiveness. Similar problems are likely to be faced by India's IT exports. During 2010, India's leading software firms Wipro and Infosys, along with the popular mobile handset manufacturing firm Nokia, increased wages substantially to counter the adverse effects of inflation (Goyal 2010). Indeed, high salary hikes in India after its recovery from the global financial crisis may well be on account of inflation ruling at double digit level and the necessity to negate its effects on employee purchasing power. These increases, however, can have serious implications for both countries in their respective areas of comparative advantages in global markets as they get reflected in higher costs of production and higher prices for traded goods.

Environment

Environmental problems faced by China and India have two dimensions. The first is the intensive pollution caused by rapid industrial expansion and urbanisation leading to degradation in the quality of natural resources such as air, water and forestry. The second is the threat to environment arising from global warming and climate change.

Analysing the findings of the Yale and Columbia Environmental Performance Index of 2008 for different environment indicators in China and India, Bardhan (2010) points out that while both fare poorly in almost all indicators, they are particularly worse off in sanitation and air pollution. Access to safe drinking-water facilities and water contamination appear to be more serious problems in China, along with environmental degradation of fisheries. India, on the other hand, suffers seriously from problems of regulation of pesticides and the protection of biodiversity and natural habitats.

Both sanitation and air pollution are major problems for both countries. These have been aggravated by rapid growth in population, urbanisation and industrial expansion. Lack of access to adequate sanitation facilities has become a serious problem in urban areas with civic facilities unable to increase as fast as the rate of growth in urban population. On the other hand, outdoor air pollution has increased through energy-intensive industrialisation depending heavily on coal and a rise in the number of vehicles. Large emissions of toxic chemicals like carbon monoxide, sulphur dioxide, nitrogen dioxide and particulate matter in the air has led to the occurrence of acid rain, creating serious public health problems (IEA 2007). China and India's air pollution problems are not limited to outdoor air, however. Indoor air pollution has been remarkably high in both countries due to extensive use of traditional biomass (fuelwood, dung and agricultural waste) in cooking.

Air and water pollution in China and India have reached levels where they are inflicting serious damages on people's lives. Aggregate costs of air and water pollution in China are estimated at almost 6 per cent of GDP per year in China, while in India human health costs from water only are expected to be almost 4 per cent of GDP (Bardhan 2010). Several Chinese cities (e.g. Lifen, Kaifeng, Panzhihua, Datong, Beijing, Shanghai, Xiamen, Chongqing) are among the world's most polluted cities. Indian cities figuring in this category are Delhi, Mumbai and Kolkata. Estimates by the OECD (2007) point to health damage from air pollution in China rising to as much as 13 per cent of GDP by 2020. With coal – the main driver of air pollution in China – continuing to remain the main source of energy in the foreseeable future, nitrogen and sulphur emissions are unlikely to reduce. China also has to contend with high costs of indoor air pollution arising from use of traditional biomass, particularly in rural areas. Both biomass and coal are responsible for widespread respiratory diseases, while smoke from biomass is also known to cause lung cancer (IEA 2007). These problems are acute in India as well, where traditional biomass continues to remain the major source of energy in rural households. The IEA (2007) expects biomass use in India to increase over time primarily because it will continue to remain a popular and affordable fuel among rural households, although its urban use may decrease. On the other hand, as with China, high reliance on coal in the coming years will ensure larger emissions of nitrogen and sulphur increasing outdoor air pollution. The prospects for both countries on air pollution appear distinctly gloomy, given their nature and pattern of energy consumption and also the growing number of vehicles on city roads.

In addition to air pollution, both countries are concerned over the alarming levels of pollution experienced by some of their major rivers and water resources. Widespread discharge of industrial waste, along with the deposition of municipal sewage, has resulted in extensive water contamination in China and India. Northern China is a heavily affected part of China in this respect, where 70 per cent of the waters of the Hai-Luan, Huai and Huang rivers are unfit for human consumption (Bardhan 2010). Tibet, Xinjiang and Qinghai provinces in the relatively less-developed west of China have large amounts of industrial waste water that does not comply with official discharge standards (Wu 2009). In India, the River Yamuna, flowing through the national capital region of Delhi, is one of the most polluted rivers and has suffered heavily from deposition of industrial waste and sewage. Almost 20 per cent of urban waste water in India is discharged untreated, leading to widespread contamination (Wu 2009).

The long-term environmental challenges facing the two countries relate to their emergence as world's leading emitters of carbon dioxide (CO_2). China's CO_2 emissions have been rising sharply since 2003 (Figure 2.5) and were estimated at 6,538 million tonnes in 2007. The annual rate of growth in China's emissions during 2001–7 has been 9.9 per cent, which is just double that of India's growth of 4.5 per cent during the same period. At 1,612 million tonnes of CO_2 emissions in 2007, India was the third largest emitter in the world. China, however, has overtaken the US to become the world's largest carbon emitter. At their respective volumes of emissions, the two countries accounted for almost 28 per cent of global carbon dioxide released in the atmosphere in 2007. In per capita terms, though, emissions in both countries continue to be much less than those in advanced economies.

The IEA's estimates of carbon dioxide emissions from energy use, beginning from a base year of 2005 and projected up to 2030, show emissions from China increasing to 8.6 billion tonnes in 2015 and 11.4 billion tonnes in 2030 in the reference scenario (IEA 2007). Emissions from India are projected to increase to 1.8 billion tonnes and 3.3 billion tonnes respectively during these periods. Though China will clearly remain the leading country in carbon emissions, India, despite experiencing large growth, is expected to remain below the US and Europe in emissions. The reference scenario of the IEA expects China to contribute 42 per cent and India 14 per cent of the total increase in global carbon dioxide emissions during 2005–30. It is evident that sustained use of fossil fuels – particularly coal – in industrialisation and primarily in electricity generation,

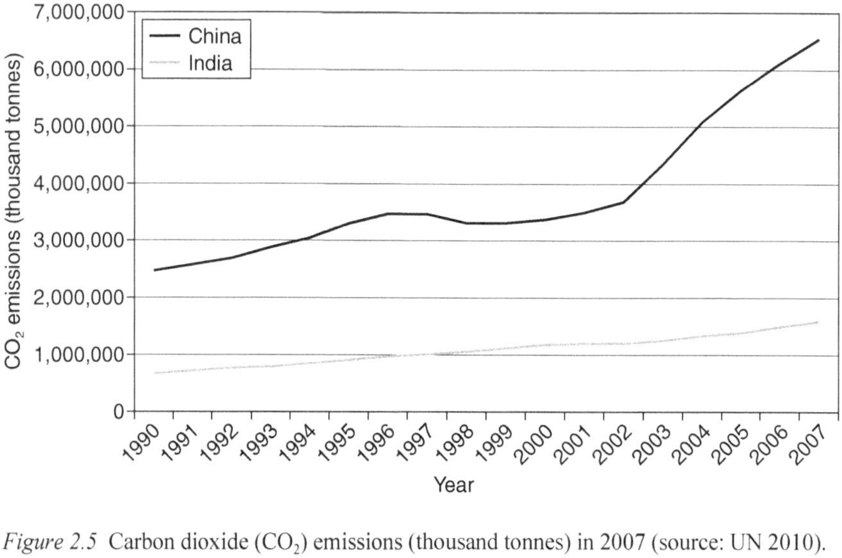

Figure 2.5 Carbon dioxide (CO_2) emissions (thousand tonnes) in 2007 (source: UN 2010).

will not only contribute to greater air pollution locally but will also make China and India the biggest contributors to global deposition of carbon dioxide. Indeed, by contributing handsomely to the carbon dioxide inventory, China and India's historical shares in emissions over the next few decades can become as much as those of the OECD countries.

There is little doubt about pollution and environmental concerns being serious worries for both countries. Undoubtedly, both would benefit from mutual cooperation in this area. Fortunately, the history of bilateral cooperation in this respect is encouraging. Beginning from a collaboration agreement on the environment signed in 1993, both countries have had research collaborations on ecosystems and biodiversity and environmental changes (Bawa *et al.* 2010). There have also been recent agreements to monitor glaciers and also in the fields of energy conservation and afforestation. The most significant step in jointly addressing climate change, however, was taken in October 2009, when both countries signed an agreement for cooperation on climate change with specific action points.[17]

Two core points of the October 2009 agreement are 'increasing dialogue, communication and pragmatic bilateral collaboration in addressing climate change' and aiming for greater collaboration in 'energy efficiency, renewable energy, clean energy technologies, sustainable agriculture and afforestation'.[18] The key operational features of the agreement include periodic ministerial consultations, the establishment of a working group for reviewing international negotiations as well as cooperative projects, cooperation on developing mitigation policies and projects in energy conservation and efficiency, renewable energy, clean coal, methane recovery and utilisation, afforestation and management of forests and eco-systems, transportation and sustainable habitat. Joint research and development, public–private partnerships and demonstrations of technologies are the declared modes of collaboration in the defined areas. Improving energy efficiency can play a major role in reducing emissions. It is encouraging that both countries have decided to cooperate in this area, since China and India's efficiency levels are still much lower than those of the OECD countries (Wu 2009).

Land and real estate

Labour and capital in China and India are factors of production that are discussed more than land. But in both countries, land is increasingly emerging as a serious challenge with respect to growing demand for shelter for more people. As discussed earlier, urbanisation and growth in city populations has increased demand for housing, which in turn has intensified the search for land. Beyond cities, expansion of industries and new economic activities have increased demand for land. Unlike labour and capital, the stock of land is finite and divided between multiple uses. These uses are distinct between rural and urban lands, with the former devoted mostly to farming and the latter to commercial and industrial activities. With demand for urban land increasing rapidly, urban outgrowths have entrenched into rural areas and acquisition of rural land for urban use has become imperative. Such acquisitions have become major sources of social and political tensions in both countries.

No land in China is privately owned. While urban land belongs to states (*guoyou tudi*), rural land belongs to collectives (*jiti tudi*). Both sets of lands are leased out to individuals for different uses. The system of leasing began in the 1980s at a time when China began industrialising aggressively by building large economic zones. Urban land can be leased out by municipal land bureaus for both residential and commercial purposes, with different lease periods. Residential leases are usually up to 70 years, while industrial and commercial leases are for 50 and 40 years respectively (Su 2008). Similarly, agricultural land is also leased out to individual households for farming. The lease periods are 30 years, 30–50 years and 30–70 years for arable lands, grassland and forest respectively (Yang 2008). Households are also allowed to transfer their land-use rights through further leasing or subcontracting.

Unlike China, in India the state does not have monopolistic ownership of land. But there are several ambiguities regarding land titles. This is particularly critical in rural areas, where absence of land records specifying ownership of land creates several problems. As Morris (2010) points out, ownership of property in India is usually established by the sequence of earlier transactions, since the state does not certify a title to ownership of the property. The rather tenuous mode of establishing ownership rights leaves considerable scope for litigation.

India is also experiencing the problem of limited supply of land following industrialisation and urbanisation. As in China, where land bureaus regulate supply of urban land, in India too, large chunks of real estate in cities are owned by municipal development bodies and housing boards. To an extent, this imparts a monopolistic dimension in India's land market as well, with government agencies controlling substantive parts of city space. Moreover, state agencies in both countries can acquire land on 'public interest' or 'public purpose' grounds. While the Land Administration Law of 1998 empowers local governments in China to acquire land from rural collectives 'in the public interest', the Land Acquisition Act of 1894 enables governments in India to acquire land 'for public purpose'.

Land availability and the high price of real estate have become serious issues in both countries. Many of the problems arise because of imperfections in land markets. In China, pressures on land began arising through rapid industrialisation and the need for manufacturers to have more capacity. Over time, as the supply of state-owned urban land began reducing owing to higher demand from industry, local governments had to acquire land from rural collectives. Compensation paid to farmers for acquiring rural land was often insufficient as local governments competed with each other to allot cheap land to industry. At the same time, greater demand for housing in expanding cities encouraged local governments to sell state-owned land at high prices to developers, who in turn passed on the prices to consumers, leading to a sharp rise in real estate prices. Revenues from land have been major sources of earnings for local government in China.

Lack of adequate land space in Indian cities has resulted in high prices of real estate, as the stock of houses within city limits has increased much less than the increase in demand for such houses. Indian cities suffer from restrictive laws on conversion of land from one particular use to another. High conversion costs have often prevented developers – particularly those without deep pockets – to stay away from acquiring residential lands in cities, even if the owners are willing to sell. This has not helped in augmenting the housing stock. Most of the new housing in Indian metropolises such as Delhi and Mumbai occurs well away from the city cores, on the outer limits of the cities, owing to easier availability of land. The heavy demand for new houses, though, has seen them being sold at a premium notwithstanding the distance of such housing from the city centres and the lack of adequate transport links.

High demand for houses has not been accompanied by simplification of procedures for acquiring property. According to the 'Doing Business' database of the World Bank,[19] most Indian cities and state capitals – Ahmadabad, Bhubaneshwar, Chennai, Delhi, Jaipur, Kolkata, Mumbai, Patna – have multiple procedures, requiring on average around 40 days for completing all the formalities. In some cities, such as Bhubaneshwar (126 days), Guwahati (84 days), Kolkata (107 days), Ludhiana (67 days) and Patna (87 days), the time required can be much longer. Not only does acquiring property require time, navigating through the procedures involves substantial costs, which can be as high as 25 per cent of the property value even in the new urban township of Noida – a part of the National Capital Region of Delhi. The 'Doing Business' database shows these costs to be essentially on stamp duties (money paid to local governments for registering property) and on lawyers' fees for successfully completing each formality. Chinese cities, in comparison, have a larger number of procedures involved in registering property, with Nanning (12), Shenyang (12), Urumqi (11), Chengdu (11), Hohhot (11), Beijing (10), Lanzhou (10) and Nanchang (10) being some of the more difficult ones. On average, completion of all formalities requires at least 50 days, with Lanzhou and Guiyang requiring as many as 78 and 77 days respectively, and Beijing almost 60 days. The transaction costs, though, as reported by the 'Doing Business' database, are much less in Chinese cities despite more procedures. This is due to absence of lawyer's fees and lower stamp duties. In most Chinese cities, however, buyers have to pay deed tax and business tax. Thus while stamp duties on registration are an important avenue for filling local government coffers in India, various other taxes do so in China.

Land acquisition and forcible seizure of houses for demolition have been serious problems in China. A recent survey conducted by the Chinese Academy of Social Sciences (CASS) found that, out of the 1,564 villages studied for instances of land confiscation, the number of confiscations had increased from 20 in 2000 to 180 in 2010. Highlighting the disturbing rise in confiscation and forced acquisition, the report mentions that conflicts over land are threatening the stability of China's rural society (Wang 2011).[20] Apart from loss of property, acquisition involves the problem of compensating farmers, who usually do not figure in land transactions as the latter are finalised between collectives and local governments. The survey released by CASS mentions that almost 70 per cent of the farmers considered the compensation paid for land too low, with 38 per cent indicating that they did not have any say in deciding the compensation (Wang 2011).

Farmers are unhappy over compensation not only in China but also in India, where compensation packages, including the potential value obtainable from the future use of acquired land, have hardly been forthcoming. Neither country has been able to develop well-established frameworks for compensating victims of disposed land. They are unlikely to do so until incentives are clearly indicated. Local government officials in China have incentives in awarding cheap lands to businesses and selling prime land at high rates to developers. They stand to benefit in both cases: first by ensuring better career prospects by generating more business, and second by earning more revenue for their provinces. Land transactions became main sources of revenue for local governments after the introduction of a new taxation system in 1994 that required them to share several taxes with the central government and that has led to a decline in their tax revenues (Su 2008; Wang 2011). They therefore do not have incentives for paying more compensation to farmers, and foresee greater benefits in acquiring rural land at cheap rates and selling it at higher prices. In India, on the other hand, the state has on several occasions tried to acquire land from farmers in order to make it available to industry. This has been particularly evident during India's policy of building special economic zones (SEZs) through private initiative, where different states have been trying to procure land for private businesses. Though the quality of compensation for farmers has widespread political significance, few developers have sufficiently deep pockets to agree to generous compensation. Government efforts to negotiate between farmers and industries have been unsuccessful on several occasions through information asymmetry and a lack of adequate information for deciding compensation.

With land markets in both countries suffering from lack of transparency, corruption has increased greatly. Most of this has arisen from the scarcity of land and from rent-seeking opportunities associated with such scarcity on the part of local government officials and agencies. The discipline inspection wing of the Communist Party of China (CPC) has expressed concern over rising corruption in the housing sector in the form of irregular possession of apartments, renting of apartments, demolition of buildings and land requisition (Yan 2011). In India, up to now, an action agenda for tackling corruption in a variety of land and housing scams all over the country has yet to be formulated. Both countries are dependent upon the good earnest and sincerity of provincial and state governments and land bureaus (China) and municipalities (India) for curbing corruption. In both China and India, provinces and states have the final say over land. They have large stakes involved with these lands that are connected to their financial solvencies. This is clear from high rates of stamp duty in Indian states. While the rates might have helped in filling state coffers, they have also resulted in the misquoting of property transaction prices, as both parties involved in the transactions wish to pay lower taxes. These and other inefficiencies adversely affecting land markets in both countries, including artificial increases in prices, speculation and corruption, cannot be curbed unless states and provinces can be convinced that this must be done. The success of the latest housing policy released by the State Council in China, aiming to reduce the bubble in housing prices, depends critically upon the role of local governments in implementing the measures for curbing speculation. The same holds true for the implementation of property taxes in Chinese cities such as Shanghai for high-end property. Both China and India realise that their lands have become much more complex issues, courtesy of urbanisation and population growth, than they had visualised. Managing these complications is no longer possible through unified national policies even in China, and far less so in India.

Collaboration: incentives and problems

There are several common development challenges that provide India and China with grounds for collaboration. The preceding sections have discussed some of these. There are many more, particularly in areas of health and education, where both countries are trying hard to overcome gaps between desired and actual standards. Income inequalities and unbalanced regional growth are equally pressing concerns.

Should China and India collaborate in alleviating common concerns just because these are common to both of them? From the wider vantage point of large developing economies, many have problems that are similar to those facing China and India. Simply suggesting that all these countries, including China and India, should collaborate bilaterally or collectively in finding common solutions is probably wishful thinking. There could be political and systemic differences between countries, such as between China and India, which might cause them to withhold collaboration. Besides, though the manifestations of problems may be similar among countries, their origins may be different. Land markets, for example, are distorted in both countries, but these distortions have taken shape through circumstances that are unique to both. Urban growth is more migration-induced in China, while in India it is sustained by the natural increase in urban population. But despite differences in origin, the outcomes of rapid urbanisation such as congestion, slum growth, pollution and pressure on housing are similar in both countries. While consumers in both countries are suffering from spikes in global energy and commodity prices, overall inflation is also drawing considerable momentum from domestic factors, which include (apart from greater injection of cash flows) supply bottlenecks that are more pronounced for India than China. Thus, collaborating with the objective of finding common solutions reproducible in both countries may not always be feasible, owing to differences in domestic conditions.

The incentives for collaboration in common challenges stem from two factors. The first is the urge to learn and know how the other is addressing the same problem. Slums, for example, feature in almost all major Indian and Chinese cities. These are results of explosive growth in urban populations, which might have been driven by relatively different factors in China and India. But irrespective of the determinants, slums are stark realities in the city landscapes of both countries. Providing better lives for slum dwellers and eradicating urban inefficiencies arising from slums are common challenges. Similarly, air and water pollution, despite varying in nature and intensity, are serious problems for both countries manifesting themselves in extensive health hazards. These commonalities should ideally inspire experts and agencies from both countries to greater communication and cooperation. The second – and probably less-discussed and less-comprehended – incentive for collaboration is the ineffectiveness of solutions yielded by mainstream models and explanations for fixing problems in China and India. It is difficult to explain the patterns of growth in both these countries through mainstream economic explanations. As Basu (2009) points out, explaining growth in both these countries has been a major intellectual challenge for mainstream economics, which has foundations based on Western development experiences. The downsides of such growth, therefore, are equally unlikely to be explained and resolved by mainstream theoretical constructs. For both China and India, it is important to realise that not only are their problems unique, but they are also strikingly indigenous, requiring 'home-grown' solutions.

An unusual aspect of China's and India's economic rise – something rather baffling for most – is the divergence between growth and development that they exhibit. As the world's second and eleventh largest economies (second and fourth largest if GDP on PPP basis is considered), they are unquestionably among the world's most significant economies. But despite being stark in economic size, they have progressed much less on human development and figure among the world's 'medium' human development countries. Not only do the world's other major economies, most of which are G7 members, show progress on human development that is commensurate with their economic size, but large emerging market economies like Brazil, Mexico and Russia also score higher on human development than China and India (South Africa and Indonesia being a couple of exceptions). The gaps that have emerged between growth and development trajectories in the two countries explain the complex – and on many occasions common – challenges facing them despite rapid economic progress. As countries nursing such remarkable contrasts between growth and development as have hardly been noticed among the world's major economies, China and India are in a distinct league defined by their own contrasts. This underscores a further rationale for their cooperation on common problems.

The overriding obstacle in collaboration is clearly the 'trust deficit' shrouding perceptions on both sides. In a generic sense, although commercial engagement between China and India has been on an upswing the scale of engagement could have been even higher had the 'trust deficit' been less. The prevalence of such a deficit is rather unusual between two countries that have had copious exchanges of people, commodities, culture, ideas, thoughts and knowledge for centuries. Indeed, history shows the two countries to have had far greater interactions in various spheres with each other than with other countries. Unfortunately, the positive history of centuries has been almost completely undermined by the much briefer but significantly acrimonious period that followed military hostilities in 1962. The last decade has seen business and commercial exchanges improving owing to flourishing trade. But rising trade has failed to eradicate the trust deficit, which has remained strong because of the persistence of differences on territorial issues and contentious problems like Tibet and Arunachal Pradesh. While there are understandable difficulties in moving ahead on outstanding issues, the atmosphere surrounding them has been vitiated by exaggerated alarmist postures. The mainstream media on both sides, barring a few exceptions, has contributed significantly to the growth and maintenance of the trust deficit by making no efforts to curb the expression of hardline views. During his visit to India in December 2010, the Chinese Premier urged the Indian media to play a more constructive role in promoting friendship between the two sides, particularly on sensitive matters like the border dispute.[21] Reflections in the Chinese media on unresolved issues with India have also not been particularly positive. It is important for the media on both sides to realise that clouding perceptions will only complicate matters between the two countries, which are trying to move ahead on the basis of pragmatic concerns.

Beyond the trust deficit, there are typical systemic and structural issues that can be roadblocks to collaboration between the two countries. Systems and functions in both countries are not only different from each other, but also inherently complex. Because of different pre-independence histories and political systems, institutions have evolved in different ways. These are reflected in the manners in which business rules, procedures, attitudes and approaches have shaped. The legal systems in both countries, for example, are different in their own ways. China has a mixed legal system that combines features of traditional Chinese law with a communist legal system and civil law. India, on the other hand, follows common law. Both countries, despite having moved to a market-based principle of exchanges in several spheres, continue to have informal networks that are crucial in facilitating business and interfaces. For both Chinese and Indian individuals and agencies, it is not easy to know how these networks perform on the other side. Provincial governments play important roles in facilitating and establishing businesses in China. In India, state governments can at best be facilitators only. For Chinese and Indian scholars, experts and also students interested in knowing more about both countries, the respective statistical systems and data maintenance standards may not be easy to follow and compare. Chinese statistical practices have been largely modelled on the erstwhile Soviet systems of maintaining data. India has been more aligned to the practices followed by Western agencies and institutions. The differences are noticeable not only in statistics but also in accounting and invoicing practices. On top of these difficulties, there are typical problems with respect to languages, with English and Mandarin not yet finding deep roots in China and India respectively. The number of people speaking English in China is far more than the number of people speaking Mandarin in India. However, the English spoken in China is largely functional and more attuned to purposes of business and commerce. This, though, is expected to change over time as generations of Chinese students used to being taught English in schools and with greater proficiency in the language enlarge the English-speaking population. In India, though, Mandarin has only lately been included in the school curriculum. It will be a long time before India has a large population conversant in Mandarin. Food habits and religious and cultural practices also are vastly different between the two countries. Understanding these habits and practices for the average Chinese and Indian with respect to their counterparts becomes even more difficult as habits vary sharply between different regions of the individual countries themselves.

All the above underline differences and contrasts which create typical 'information asymmetries' about each other, as discussed in Chapter 1, and can become issues in promoting and fostering collaboration. However, the history of business has numerous examples of overcoming systemic and cultural asymmetries. For India and China, information asymmetries, in terms of lack of adequate knowledge and perceptions about each other's governance, administrative systems, business practices, legal structures, political institutions, cultural traits and social habits, are compounded by the 'trust deficit'. Thus it is not only a problem of not knowing each other very well: it is also a problem of whether both want to know each other that well, given that there is a sense of political and security-related discomfort with each other. While information asymmetries can be gradually overcome through greater interfacing between agencies and people-to-people contact, the positive intensity in such interfacing and exchange may be lacking if the trust deficit prevails.

3 Competition

Present and future

As two of the world's largest and most populous economies, China and India encounter a rather unusual problem. Their growth rates are among the fastest in the world. Yet they have large numbers of poor people who have not benefited from these high growth rates. Indeed, as the world's largest developing countries, both are in the ironical situation of being labelled economic superpowers while they grapple with chronic development challenges.

The apparently paradoxical outcome of being developing economies and yet the world's major economic powers has resulted in both searching for means for maintaining their rapid growth, as growth is seemingly the only answer to the outstanding problems of poverty and low incomes. Both, however, realise that maintaining high and broad-based growth requires access to much greater reserves of natural resources than those available to them. Furthermore, growth requires moving into new markets and expanding diplomatic and strategic relationships in a manner that furthers long-term economic objectives. What all these also imply is that China and India can hardly avoid competing with each other in their race for resources, markets and allies.

This chapter focuses on some of the major spheres of competition between China and India in their quest to maintain high growth and make their people integral parts of the growth process. With both countries competing for strategic space in a globalised world, it is inevitable that they will compete for financial assets and natural resources. Such competition may not only produce friction, some of which might be short-lived, but can also yield inefficient outcomes. The chapter examines the nature of Sino-India competition with respect to obtaining access to energy and water resources, forging bilateral trade agreements and deploying foreign aid as key aspects of their competitive interface. It also discusses friction in trade that has been a rather regular feature of the bilateral economic engagement.

Energy

The steadily rising growth trajectories in China and India have resulted in energy resources playing increasingly important roles in their growth processes. High economic growth creates a virtuous and mutually reinforcing cycle of greater production and consumption. Both producers and consumers require more energy for maintaining growth momentums. Demand for energy resources has grown enormously in the two countries as they have surged ahead on their rapid growth paths. Indeed, in the year 2009 China and India were the second and fourth largest primary energy consumers in the world, with the US and Russia being the first and third respectively.[1] There are considerable differences between the two countries in the volume of energy consumed, with India's primary energy use being just a little more than one-fifth of that of China. Despite the gap, which reflects the difference in the long-term growth rate trajectories between the two countries, the varying intensity in energy demand produced by such growth and the ability to respond to the ensuing demand, China and India are expected to be the world's top energy consumers in the years to come. The International Energy Agency (IEA) expects China and India to contribute to 36 per cent and 18 per cent respectively of the projected growth in global energy use during the period 2008–35 (IEA 2010). In the medium term, China is expected to replace the US as the world's largest energy consumer. India is projected to be the third largest consumer, though at a fair distance.

Discussions on energy usually begin from oil. It is pertinent to study the nature of oil consumption in the two countries. During the period 1999 to 2009, China's oil consumption[2] has experienced an increase of 93 per cent from 209.6 million tonnes to 404.6 million tonnes. The same period saw India's oil appetite increasing by 48.1 per cent, reflecting a rise in consumption from 100.3 million tonnes to 148.5 million tonnes. Relatively faster growth and economic expansion in China has resulted in its becoming a comparatively bigger oil consumer than India; China's oil consumption was 2.7 times more than India's in 2009 as against 2.1 times in 1999. But bilateral comparisons should not obliterate the fact that oil consumption in both countries during the mentioned period grew at much higher rates than those in the Asia-Pacific (25.4 per cent) and the entire world (10.2 per cent). No other emerging market economy has experienced as much growth in oil consumption as China and India in the last decade. Brazil's oil consumption increased from 92.5 million tonnes to 104.3 million tonnes, while Russia's remained almost unchanged at around 126 million tonnes. China and India's emergence as two of the world's largest and fastest-growing oil consumers during this period is a reflection not only of their high economic growth, but also of the fact that such growth has been heavily energy-intensive and has increased the dependence of both economies on oil. Forecasts on average annual oil consumption growths in the two countries (measured in million barrels per day) show 0.4 per cent growth in China and 0.1 per cent growth in India during 2007–15 (ADB 2008). Growth in oil consumption is expected to continue unabated in both countries over time.

The structure of energy consumption in China and India, compared with other large developing country and emerging markets, reveals interesting differences. Consumptions in both countries are overtly dominated by coal and oil (Table 3.1). While natural gas has begun emerging as an important source of energy, its relative use is still far less than coal and oil. Together, coal and oil account for

Table 3.1 Energy consumption structures of major emerging market economies

	Oil (million tonne)	*Coal (million tonne oil equivalent)*	*Gas (million tonne oil equivalent)*	*Nuclear energy (million tonne oil equivalent)*	*Hydel power (million tonne oil equivalent)*	*Total (million tonne oil equivalent)*
Argentina	22.3	1.1	38.8	1.8	9.2	73.3
Brazil	104.3	11.7	18.3	2.9	88.5	225.7
China	404.6	1,537.4	79.8	15.9	139.3	2,177
India	148.5	245.8	46.7	3.8	24	468.9
Indonesia	62.0	30.5	33.0	–	2.7	128.2
Mexico	85.6	6.8	62.7	2.2	6.0	163.2
Russia	124.9	82.9	350.7	37.0	39.8	635.3
South Africa	24.3	99.4	–	2.7	0.2	126.8
Turkey	28.8	27.2	28.9	–	8.1	93.0

Source: BP (2010).

Note
The estimates are for the year 2009.

89.2 per cent and 84.1 per cent respectively of China's and India's total energy consumptions. Other than South Africa, none of the other emerging markets show such overt dependence on coal and oil. Between the two fossil fuels, coal is a more important source of energy in China and India.

The insatiable hunger for coal in China and India is largely due to electricity in both countries relying on coal-fired thermal power generation. Conventional coal-based thermal power accounts for more than 80 per cent of electricity generated in both countries (EIA 2010a, 2010b). Hydro power is the next major source of electricity, accounting for around 15 per cent of power generated, followed by nuclear and renewable sources like wind and solar. Electricity generated from nuclear, wind and solar energy is still insignificant. The reliance on coal as the major source of electricity has ensured that both countries remain leading coal consumers in the world. Between them they consumed 54.4 per cent of the total global coal consumption in 2009. In the medium-term future as well, they are expected to remain major global consumers of coal and are projected to account for 82 per cent of the increase in global coal demand by 2030 (Palit 2010b).

Both China and India have ample coal reserves and have been trying to deploy these as effectively as possible to meet the rising demand for electricity emanating from high economic growth. Different estimates suggest that 13–14 per cent of the world's mineable coal reserves are located in China (Zhao 2009; Palit 2010b). As Table 3.1 indicates, China's current levels of coal production and consumption are far higher than those of India; India is currently producing only 13.6 per cent of what China produces and consuming around 16.0 per cent of China's consumption. While lower consumption can probably be explained by the difference in the size and rate of expansion of the two economies, lower production can be explained by India's sub-optimal mining operations that have failed to take off on account of an absence of adequate incentives for encouraging private enterprise in mining. Ironically, both China and India, notwithstanding their large underground reserves, have begun importing coal, with India also importing coal from China. In China's case, transport costs of shipping coal from inland sites to coastal provinces have been a deciding factor for imports, while for India the mediocre quality of home-produced coal has necessitated imports. In a way, this has turned out be advantageous for coal-exporting economies such as Australia, which have been able to maintain mining operations by making them export-intensive, thereby avoiding environmental penalties (Rosenthal 2010). The imperatives driving both countries to imports were discussed earlier in Chapter 2.

Both countries are keen to reduce their dependence on coal as a primary source of energy given their commitments to reducing carbon emissions and carbon-intensity in production. The spate of coal imports forced by a strange combination of high demand and quality imperfection (and in India's case by the inability to expand mining capacities) is not an encouraging development since it increases vulnerability to fluctuations in global commodity prices, with adverse implications for inflation at home. Moreover, coal mining is a labour-intensive process generating large numbers of unskilled and semi-skilled jobs in both countries. Neither country would like to cramp its job market and would wish to augment domestic mining capacities in the foreseeable future rather than relying on imports. This has to be balanced against compulsions emanating from self-imposed targets of climate policy in both countries. But given rapid economic growth and the concomitant demand for energy, particularly electricity, reducing reliance on coal cannot be immediate. It will take time before gas, hydro and nuclear, along with other renewable sources, become dominant sources of energy.

From a supply perspective, given the untapped reserves higher coal demand is not as much a concern for China and India as are similar prospects for oil and gas. Both countries are endowed with abundant coal reserves. The reserve–production (R/P)[3] ratios for coal in China and India are 38 and 105 respectively, indicating that, despite exponential increases in demand, there are enough unexploited reserves to cater to the growing demand, provided they can be extracted. It is not the same with oil and gas, however. Indeed, increasing demand for oil and gas and lack of access to adequate reserves of both fuels is a matter of grave concern for both China and India. It is in their quest for new sources of gas and energy that both countries find themselves competing in similar domains.

Geographically, the world's largest oil reserves are in the Middle East (102.0 '000mt; 56.6 per cent)[4] followed by South and Central America (28.5 '000mt; 14.9 per cent), Europe and Central Asia (18.5 '000mt; 10.3 per cent), Africa (16.9 '000mt; 9.6 per cent), North America (10.2 '000mt; 5.5 per cent) and Asia-Pacific including China and India (5.6 '000mt; 3.2 per cent) (BP 2010, p. 6). Given the geographical distribution of proven oil reserves, China and India are at a disadvantage in the sense of not housing major sources of oil in their domestic territories. This is, of course, excluding the possibility of ongoing and future exploration initiatives throwing up new finds. But on the basis of the current spread of reserves, the rest of the world holds much more oil compared to that held by the world's two largest and fastest-growing economies. Lack of access to adequate crude oil at home has forced both to rely on imported supplies. During 2009, China and India imported 51.8 per cent (203.5 mt out of 392.5 mt) and 80.5 per cent (145.8 mt out of 181.2 mt) respectively of their total crude oil requirements. At this level of imports, they were the second and fifth largest net oil importers in the world (EIA 2010b). Given the rapid economic growth in the two economies, and particularly the expansion which such growth has induced in the transport sectors of both in terms of increase in number of vehicles, oil demand and oil imports are expected to increase further for both in future (Zhao 2009). Demand for imports will also increase since both countries are building and maintaining strategic petroleum reserves (SPRs), which are intended to be cushions for managing potential supply disruptions.[5]

The oil import structure of both countries in terms of source of imports shows considerable similarity. The Middle East is the main source of imports for both, within which Saudi Arabia accounts for the largest imports followed by Iran, Iraq and Kuwait. Africa is the second largest source of oil imports for both, with Angola and Sudan being major sources for China and Nigeria and Angola the leading sources for India. Venezuela is also an important source of imports for both. Geographical proximity and lower cost of transportation has influenced sourcing pattern of imports for both countries. This is reflected in Russia and Kazakhstan featuring among oil import sources for China, India sources around 70 per cent of oil imports from the Middle East as compared with around 50 per cent for China (EIA 2010a, 2010b).

Natural gas is yet to emerge as being as significant as coal and oil in China's and India's energy use. The countries consumed 79.8 and 46.7 mtoe of gas in 2009 (see Table 3.1), which was 3.7 per cent and 10.0 per cent of their total energy consumption. Compared with Russia, where 55 per cent of energy used is contributed by gas, or Argentina and Mexico, which also rely considerably on gas, China and India are yet to deploy gas as effectively as they would wish. As with oil, China and India also have a resource disadvantage in gas, since they are not endowed with large reserves. The Asia-Pacific has only 8.7 per cent (16.24 tcm)[6] of the world's total gas reserves (187.49 tcm), while the Middle East and Europe and Central Asia have 40.6 per cent (76.18 tcm) and 33.7 per cent (63.09 tcm) of the reserves respectively (BP 2010, p. 22). Africa also holds 7.9 per cent (14.76 tcm) of total gas reserves, with Algeria, Egypt and Nigeria being the main sources (ibid.). With demand for gas increasing in both countries, domestic production of gas in China and India has fallen short of consumption requirements, forcing both to become net importers. During 2009, gas productions in China and India were 85.2 and 39.3 billion cubic metres (bcm) respectively, while consumptions were 88.7 and 51.9 bcm (ibid., pp. 24, 27). With both countries, particularly China, planning to utilise gas more intensively in future as an alternative for coal for curbing pollution, demand for gas is expected to rise sharply, thus increasing the demand for gas imports. China has been relying primarily on Australia, neighbouring Central Asia, Middle East and Africa for importing liquefied natural gas (LNG). India's LNG imports also show a similar sourcing pattern, though its biggest supplies come from the Middle East and Australia.

The paucity of adequate oil and gas resources, coupled with increasing demand for these fuels generated by rapid growth and industrialisation, has resulted in both countries stepping up efforts to access resources overseas. Many of these efforts have centred on exploration and production (E&P) activities. For both countries, such efforts have been led by state-owned energy corporations. The latter for China have been the China National Petroleum Corporation (CNPC), the China Petroleum and Chemical Corporation (Sinopec) and the China National Offshore Oil Corporation (CNOOC). For India, the leading corporation guiding overseas investment activities has been OVL (the Oil and Natural Gas Corporation (ONGC) Videsh Limited), followed by Oil India Limited (OIL) and the Indian Oil Corporation Limited (IOCL).

China's overseas ventures

Both the scale and the scope of China's overseas energy ventures have been bigger than those of India. During the period 1995–2006, Chinese state oil corporations, particularly CNPC, reportedly invested more than US$27 billion in

E&P projects spanning several countries in the Middle East, North Africa, Central Asia and Latin America (Zhao 2009). Chinese investments in overseas oil assets have increased particularly sharply after the financial crisis, with China utilising its relative immunity from the downturn to acquire large chunks of energy assets at low prices. Indeed, during the period from October 2008 to December 2009, Chinese companies reportedly invested US$17 billion in the acquisition of oil and gas assets (EIA 2010b). The downturn has also encouraged China to enter into several loan-for-oil deals with prominent oil-rich countries such as Russia, Brazil, Kazakhstan, Ecuador, Turkmenistan and Venezuela (EIA 2010b). The deals involve China extending soft loans enabling the recipients to build upgraded oil infrastructure (e.g. the East Siberia Pacific Ocean oil pipeline) or execute other projects in exchange for oil exports to China. China has also deployed similar 'oil for infrastructure' credit facilities in African countries such as Angola (Vines *et al.* 2009).

Production from overseas oil ventures involving equity investments by Chinese firms, particularly CNPC, has become an increasingly important source of oil supply for China, with such output projected to exceed more than 1 million barrel per day by the middle of the current decade (Zhao 2009). CNPC, which currently holds 70 per cent of the aggregate equity investments made by Chinese companies in overseas oil assets, plans to invest US$60 billion for expanding overseas capacities with particular attention on securing sour and high-sulphur crude oil from the Middle East (EIA 2010b).

In another significant development that is likely to favourably influence China's oil supplies in the long term, the transnational oil pipeline bringing oil from Kazakhstan and Russia has become functional since May 2006. Completion of the ongoing East Siberia Pacific Ocean oil pipeline will make East Russia another critical source of China's oil imports. Central Asia has also emerged as a key source of China's natural gas imports, which come into China through the Central Asian gas pipeline. Another country that has received close Chinese attention for sourcing oil is Myanmar, not in terms of oil reserves but as the conduit for a pipeline providing quicker transportation option (EIA 2010b). Myanmar, of course, is an ample reserve of gas and has been a point of competition between China and India, as discussed later in this chapter.

India's overseas ventures

Acquisition of both new oil blocks and existing oil assets has featured prominently in India's overseas energy strategy. OVL has been playing the lead role in this regard, scouting resources deep and wide in several countries, and currently has operations in 13 locations in Africa, the Middle East, Central Asia, Southeast Asia and Latin America. In Africa, OVL has been active in exploration and production activities in Nigeria, Sudan, Libya and Egypt. The Middle East, which has traditionally been India's largest source of oil imports, has OVL's footprints in Iran, Iraq and Syria. The Sakhalin oil and gas field in Russia has been eyed closely by both Indian and Chinese oil companies, and OVL is active here.

Russia has also witnessed one of OVL's biggest acquisitions of existing oil assets.[7] Vietnam and Myanmar have been OVL's interests in Southeast Asia, while in Latin America Brazil, Colombia, Cuba and Venezuela have seen considerable E&P activities by OVL. In addition to OVL, OIL has also been active in E&P projects in Libya, Gabon, Nigeria and Sudan (EIA 2010a).

The Middle East is expected to remain India's most critical source of energy in the foreseeable future. Indian firms have invested around US$10 billion in Iran for developing gas and liquefaction facilities in the country in exchange for generous supplies of LNG, amounting to not less than six million tonnes per year (Sheikh 2009). In a significant development expected to make a major difference to India's gas supplies, India has finalised a multi-country US$10 billion gas pipeline facility that will transport gas from Turkmenistan via Afghanistan and Pakistan (Times News Network 2010).

The competition between China and India with respect to accessing new energy resources is visible in Central Asia as well as Africa and Southeast Asia. Central Asia witnessed the race fairly early on when, in August 2005, CNPC and ONGC competed to take over Petrokazakhstan, a Canadian company with large oil assets in Central Asia. CNPC won the bid. China also made headway in securing oil supplies from Russia by extending a generous loan of US$6 billion when Russia was seeking funds to re-nationalise one of the main subsidiaries of its oil major Yukos and was in talks with both China and India (Bush 2005). The competition for securing oil assets has seen China emerging successful on more occasions, something that is due not only to its greater financial clout, but also its focused and emphatic policy in acquiring oil assets backed by proactive oil diplomacy (Zhao 2009). India is yet to develop powerful agencies such as China's Energy Leading Group, headed by the Chinese Premier, to implement a holistic energy policy.

For Africa, the race for resources between the two Asian giants has come as an unexpected bonanza. Energy-rich African countries see the race as a process that enables them to access precious financial resources and also provides the opportunity to build new infrastructure assets. In addition to the long-term forward oil contracts they have with African countries for physically lifting oil,[8] both China and India have been shifting to ownership of oil assets in these countries with a view to ensuring long-term energy security. These asset ownerships, arising from grant of access to new E&P activities awarded by African national governments, also involve investments by China and India in host country infrastructures.[9] The process reflects the evolving structure of oil geo-politics where oil-exporting countries look forward to the realisation of considerable benefits from resource extraction.[10] China has extended development loans for participation in the energy development infrastructure in Chad, Gabon and Angola. Angola and Sudan are successful examples of the 'oil-for-infrastructure' arrangements. However, these can also create certain difficulties, as discovered by both Chinese and Indian firms in Nigeria, where none of the infrastructure projects linked to acquisition of oil blocks offered at discounted rates have actually taken off, on account of domestic political constraints (Vines *et al.* 2009).

India's long history of diplomatic relationship with Africa should encourage it to conceive an energy model where it also focuses on long-term industrial development in host countries, in addition to a narrower purpose of resource extraction (Sheikh 2009). From an Indian vantage point, this is important since there are occasions where China has been able to comprehensively surge ahead of India in the run for resources. The ONGC's attempt in 2004 to bid for an oil block in Angola did not succeed as the bid was won by a consortium led by Sinopec. In early 2006, CNOOC beat ONGC to acquiring contractor rights in an oilfield in Nigeria. Most watchers of the Sino-Indian rivalry in Africa will correctly opine that China's ability to spend more has given it a head-start over India in the race for resources.[11] However, there is also the view that India's state-owned energy companies are more risk-averse and cautious in investing in Africa as opposed to China, owing to the greater questions that they are required to answer on how they spend public money (Vines *et al.* 2009).

Diplomacy has been playing and is expected to play a critical role in China and India's quest for new energy resources. Both China and India have been organising high-level summits with top African leaderships.[12] But the quality and effectiveness of oil diplomacy in making new advances is clearly visible in Myanmar in Southeast Asia – a strategically located country having contiguous borders with both China and India and endowed with significant untapped gas reserves. Gas reserves in Myanmar can satisfy the considerable demand for energy in western provinces of China and the northeastern and eastern states of India. These are landlocked regions in both countries that are relatively less developed, lacking economic prosperity, and it is imperative to address the long-term development concerns of these regions. However, as noticed earlier on other occasions, China's diplomatic overtures in Myanmar have been more successful than India's in lobbying with the host government for securing oil assets. In December 2005, PetroChina successfully overcame competition from Indian energy firms in securing rights for extracting natural gas from Myanmar's most well-endowed gas field owned by Daewoo International of Korea (Dalliwall and Clarke 2008). This enables PetroChina to build a gas pipeline from the Shwe field for supplying gas to its western province of Yunnan. Interestingly, Indian firms OVL and Gas Authority of India Limited (GAIL) have held 30 per cent controlling stakes in the field since 2002.[13] This was therefore an interesting situation where, despite prior ownership of critical gas assets, India faced the prospect of not being able to obtain optimal benefits from such ownership. Failure to match up to more proactive Chinese diplomacy was one of the main reasons behind India finding itself in such a piquant situation. This diplomatic shortcoming has also been visible in India's limited success in pushing an alternative pipeline for transporting gas from Shwe to Kolkata in India's eastern state of West Bengal, passing through Bangladesh. In a similar vein, India's unsuccessful attempt to secure Central Asian gas supplies through the Iran–Pakistan–India pipeline shows its inability to conduct energy diplomacy in a meaningful manner. In contrast, China's energy diplomacy has been more robust and pragmatic, and it has been able to influence the policy decisions of energy-rich countries in its favour. Indeed, it is not a coincidence that China's vetoing of a Security Council resolution against Myanmar in 2007 was followed immediately by the Myanmar government's award of a major exploration contract to a Chinese firm that had been outbid by its Indian counterpart (Zhao 2009).

While both countries realise the opportunity costs involved in competing for natural resource assets in third countries and have begun collaborating on a case-by-case basis as explained earlier, a race for resources and diplomatic machinations for securing these resources are unavoidable on occasions. The domain of the race is expected to expand from oil and gas to coal as Chinese and Indian firms contest for acquiring coal mines in third countries.[14] The inevitable shortfall between rising demand and inadequate supplies is expected to reflect in considerable energy competition in the short run.

Water

The competition on accessing water resources has a different dimension than that for energy. For energy, the competition is apparent in third-country markets and regions as both China and India rush to tap new reserves in those parts of the world where they are available. For water, however, the geographical domain of competition is much closer to home. Both countries are concerned over access to water resources that are shared by them in different proportions. Geography has ensured that the competition over water remains confined to the immediate neighbourhood of both countries, with obvious ramifications for such competition in other parts of the larger neighbourhood.

Several major rivers common to China and India originate from the Tibetan plateau in the Greater Himalayas, which is also popularly referred to as the 'Water Tower of Asia'. The nine largest Asian rivers, including the Yangtze, Yellow River, Mekong, Brahmaputra and Indus, take off from the Tibetan plateau. Rivers arising from the Tibetan plateau are sources of fresh water for around a quarter of the world's population (Zha 2010). Transboundary rivers for China and India flow downstream from the Tibetan plateau through various parts of India to end in the Arabian Sea or the Bay of Bengal. The biggest among these is the Brahmaputra – the world's fourth largest river, with a course of almost 3,000km – originating in the northern Himalayas near Mount Kailash in the Tibetan plateau. One of the world's major transboundary rivers, the Brahmaputra's waters are shared by China, India and Bangladesh. Floods originating from the higher Brahmaputra in Tibet often catch downstream territories by surprise, leading to loss of resources and damage to crops. The Ganges, another major river in India, also has its origins in the Himalayan glaciers, though it is not a transboundary river between China and India. The Indus, Sutlej, Ghaghara and Torsa are some of the other rivers flowing through both China and India (Table 3.2).

The waters of the Brahmaputra have emerged as a serious point of contention between China and India. They reflect tensions that are witnessed

Table 3.2 Transboundary rivers for China and India

Name	*Course in China*	*Course in India*	*Other country*
Indus	Tibetan plateau in Western China in Tibet Autonomous Region	Ladakh district in Jammu and Kashmir	Pakistan
Sutlej	Tibet Autonomous Region	Himachal Pradesh and Punjab	Pakistan
Brahmaputra (also known as Yarlung Tsangpo, Dihang, Jamuna)	Tibet	Arunachal Pradesh, Assam	Bangladesh
Ghaghara	Tibetan plateau	Bihar, Uttar Pradesh and Uttarakhand	Nepal
Torsa	Tibet	West Bengal	Bhutan, Bangladesh

Source: Compiled from www.en.wikipedia.org.

between states in various parts of the world over the sharing of a regional public good like water.[15] India accounts for 58 per cent of the Brahmaputra basin while China accounts for 20 per cent (Vignesh 2010). India's concerns emanate from the fact that the origin and higher course of the river lies outside its territorial boundaries. As a result, disruptions in upstream water volume, which are beyond its scope of control and intervention, can have major consequences for lower downstream segments. Due to lack of a proper mechanism for sharing hydrological data, India has often suffered the adverse consequences of floods. The situation is much better now following an agreement between the two countries in 2002 over water level, discharge and rainfall (Hodum 2007). Bigger concerns for India, however, relate to China's plans to construct a dam across the Brahmaputra. China's proposed construction of a 510 MW hydro power plant on the Brahmaputra at Zangmu in Tibet (expected to be followed by a few more, similar plants) has caused considerable anguish in India (Bagchi 2009). India fears that the construction will be the beginning of a grand plan by China to divert more water from the Brahmaputra to its own territories. China's assurances that the project does not intend to divert and store water and will not affect downstream flows have failed to assuage India's worries. As a lower riparian state for the Brahmaputra, displacement of local populations and disruptions in water flows following potential interventions upstream are expected to remain anxieties for India and sources of tension between the two countries.

The larger competition over accessing resources in the 'Water Tower of Asia' can become intense on account of two specific constraints being faced by both China and India. As the world's two largest and most populous countries situated in the Himalayan river basin, they are facing growing demand–supply imbalances in freshwater sources. The imbalances are inevitable outcomes of rapid growth and structural changes in their respective economies, which have witnessed not only large-scale industrial expansion but also vast modernisation of farming techniques that are often water-intensive. Research on projected water requirements indicates that over the period 2005–30, annual water demand in China and India will increase by 61 per cent and 58 per cent respectively (WRG 2009). The sources of demand will vary between the two countries, with 56.4 per cent of the incremental demand in China coming from industry as against a much smaller 19.0 per cent incremental industrial demand from India. Agriculture is projected to contribute the maximum incremental water demand – 72.2 per cent – in India, while in China it is expected to account for 33.5 per cent.[16] The remaining increase in demand is on account of higher municipal and domestic consumption requirements. In India, irrigation requirements in agriculture are expected to be the prime mover of water demand.[17] This has fairly serious implications for supply and availability of groundwater reserves. The large increases in demand in both countries are accompanied by projections of water availability experiencing sharp declines. Per capita water availabilities are forecast to reduce from 2,150 at present to 1,860 by the year 2030 for China and from 1,730 to 1,240 over the same period for India (SFG 2010). While for China the reduction implies a decline of 13.5 per cent in availability of water for each individual, for India the reduction is a more worrying 28.4 per cent. The prospects, though, are not much brighter for China, which, despite having a fifth of the world's population has only a quarter of the average global per capita water supply (Zha 2010).

Both countries suffer from irrigation deficiencies that can be traced not only to inadequate deployment of resources in irrigation, but also to scant attention to conservation. Bardhan (2010) points out that public policy focus in both countries is steadily shifting towards better management and conservation of water resources as opposed to constructing large dams and irrigation projects. While that is a welcome tendency at the macro-level, what is somewhat worrying is the growing competition among farmers in both countries for access to groundwater resources. Tube wells, particularly in northern China, are now mostly privately owned. In India, too, there is a growing tendency towards individual well ownership due to the growth of a lucrative water market (Villholth 2009). For both countries, it is important to put in place regulatory mechanisms for limiting user rights to ensure that private ownership of water resources does not lead to over-extraction (Bardhan 2010),[18] particularly in river basins fed by water from Himalayan glaciers, which are the main bone of contention between the two countries.

The main reason behind the reductions in per capita availability of water is lower water flows in rivers originating from the Himalayan glaciers, which are expected to deplete on account of global warming over a period of time. While the depletion will occur over several decades, some impact is expected to be felt by the middle of the current century, with the Yellow River in China and the Ganges in India being among the worst affected (SFG 2010). In addition to depletion in natural volume of water, availability is also expected to decline on account of pollution, contamination and inefficient water management in both countries. Matters are not going to be helped by extensive deforestation leading to the drying up of lakes and water bodies. Scarcity of water has adverse implications for agricultural production, thereby affecting prospects for livelihoods. The difficulties are relatively greater for India, as its farming sector continues to be the largest provider of livelihoods, notwithstanding a steadily shrinking share in national output.

The demand–supply imbalance will keep both countries vigilant regarding possibilities for accessing new water supplies as well as preserving existing ones. The upper riparian–lower riparian contestations between China and India are similar to identical frictions between India and Pakistan over the waters of the Indus, of course with roles reversed. Pakistan has expressed concerns over India's efforts to build dams in Jammu and Kashmir, which it feels will reduce water supply to Pakistan.[19] For China, the imperatives are clear: accessing larger water resources, particularly for its arid north and northwestern regions, which have been traditionally economically backward and have been identified for a vigorous industrial push to ameliorate regional imbalance. Even without industrial compulsions, water scarcity in these regions is a serious issue given that almost half of China's population lives in northern areas, which also grow several food crops (e.g. wheat and vegetables) and yet have just a quarter of the per capita water availability of the south (Jiang 2011). China's plans to transfer water from the south to the north of the country have been the subject of intense debate within the country itself (Zha 2010). Whether China's plans to achieve greater self-sufficiency in water will aggravate existing tensions with India will be revealed only over time. But both should try to take note of mutual economic compulsions and probably forge a common front for addressing the problem, rather than effecting overarching individual solutions which might produce considerable negative externalities.

Access to new markets

As the world's largest and fastest-growing economies, China and India have been working hard on building external economic relations, with particular emphasis on trade and investment linkages. Despite having large domestic economies with strong contributions from domestic consumption and investment to GDP growth, trade has been significant for overall economic progress, particularly for China, which is one of the largest economies in world trade. With an average trade–GDP ratio of 58.6 per cent during 2007–9, China was ranked first and second respectively in global merchandise exports and imports in 2009, and was also ranked fifth and fourth respectively in world exports and imports of commercial services in the same year (WTO 2010). India, despite being far behind China in terms of significance in global trade, has nonetheless come a long way from being an inward-looking, import-substituting economy to notch up an average trade–GDP ratio of 46.2 per cent during 2007–9. India ranked twenty-first and fourteenth in world merchandise exports and imports respectively in 2009 and was ranked twelfth in export and import of commercial services in the same year (WTO 2010).[20]

Both China and India realise the importance of expanding trade by accessing new markets. The realisation has been driven primarily by the lack of progress at the WTO and the stalemate over the Doha Development Agenda (DDA; China's and India's posturings on the DDA at different points in time during the last decade is discussed at length in Chapter 5). But unfulfilled expectations from the multilateral trade framework and limited progress in securing additional access in developed country markets have encouraged both to pursue bilateral and regional trade agreements vigorously. In the process, both have run into a mutually competitive process of negotiating trade and economic agreement pacts with the same partners in different parts of the world.

India and China have a fairly long history of participating in regional trade agreements, as is evident from both figuring in the Asia-Pacific Trade Agreement (APTA), which was the erstwhile Bangkok Agreement. Though the APTA is political and diplomatically symbolic rather than being a sweeping economic agreement, it is the only agreement linking both South and East Asia, and involving both China and India. Beyond the APTA that represents a larger Asia-Pacific trade architecture in scale and scope, India has shown a relatively greater zeal in pushing and striking trade deals. India's efforts in this respect have focused on countries in Africa, Latin America, the Middle East, Southeast Asia, South Asia and East Asia. China's trade negotiations have been mostly in Southeast, South and East Asia with sporadic efforts in Latin America and Europe. India's greater activity in pursuing trade deals (or, conversely, China's relatively less vigour in pushing bilateral trade talks) is probably on account of India's rather recent, maybe six- or seven-year-old realisation that it needs to step up trade for accelerating growth, and that bilateral trade pacts are best options for accessing new markets. This is in contrast to China's more selective choice of markets for trade deals given its already substantive presence in world trade and the major markets of the world. The current FTA (free trade agreement) engagements of both countries, however, show a fairly uniform choice of partners geographically (Table 3.3).

As Table 3.3 indicates, Asia has been a key area of activity for both countries in negotiating trade deals. Geographical proximity has determined a part of these negotiations, as is evident from China's trade pacts with Hong Kong, Macao and Taiwan, as well as India's initiatives with South Asian and Middle Eastern countries. Southeast Asia has been a common foray for both countries, and not without reason: Southeast Asia or the Association of Southeast Asian Nations (ASEAN) is a significant economic zone for both. The region has been the economic hub of Asia and a key part of the Asian economic success saga comprising both mature high-income economies such as Singapore, robust middle-income and export-oriented economies like Indonesia, Malaysia, the Philippines, Thailand and Vietnam, and low-income but promising economies with captive unexploited resources such as Cambodia and Laos. The region is also a conduit for the heavy shipping traffic through the Strait of Malacca. Both

Table 3.3 Regional and bilateral trade agreements by India and China

India		
Region/country	*Agreements concluded*	*Agreements being negotiated/studied*
1 Asia-Pacific	APTA	Australia, New Zealand
2 Southeast Asia	ASEAN (goods), Singapore, Malaysia, Thailand	Indonesia, Vietnam
3 South Asia	South Asian Free Trade Agreement (SAFTA), Afghanistan, Bhutan, Nepal	Bangladesh, Maldives
4 East Asia	Korea, Japan	Japan, China, Mongolia
5 Middle East		Gulf Cooperation Council (GCC) countries
6 Africa	South African Customs Union (SACU)	Mauritius
7 Latin America	MERCOSUR, Chile	
8 Europe	Finland	European Union (EU)
China		
1 Asia-Pacific	APTA, New Zealand	Australia
2 Southeast Asia	ASEAN (goods and services), Singapore	
3 East Asia	Hong Kong, Macao, Taiwan	Korea, Japan
4 South Asia	Pakistan	India
5 Middle East		GCC
6 Africa		SACU
7 Latin America	Chile, Peru, Costa Rica	
8 Europe		Iceland, Norway, Switzerland

Source: Regional Trade Agreement (RTA) Database, WTO; Department of Commerce, Ministry of Commerce and Industry, India; China FTA Network, Ministry of Commerce, People's Republic of China (PRC); Jiangyu (2010).

Note
The agreements listed as being negotiated or studied are at various stages of discussion, ranging from those at a fairly mature stage to those where only feasibility studies have taken place, or where MOUs have been signed on specific trade aspects.

China and India are conscious of the economic significance of ASEAN and have been trying to engage it as a grouping as well as bilaterally with individual members. Both countries have had formal trade agreements with Singapore (Table 3.3) and in addition India has bilateral pacts with Malaysia and Thailand and is in the advanced stages of negotiating an FTA with Indonesia. In addition, both have signed trade agreements with ASEAN. China's agreement with ASEAN covers both goods and services while India's, up to now, covers only goods; negotiations are taking place on expanding the agreement to include services. The India–ASEAN goods agreement was announced on 19 August 2010, while the China–ASEAN goods pact was announced on 21 September 2005 and the services agreement was formalised on 26 June 2008.

India and China's aggressive pursuit of regional agreements, particularly in the context of such deals in Asia, has been argued to have been driven by the 'domino effect' or 'fear of exclusion' (Jiangyu 2010).[21] Neither China, nor India, is willing to be cramped for market space in an Asian region that is expected to be the main economic hub in the world in the years to come. As a result, they are eager to formalise relationships with partners in the region as fast as possible. However, the rush for these arrangements is not always accompanied by careful assessment of economic gains. Empirical research on industry-specific comparative advantages between ASEAN and China, and ASEAN and India, reveal that gains from specialisation might be limited on several occasions. Okamoto (2010) finds little possibility of inter-industry specialisations between Thailand and the Philippines and China and India, notwithstanding greater economic cooperation, due to similarity of trade structures between the countries. For India in particular, the FTA with ASEAN might not produce significant market access gains at the outset; the degree of reduction in Indian tariffs will be much more than that for their ASEAN counterparts, as at the time of commencement of the FTA, ASEAN tariffs were at a much lower base than India's (Palit 2009). For China, one of the main motivations for striking a trade deal with ASEAN was obtaining the market economy status, which it has been denied at the WTO until the middle of the current decade.[22] Indeed, China actually granted relatively more preferential market access to ASEAN exports in the FTA than it obtained for its own exports in ASEAN markets, primarily in view of the long-term integration benefits it was considering.[23]

Till now, in the race for market access in ASEAN and East Asia, China has been ahead of India as far as securing meaningful bilateral agreements is concerned. India's negotiations have been fraught with delays. Both China and India signed the framework agreements on comprehensive economic cooperation within a year of each other – November 2002 and October 2003 respectively. However, while the China–ASEAN FTA was formalised in September 2005, the India–ASEAN deal could be settled only in August 2009. The delay has caused India loss of potential economic space in Southeast Asian markets, where it was already trailing China, thanks to the latter's long and deep industrial and trade linkages with the region. Nonetheless, for India, closer engagement with the new ASEAN members – Cambodia, Laos, Myanmar and Vietnam (CLMV) – through a homogeneous FTA encompassing progressive reduction in barriers to market access underlines secured entry into ASEAN markets (Zhao 2007). On the other hand, China's trade talks have also occasionally run into delays, a notable example being those with Australia, which began in May 2005 but are yet to be concluded (Gao 2009). For both countries, however, forging FTAs with Asian partners that have large home markets or are gateways into bigger regional economic segments appears to have been a major imperative. This imperative will get stronger if multilateral trade talks fail to break the deadlock.

Aid and development assistance

A couple of decades ago, it would have been rather far-fetched to imagine that China and India would emerge as major donors of development assistance. As the world's largest developing countries they are expected to be recipients of development assistance, not donors. Furthermore, barring Japan and South Korea,[24] aid and development assistance has traditionally been associated with the advanced economies of the West, primarily the Organisation of Economic Development (OECD) countries. Emerging Asian economies are hardly expected to figure in the league of rich OECD nations and contribute to the global pool of overseas development assistance (ODA).

However incredible it might appear, China and India have indeed become major sources of assistance for low-income developing countries. China, though, is far ahead of India in the sheer scale of its aid programme. China is estimated to have spent around US$27.5 billion in 2006 and US$25 billion in 2007 in foreign assistance, and the Chinese government has supported projects in Africa, Latin America and Southeast Asia (Lum *et al.* 2009). This was, indeed, more than the US$24 billion foreign operations budget of the US in FY2008 (Kilby 2010). China has expanded its aid activities at a rapid pace during the last decade, from less than US$1 billion in 2002 to match the US and other top OECD donors (Moxley 2010). India's foreign aid and development assistance has, until now, been much less. Its total aid and assistance including the loans and guarantees extended by the Exim Bank of India were around US$13.7 billion in FY2008.[25]

There is a methodological issue in comparing the nominal sizes of Chinese and Indian development assistance with that of other major donors, particularly the OECD countries. This is due to the definition of ODA employed by OECD, which does not capture the full scope of Chinese and Indian aid programmes. Neither country is a member of the Development Assistance Committee (DAC) of the OECD and, as a result, neither follows the OECD practices of defining and documenting aid and development assistance.

The OECD defines ODA as financial flows from official agencies in donor countries to developing economies with a primary anti-poverty, or at least development, focus. The flows are usually concessional with at least 25 per cent being grants.[26] Interpreted in this sense, the Chinese aid and development assistance is unlikely to qualify as typical ODA. A considerable part of Chinese aid flows to developing countries in Africa, Latin America and Asia is not specifically focused on eradicating poverty, nor is this aid in the form of humanitarian and debt relief. Most Chinese aid flows are project-based, focusing on the creation of infrastructure or the extraction of natural resources. They often involve participation of Chinese state-owned enterprises (SOEs) in the execution of the projects. These activities obviously do not qualify as ODA according to the OECD nomenclature. Among major OECD donors, it is only Japanese aid, with its emphasis on infrastructure and functional links with donor economy interests, that comes close to the Chinese aid programme (Lum *et al.* 2009). Furthermore, neither China nor India is fussy about conditionalities in aid, unlike OECD donors, which insist on recipient countries satisfying several political and civil conditions.

As Table 3.4 indicates, the recipients of Chinese and Indian development assistance are largely common, with both countries extending assistance to not only least developed countries but also low- and middle-income countries in different parts of the world. In this respect, there is bound to be an element of competition between China and India as far as reaching out to the same group of developing countries is concerned. Up to now, both have tried sticking to their respective strengths in extending development assistance. China has relied on the large capacities of its SOEs for deploying funds in various infrastructure projects in developing countries, including Angola, Congo, Ethiopia, Gabon, Sudan, Niger, Nigeria and Zambia in Africa; Brazil, Chile, Columbia and Venezuela in Latin America; Myanmar, Thailand and Vietnam in Southeast Asia; and Afghanistan and Pakistan in South Asia.[27] These investment-based projects are in addition to grants and concessional loans that China has extended to some of these countries and the others mentioned in Table 3.4 at different points in time. On account of larger investible surplus and the ability to implement projects efficiently, infrastructure projects owned and implemented by Chinese firms in low-income countries have emerged as a key feature of China's development assistance programmes. India, however, has been following a different policy. In terms of capacity to fund projects in other countries, it has limitations compared to China, just as it has in the ability to execute such projects. Unlike China's, most of India's outbound investments have been by private Indian firms without directives from state agencies. Nonetheless, the scale of China's state policy-induced investments is much larger. India has followed a more low-profile approach in this respect by relying more on extending credit lines to developing countries and capacity-building through technical and economic cooperation.

India's credit lines have been among its most popular measures for connecting to developing countries. These lines are extended by the Government of India through the Exim Bank of India. Meant for heavily indebted poor countries (HIPC), low-income and least developed countries (LDCs) as well as middle-income countries,[28] the credit lines imply concessional loans for importing goods and services from India as well as exporting project goods from India. The credit lines include grants varying from 36 per cent to 54 per cent of their total values depending upon income status (middle, low, HIPC) of

Table 3.4 Beneficiaries of Chinese and Indian development assistance

	China	*India*
Africa	Angola, Congo, Gabon, Ethiopia, Equatorial Guinea, Mozambique, Kenya, Liberia, Madagascar, Niger, Nigeria, Rwanda, Sierra Leone, Sudan, Uganda, Zambia	Angola, Cameroon, Chad, Congo, Ethiopia, Gambia, Ghana, Kenya, Lesotho, Madagascar, Mali, Mauritius, Mozambique, Niger, Rwanda, Seychelles, Sierra Leone, Sudan, Suriname, Tanzania, Zambia
Latin America and the Caribbean	Bolivia, Brazil, Chile, Columbia, Costa Rica, Cuba, Grenada, Peru, Venezuela, Uruguay	Columbia, Ecuador, Guyana, Honduras, Jamaica, Peru, Venezuela
Southeast Asia	Indonesia, Myanmar, Cambodia, Laos, Philippines, Thailand, Vietnam	Cambodia, Myanmar, Laos, Vietnam
South Asia	Afghanistan, Bangladesh, Nepal, Pakistan, Sri Lanka	Afghanistan, Bangladesh, Bhutan, Nepal, Pakistan, Sri Lanka

Source: Lum *et al.* (2009); Chanana (2009); Exim Bank of India.

Note
The above list of countries is not entirely exhaustive.

the recipients. Offered usually on a project-specific basis, the credit lines ensure that borrowers source around three-quarters of the project's goods and services pertaining to the contracts covered by the loans (Exim Bank of India 2009a, p. 3). A key advantage of these credit lines for both importers and exporters is a deferred credit facility. India currently has 132 operational credit lines in different parts of the world aggregating to around US$5.9 billion of concessional finance.[29] Several of these are operating in countries where Chinese firms have invested and are implementing projects, such as in Angola, Ethiopia, Niger, Sudan (Africa); Columbia, Venezuela (Latin America); Myanmar, Vietnam (Southeast Asia); Nepal, Sri Lanka (South Asia). In several instances, the common emphasis on infrastructure-building is visible though the sectors are different. In Myanmar, for example, Chinese investments are visible in nickel ore mining and oil and gas pipelines, while the Exim Bank of India's credit lines are for railway infrastructure upgrading, urban transport linkages and refineries (Exim Bank of India 2009b and Lum *et al.* 2009). Similarly, Sri Lanka has benefited from the emphasis of both countries on infrastructure, with Chinese firms investing in sea port facilities in Sri Lanka and India extending credit lines for new rail linkages. In more distant Africa, while Angola has Chinese investments in housing and related infrastructure, India's credit lines support textile projects and sugar plants (ibid.).

Another aspect of India's development assistance – qualitatively different from China's – is its efforts to extend technical and economic cooperation. While the credit lines are designed to address project-based requirements of developing countries with the idea that such requirements also provide markets for Indian exports, the Indian Technical and Economic Cooperation (ITEC) programme focuses primarily on building capacity through training. The programme, which is now almost five decades old, has historically helped India in connecting to large developing country groupings such as the G77. African countries have been a major focus under the corollary of the programme – the Special Commonwealth African Assistance Programme (SCAAP). With a coverage of 158 countries, the programme has been India's flagship mode of becoming a stakeholder in the development ambitions of low-income countries.[30] Available estimates indicate that during the last five decades when the ITEC has been in operation, around US$1 billion has been transferred by India to other developing countries through the programme, in the form of training, project aid, technical assistance, humanitarian assistance and study tours (Kragelund 2010). One of the most attractive components of the programme has been the capacity-building opportunities it offers in areas where expertise is conspicuously limited in almost all parts of the developing world. These include information and communication technology (ICT), entrepreneurship, linguistics, rural development, mining, renewable energy and allied areas (Verman 2010).

Foreign aid and development assistance have traditionally been employed by countries for obtaining strategic gains, and China and India are no exception. As both countries assume greater roles in international affairs, it is imperative for them to build close alliances with the developing world. As the largest developing countries themselves, China and India realise the importance of remaining connected with the developing world for strategic and economic benefits. Aid is critical in generating and sustaining this strategic leverage. Both countries have been employing aid accordingly. The domain of employment for both is also largely common. India's aid activities, which have been limited compared to China's until now, and mostly confined to capacity-building, have slowly begun assuming larger proportions particularly in Africa and South Asia, where India aims to match the Chinese quest for new markets and energy resources (Ramachandran 2010).[31] South Asia is particularly a region where economic underdevelopment and geo-strategic motivations have encouraged first China and then India to sharply ramp up development assistance (P.S. Palit 2010). As India's growth moves on to a higher trajectory, it might be tempted to expand the size of its aid programme to draw closer to China's. That would, however, accelerate a race, which is already on between the two countries, to garner strategic dividends from different parts of the world.

Bilateral trade friction

Trade in modern times has been characterised by two opposite trends. The introduction of a rule-based multilateral trade system managed by the WTO since the mid-1990s has seen tariffs imposed by countries on other country exports coming down progressively. This has happened because of the WTO guidelines urging members to extend Most Favoured Nation (MFN) treatment to each other and encouraging greater access for products in each other's markets. At the same time, there has been a rising tendency on the part of members to use protection instruments available within the WTO, such as anti-dumping duties, countervailing duties and other safeguarding measures. What is particularly noteworthy is the increasing tendency on the part of emerging market and developing countries to impose these measures on other developing country exports. Bown (2010b) draws attention to this growing 'South South' phenomenon in the world of anti-dumping duties, where China has been at the receiving end on most occasions with 2.6 per cent of its products subject to anti-dumping duties in 2009. On the other hand, among developing countries, India is found to be the most frequent user of restrictive market access policies. At the end of 2009, almost 3.0 per cent of India's imports (in value terms) were subject to various restrictive measures (Bown 2010b).

The above dynamics highlight contrasting features about China and India in the global club of traders. China entered the WTO after more than a decade of negotiations. Its entry was accompanied by extensive commitments for providing market access and led to substantive reductions in tariffs. While the Chinese domestic market became more accessible to exports as a result, several countries, particularly developing economies, were alarmed at the prospect of cheap Chinese exports flooding their markets. This was because, as a member of WTO, China had to be awarded MFN treatment. However, there was a discriminatory measure acting against China in the form of China-specific safeguards to which member countries could resort in the event of a surge in Chinese imports. Furthermore, the WTO's refusal to grant full market economy status to China makes it an easy target for anti-dumping actions and duties (more on China and the WTO in Chapter 5). Several developing economies have used these provisions extensively.

India, on the other hand, has always adopted a defensive posture towards granting greater market access on the grounds that cheap imports would affect the livelihoods of domestic producers of similar products. As the world's largest developing countries in the world trade system, China and India are remarkably distinct in their trade interests. As the world's largest exporter of manufactured products, China has been keen (though maybe not always as keen as its posturing might suggest) to obtain greater access to the domestic markets of WTO members. India, up to now, has remained a relatively smaller player in global trade though its role has become larger over the years, particularly in the trade of commercial services. Since exports have not been as major a driver of growth for India as for China, and also because of the political compulsions of protecting industries and producers used to operating in inward-looking circumstances, India has been keen to use the restrictive polices permitted by the WTO (Mattoo and Subramanian 2003) and has never actually been a strong advocate of faster trade liberalisation (Jianfu 2010). The implications of contrasting trade interests on the part of the two Asian giants contain the potential for friction, which has periodically surfaced in an otherwise robust domain of bilateral trade.

India, like many other emerging markets, has been wary of cheap Chinese imports affecting the competitiveness of its domestic producers. It has been regularly using the WTO's safeguard measures for protecting the domestic industry's commercial interests. China has been one of the main targets of anti-dumping actions initiated by India. From 2002, with China's entry in the WTO, until the end of 2010, India has initiated 96 anti-dumping actions against China. These 96 actions between them cover almost 200 import tariff lines.[32] In contrast, China has initiated only three, which clearly indicates the stark difference in the threat perception of the two countries with respect to imports from each other (Bown 2010).[33] Indeed, not only was China the largest target of anti-dumping investigations during this period, actions initiated against China by India were far more than those it raised against other major trade partners such as South Korea (28), European Union (27), the United States (18) and Japan (13). In addition to anti-dumping actions, India also employed China-specific safeguards on six occasions during the period 2002–9, with five of these being used during 2009 itself (Bown 2010c).

A large variety of Chinese exports have attracted anti-dumping actions from India. The following paragraphs attempt to provide a broad idea of these exports. The exports have been sub-divided into broad product categories with examples of specific tariff lines in different categories. Owing to a lack of complete information on disaggregated tariff lines at the lowest level of commodity classification, the illustration should not be taken as entirely exhaustive. The report has been prepared on the basis of anti-dumping actions reported in Bown

(2010b) and matching the corresponding tariff lines with the Indian Trade Classification (Harmonised System) of tariff lines prepared by the Directorate General of Commercial Intelligence and Statistics (DGCI&S), Ministry of Commerce and Industry, Government of India. The period covered is 2002–10.

1 *Organic chemicals* such as antibiotics (e.g. penicillin, rifampicin and its salts); vitamins (e.g. vitamin A, vitamin E, vitamin B12 and its derivatives); acids, alcohols and their derivatives (e.g. citric acid, pentaerythritol, sodium formaldehyde); heterocyclic, nitrogen function, diazo (or azoxy), carboxyamide-function, amine-function, organo-sulphur, sulphonamides, organo-inorganic and other organic compounds (e.g. morpholine, paranitroaniline, azodicarbonamide, coumarin, cefadroxil and its salts, diclofenac sodium, saccharine and its salts); cyclic hydrocarbons, phenols (e.g. cresols and their salts), ethers, polycarboxyclic acids (e.g. maleic anhydride), nucleic acids and their salts, sulphonamides, esters or inorganic acids of non-metals (e.g. phosphorus-based chemical compounds and salts, including parathion, phosphorothioic acid, diethyl and dimethyl sulphate).
2 *Inorganic and other chemicals* (e.g. carbon black, phosphorus-based chemicals, chlorides and chloride oxides, sulphates, polyphosphates, caustic soda, tetraborate (refined borax), titanium oxide, phosphoric acid, reaction initiators, pickling preparations, anti-knock preparations, pesticides).
3 *Photographic/cinematographic products* (e.g. photographic plates and film).
4 *Tanning or dyeing extracts* (e.g. pigments based on titanium dioxide).
5 *Plastic and plastic articles* (e.g. floor and wall/ceiling coverings, self-adhesive plates and sheets, polyethylene and PVC plates, sheets, films and strips, polypropylene articles for stationery and other purposes, polyvinyl chloride resins, cellulose and its derivatives, polyethers, unsaturated polyesters).
6 *Rubber and rubber products* (e.g. pneumatic bus and radial tyres (new and used), tyre flaps, inner tubes, rubber accelerators, plasticisers, seamless tubes and pipes).
7 *Wood, paper and ceramic products* (e.g. wooden fibre boards, glazed paper, glazed ceramic tiles.
8 *Textile and textile products* (e.g. raw silk, single and multiple viscose rayon yarn of different sizes, woven silk fabric, synthetic filament yarn, woven fabrics of flax).
9 *Iron and steel* (e.g. stainless steel products (including hot rolled and cold rolled flat products made of different alloys), cast iron pipes).
10 *Glass and aluminium products* (e.g. glassware used for table/kitchen/toilet, glass fibre and articles, aluminium plates).
11 *Machinery and mechanical appliances* (e.g. ball bearings, compressors, rolls for rolling mills, lithographic plates for printing, pumps for liquids, injection-moulding machines, sewing machines and sewing machine needles, tyre curing presses, plastic processing machinery, power-steering gear system, circular weaving machines).

12 *Electric machinery and equipment* (e.g. fluorescent lamps, drafting tables, micrometers, lamp parts, colour television picture tubes, prepared unrecorded media for sound or other recording purposes such as DVDs, compact discs and blank master discs, telephone apparatus, transmission equipment).
13 *Vehicle parts and accessories* (e.g. road wheels and parts).
14 *Optical, photographic and measuring instruments* (e.g. spectacle lenses).

As the above illustration indicates, practically all varieties of manufactured products exported by China to India have been subjected to anti-dumping actions. China's exports to India are discussed at length in Chapter 4. Electrical machinery and equipment, machinery and mechanical appliances, organic chemicals, inorganic chemicals, optical and photographic instruments, iron and steel, textiles (including silk) and plastic are India's major imports from China. Tariff lines from all these categories have been subject to anti-dumping actions. Chemicals, though, appear to have been subjected to more anti-dumping actions than other products, with around 30 per cent of total actions including different organic and inorganic chemicals. Machinery and appliances, iron and steel, plastics and rubber have been the other major product categories facing anti-dumping procedures. The petitioners demanding anti-dumping action include large and prominent industrial entities from India such as Reliance Industries, Larsen & Toubro, Apollo Tyres, Ceat, Jindal Stainless, Moserbaer, Osram, Aurobindo Pharma, Wockhardt, Nicholas Piramal, Kanoria Chemicals, Nirlon, Tata Iron and Steel Company, Eveready Industries, Grasim, DCM Sriram, Osram India and Wellspun Syntex. These firms have occasionally been joined by relatively small firms from the respective industries. On several occasions, the petitioners have been supported by industry associations that include the National Organic Chemical Industries Association, Optical Disc Manufacturers Association, Association of Synthetic Fibre Industries, Association of Man-made Fibre Industry of India, Automotive Tyre Manufacturers Association, Central Silk Board, Indian Plastic Ophthalmic Lenses Association, Sulphur Black Manufacturers Association, All India Fibre Board Manufacturers Association and Alkali Manufacturers Association of India.

Chinese products have been targets of anti-dumping actions in almost all major developed and emerging markets of the world. In that respect, there is little surprise in the flurry of anti-dumping actions on Chinese products by India. This, though, should not imply that Indian products do not face market access barriers in the Chinese market. Despite having much lower tariffs following extensive market access commitments given during accession to the WTO, China has rules and standards that hinder market access for international exporters on occasions when they compete with domestic industry. Indian exports have also faced these restrictions. One of the reasons behind the growing imbalance in China–India trade is the restrictions that several Indian exports face in obtaining deeper access to the Chinese market. While anti-dumping duties have been India's way of restricting access to Chinese exports, Indian exports face restrictions on market access from non-tariff barriers (NTBs) in China.[34] Table 3.5 provides some details on the nature of NTBs faced by Indian exports in the

Table 3.5 Barriers to Indian exports in the Chinese market

Product/item	*Nature of non-tariff barrier (NTB)*
1 Fish	Difficulties in complying with existing technical standards, food safety requirements and also procedures for approvals.
2 Vegetables	Phyto-sanitary measures and certification procedures.
3 Tobacco (FCV and Burley – both unstemmed and stemmed)	Environmental risk analysis and quarantine permission requirements.
4 Pharmaceuticals	Procedures for product and corporate registrations, delays in obtaining import drug licences, customs procedures, re-inspection, packaging regulations and banking procedures for remittance. Kuhrt (2009) points out issues of import drug licences are preceded by quality testing at the State Food and Drug Administration (SFDA), leading to long delays.
5 Electrical insulators	Export subsidy and low energy costs.
6 Indian films	Limiting quotas on number.
7 Wind/non-conventional energy	Local content requirement and non-recognition of international Intellectual Property Rights (IPR) regime.

Sources: (1) 'Countrywise database of NTMs/NTBs', Department of Commerce, Ministry of Commerce and Industry, Government of India; http://commerce.nic.in/trade/NTB_countrywise.pdf; (2) 'Non-tariff barriers hinder pharma trade with China', *Business Standard*, 28 January 2007, New Delhi; www.business-standard.com/india/news/%60non-tariff-barriers-hinder-pharma-tradechina%60/272830/ (accessed on 11 March 2011); (3) 'NTBs obstruct correction in trade imbalance with China', *The Financial Express*, 18 January 2010; www.ficci.com/ficci-in-news-page.asp?nid=3548 (accessed on 11 March 2011); (4) 'Dissatisfied with China on Indian exports, govt issues strong demarche', http://ieport.blogspot.com/2010/01/dissatisfied-with-china-on-indian.html (accessed on 11 March 2011).

Chinese market in terms of safeguards, certification, environmental, subsidy and other NTBs.

India's concerns about the NTBs facing its exports in the Chinese market led to it issuing a *demarche*, or diplomatic warning, to China on the matter in January 2010 (Nayyar 2011). Issued on the occasion of the Indian Commerce Minister's visit to China and the eighth bilateral meeting of the Joint Economic Group, this rather unusual step reflects India's mounting concerns over the trade imbalance and persistent complaints from its domestic producers about lack of sufficient market access. Other than addressing the NTBs mentioned in Table 3.5 for facilitating exports, India's concerns also relate to China's restrictions over the import of Basmati rice and bovine meat – two of India's major exports to other global markets. Delay in concluding negotiations on phyto-sanitary measures continues to obstruct export prospects of fruits and vegetables. Power plant equipment exports from India have been facing both tariff and non-tariff restrictions, while met-coke is encountering export duties. Another industry, where India is particularly keen on getting a foothold in the Chinese market is landing rights and up-linking facilities for Indian television channels. With state-owned enterprises (SOEs) the biggest buyers in China's domestic market, India is also keen on the SOEs securing more high value-added exports from India.

Both countries realise that one-sided trade can create problems of sustainability in the longer term and are keen on addressing the imbalance. The issue has been resonated in bilateral official pronouncements issued during the Indian Commerce Minister's visit to China in January 2010 and Premier Wen Jiabao's visit to India in December 2010.[35] Other than emphasising the importance of moving towards a balanced trade relationship, the joint statements also took note of India's specific concerns over the different NTBs and export restrictions and promised to 'appropriately handle economic and trade frictions and differences and jointly oppose protectionism in all forms'.[36] While these are welcome steps and are expected to yield results over the medium term, domestic distortions in both markets will continue to create grounds for restricting market access and resultant trade friction. Both countries are keen on protecting specific industries in their economies by employing different instruments. This is reflected not only in the bilateral economic sphere, but also in their trade relationships with other partners. India is expected to take recourse to WTO safeguards for acting against China as long as its domestic industry is threatened by cheap Chinese exports and until it can, like other WTO members, exploit China's lack of market economy status by imposing unilateral safeguards and dumping actions. China, on the other hand, is yet to fully move out of a system where its indigenous enterprises enjoy certain competitive advantages in the domestic market over foreign products, institutionalised by subsidies and fiscal incentives, greater procurement support and safeguards and certification barriers imposed on exports. The distortions reflect the fact that, despite economic liberalisation and figuring in the multilateral trade framework, China and India continue to harbour strong protective tendencies, which are distinct between the two countries. Continuation of these tendencies will provoke trade friction and limitation of market access for each other's products.

4 Trade

Engine of bilateral collaboration

During his visit to India in January 2002 – the first by a Chinese Premier in the new millennium – Zhu Rongji expressed the hope that bilateral trade, which was at US$3 billion then, would grow to US$10 billion in near future (Cherian 2002). When Premier Wen Jiabao came to India in April 2005, the two countries aimed to take bilateral trade to US$20 billion by 2008. The target was upgraded to US$40 billion to be achieved by 2010 during President Hu Jintao's visit to India in November 2006. The latest target set during Premier Wen's second visit to India in December 2010 aims bilateral trade to reach US$100 billion by 2015.[1]

The frequent upgrading of targets on bilateral trade indicates the rapidity with which such trade has been growing. The growth has been fast to the extent that it has caught even official agencies by surprise. The last five or six years particularly have seen bilateral trade achieving its target before the deadline. Trade crossed US$20 billion in 2006–7 when it was supposed to do so by 2008. It went beyond US$40 billion in 2008–9 when the target date for doing so was 2010. The current expectations are that bilateral trade will cross US$100 billion before its targeted deadline of 2015. Indeed, since trade statistics in the public domain are available only for bilateral merchandise trade, and data on bilateral trade in services is not available, the actual size of goods and services trade between the two countries is probably larger than what statistics show. In that case, the US$100 billion level might be reached even sooner.

Fast growth in bilateral trade, however remarkable, has raised questions about its structure, composition and sustainability. These questions range from whether the trade is imbalanced, and dominated by low-value primary items, to whether it is sustainable in future in its present form. Most of these are India's concerns. Since trade is expected to be the fundamental form of economic engagement between the world's two largest and fastest-growing economies in future, it is important to analyse the nuances of the bilateral trade relationship. This chapter aims to do so from an Indian perspective. It studies the trends in bilateral trade over the last decade and examines India's import and export baskets, from and to China, for identifying the specific factors determining the nature and compositions of the baskets. Thereafter it proceeds to analyse the feasibility of a bilateral trade pact between the two countries, from economic and strategic perspectives.

Trends in bilateral trade

At the beginning of the century, bilateral trade between China and India was paltry and nowhere near the level it reached by the end of the decade. Merchandise trade was just around US$2.3 billion in 2000–1 (Table 4.1). As a proportion of India's total trade, trade with China was a little more than 2 per cent. Within a decade, the dimensions of bilateral trade changed dramatically, with India's trade with China increasing to US$42.4 billion in 2009–10 and the share of such trade in India's total trade increasing to more than 9 per cent. This was a remarkable increase that made China India's second largest merchandise trade partner in 2009–10 after the United Arab Emirates (UAE).

A closer look at Table 4.1 shows the buoyancy in trade to have set in from the year 2003–4. This coincides with a virtuous upswing in the growth trajectories of both countries. From 2003, right after it joined the WTO, China stepped on to a double-digit growth cycle that was maintained till 2009. Similarly, India overcame sluggish growth of around 4.0 per cent in the early years of the decade to register growth of around 8.0 per cent thereafter. The period from 2003–4 to 2008–9 – the five years during which the Indian economy grew at an annual average rate of 8.9 per cent – saw India–China trade taking off at an almost audacious pace. Throughout this period, India's trade with China grew at a faster rate than its overall trade with the rest of the world (Figure 4.1). While India–China trade increased at the remarkable annual average rate of 52.2 per cent, India's overall trade, despite growing at a robust pace, displayed a much lower annual average growth of 29.5 per cent. The departure from this trend of Sino-Indian trade growing at a rate higher than the rate of growth in India's overall trade occurred in 2008–9, the year when India's GDP growth (at constant prices) reduced to 6.8 per cent on account of the deceleration induced by the global financial recession. Bilateral grew by only 10.1 per cent during the year, which was not only lower than India's overall trade growth of 17.9 per cent, but was also noticeably modest compared to the growth in bilateral trade witnessed in the

Table 4.1 India–China trade (2000–1 to 2009–10, US$ billion)

Year	*Export*	*Import*	*Trade*	*Trade balance*
2000–1	0.8	1.5	2.3	0.7
2001–2	1.0	2.0	3.0	–1.0
2002–3	2.0	2.8	4.8	–0.8
2003–4	3.0	4.1	7.0	–1.1
2004–5	5.6	7.1	12.7	–1.5
2005–6	6.8	10.9	17.6	–4.1
2006–7	8.3	17.5	25.8	–9.2
2007–8	10.9	27.1	38.0	–16.3
2008–9	9.4	32.5	41.9	–23.1
2009–10	11.6	30.8	42.4	–19.2

Source: Export Import Data Bank, Department of Commerce, Ministry of Commerce and Industry, Government of India.

previous five years. Bilateral trade growth dropped to as low as 1.4 per cent in 2009–10 as India's external trade shrank in the aftermath of the economic crisis. But in spite of the contraction, the growth in Indo-China trade remained positive, which was rather exceptional given that India's overall trade shrank by 4.5 per cent during the year (Figure 4.1).

The size of bilateral trade and the growth in trade appears even more robust according to the statistics provided by China Customs. The latter's estimates indicate bilateral trade to have grown from US$10 billion in 2004 to more than US$50 billion in 2008, following which the financial recession dragged down trade to US$43 billion in 2009.[2] The Customs estimates indicate bilateral trade to have increased at an annual average rate of 43.0 per cent during 2000–8. Despite the difference in size of bilateral trade reported by trade agencies on both sides, there is unanimity over such trade having increased at a phenomenal pace. While the pace of growth is indeed remarkable, particularly given the political irritants that refuse to recede in the background and yet do not appear to have thawed growth, it must also be noted that, as a share of total trade of both countries, Sino-Indian trade is still relatively small; the bilateral trade accounts for only 2 per cent and around 10 per cent of China's and India's total external trade.

The noticeable feature of bilateral trade has been its increasing imbalance. From an Indian perspective, exports to China have been increasing at a lower rate than its imports from China, thereby making the trade, at least on paper, more gainful for China. The annual average growth rates in India's exports and imports to China are 31.6 per cent and 43.2 per cent respectively during 2003–4

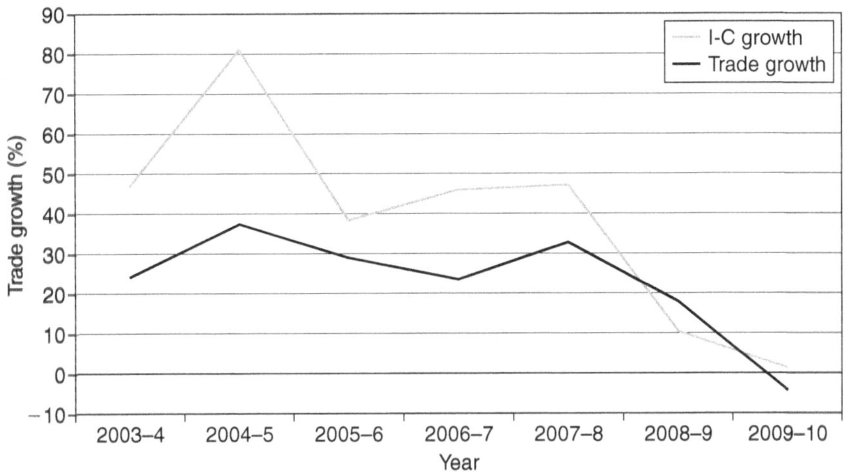

Figure 4.1 Growth in India–China trade and India's overall trade (%) (2003–4 to 2009–10) (source: Export Import Data Bank, Department of Commerce, Ministry of Commerce and Industry, Government of India; and author's computations).

to 2009–10 with import growth outstripping export by more than ten percentage points. The difference between rates of growth in export and import is even larger – around 15 percentage points given growth rates of 42.3 per cent and 57.7 per cent respectively during 2003–4 to 2007–8 – the period before the onset of financial crisis. It is also noticeable that until 2008–9, the growth rate in India's imports from China was higher than the rate of growth in its overall imports; growth in India's exports to China was roughly equivalent to its overall export growth from 2005–6 until it departed from the trend in 2008–9 (Figure 4.2).

The trade deficit, again from the Indian perspective, which was less than US$1 billion at the beginning of the century, increased to US$23.1 billion in 2008–9, and moderated to US$19.1 billion in 2009–10 (Table 4.1). As a proportion of India's total trade deficit, the deficit in trade with China has increased from 4.5 per cent in 2004–5 to 19.5 per cent in 2008–9. Though the share dropped to 16.5 per cent in 2009–10, this moderation may not signal the beginning of a declining trend. It can be explained by a greater than expected reduction in the volume of imports during the year due to recessionary conditions prevailing at home in India and the resultant lack of demand. The structural composition of India's balance of payments (BOP), since 2004–5, shows a deficit balance in its current account due to the merchandise trade deficit being higher than the invisibles surplus. The trade deficit has been enlarging since 2004–5, leading to higher deficit in the current account. While the greater trade deficit can be explained by various factors including high global crude oil prices and an inflated oil import bill, imbalanced trade with China has also been a contributor.

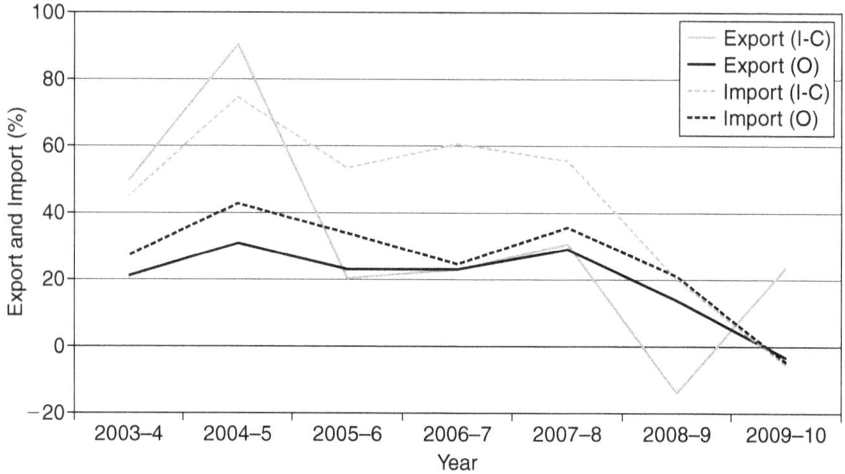

Figure 4.2 India's export and import to China and the world (%) (source: Export Import Data Bank, Department of Commerce, Ministry of Commerce and Industry, Government of India; and author's computations).

It's important to note that India's trade with China expanded, and the deficit in the trade enlarged, at a time when Indian industry was riding on a high. The early years of the last decade saw the index of industrial production (IIP) registering annual growth rates of 4.9 per cent and 2.8 per cent only in 2000–1 and 2001–2. From 2002–3 onward, there was a gradual revival in industrial output growth with the IIP growth increasing from 7.0 per cent in 2003–4 to 11.5 per cent in 2006–7 and 8.5 per cent in 2007–8. The year 2008–9 saw IIP growth dipping sharply owing to economic deceleration. However, the upward trend growth in industrial production has resumed thereafter. Manufacturing has been the main driver of IIP growth during 2003–4 to 2007–8. Annual rate of growth in manufacturing output increased from 7.3 per cent in 2003–4 to 12.5 per cent in 2006–7 and 9.0 per cent in 2007–8. The correlation between India's high trade with China, particularly its large absorption of Chinese imports, and the upswing in India's manufacturing and industrial growth, should not be overlooked.[3] Indeed, the correlation is not only with respect to industrial and manufacturing growth. This was also a period that saw robust growth in India's infrastructure industries, particularly electricity, coal, steel and cement.

It is clear that high growth in the Indian economy driven by a robust industrial sector led to an increase in India's trade with the rest of the world. India's external trade experienced an almost four-fold increase from US$146.3 billion in 2003–4 to US$576.7 billion in 2008–9. The rise was driven not only by higher manufactured exports, which increased almost three-fold from US$66.3 billion to US$189.0 billion during the period, but more by a faster growth in imports, which grew nearly five-fold from US$80 billion to US$387.7 billion, for supporting domestic industrial expansion. Trade deficit, as a result, expanded from US$13.7 billion in 2003–4 to a whopping US$118.7 billion in 2008–9. The current account in the BOP turned deficit from surplus in 2004–5 on the back of the high trade deficit and has gradually expanded from a small deficit of US$2.5 billion in 2004–5 to US$28.7 billion in 2008–9. The pattern of India's trade with China, which shows rapid growth in trade deficit on account of being driven more by imports, reflects the same trends that are visible in the current account of India's BOP for the country's high-growth phase during the last decade. Evidently factors driving India's trade with the rest of the world have also been driving its trade with China, among which domestic demand for imports is the key factor. The next section will take a closer look at India's main imports from China in order to identify their main drivers.

India's imports from China

India has repeatedly expressed concerns over the rising imbalance in its trade with China. Other than the worry over the trade assuming structurally unsustainable proportions in the long run, some of the attendant concerns also include fears over cheap Chinese imports flooding the domestic market and driving local producers out of business. Domestic industry associations have been vocal over Indian industries losing market share to cheaper imports from China. According to a survey conducted by the Federation of Indian Chambers of Commerce and Industry (FICCI), one of India's three main industry organisations – the other two being the Confederation of Indian Industry (CII) and the Associated Chambers of Commerce and Industry of India (ASSOCHAM) – Chinese imports are sold in the Indian market at prices that are 10–70 per cent less than those of their Indian counterparts.[4] Apart from industry associations, major Indian enterprises with well-spread and deep market presence have also complained about cheap Chinese imports damaging their business prospects (Pannu 2010). As mentioned in Chapter 3, concerns of these enterprises and associations have led to regular anti-dumping actions. These concerns, which have occasionally verged near paranoia over Chinese imports, require clear identification of drivers of Chinese imports. Indeed, if these imports are increasing despite inflicting injuries on Indian producers, then there must be strong 'pull' factors for such imports. A careful look at India's leading imports from China might provide useful insights and tentative answers in this regard. Table 4.2 illustrates these imports.

'Electrical machinery, equipment and parts' (HS85) dominate India's imports from China. Currently these imports account for about a third of India's total imports from China. The second leading category of imports is 'nuclear reactors, boilers, machinery and mechanical appliances' (HS84). The share of these imports has steadily increased and is now around 20 per cent of India's imports from China. HS85 and HS84 comprised more than half of India's total imports from China in 2009–10. 'Organic chemicals' (HS29), despite a steady reduction in share in total imports over the last decade, remain one of India's major imports from China. Similarly, the share of 'inorganic chemicals' (HS28) in total imports has also decreased from 2.7 per cent to 1.5 per cent over the last decade. But while chemicals (organic and inorganic) as a group have become relatively less important 'iron and steel' (HS72), 'articles of iron and steel' (HS73), 'project goods' (HS98), 'plastic and articles thereof' (HS39) and fertilisers (HS31) have increased in importance. While machinery, equipment and appliances (as represented by HS85 and HS84) and 'mineral fuels and oils' (HS27) have remained important during the entire reporting period, chemicals, 'silk' (HS50), 'pearls, stones and metals' (HS71), 'man-made filament' (HS54) and 'impregnated or coated textile fabric' (HS59) have reduced in importance in favour of iron and steel, plastic, fertilisers and project goods. 'Optical, photographic and cinematic equipments' (HS90) are also another important import category.

A clearer idea about India's imports can be obtained by perusing the data at a more disaggregated level. On the basis of statistics provided by the Export Import Data Bank of the Department of Commerce, Ministry of Commerce and Industry, Government of India, at the four-digit level of HS classification, under HS85, 'electrical apparatus for telephony and telegraphy including telephone sets with cordless handset carrier-current line system and videophones' (HS8517) was India's largest import from China in both 2008–9 and 2009–10. During these years, HS8517 accounted for 15.2 per cent and 15.8 per cent of total imports respectively. The second largest imports at the four-digit level for both years were 'project goods' (HS9801) with shares of 3.7 per cent and 6.7 per cent in total imports in 2008–9 and 2009–10. 'Flat rolled products or iron/non-alloy steel' (HS7208) were the third largest imports in 2008–9 with share of 3.3 per cent in total imports. Imported items for this category include a variety of flat-rolled steel products in coils of varying thickness. The rank and share of HS7208, however, reduced to 11 and 1.0 per cent respectively in 2009–10, which was probably on account of contraction in industrial output and lower demand for steel imports due to prevalence of recessionary conditions. A similar situation is observed for 'coke and semi/coke of coal/lignite/peat' (HS2704), which was the fourth largest import with a share of 2.9 per cent in total imports in 2008–9, but whose share dropped to only 0.1 per cent in 2009–10. 'Automatic data processing machines and units' (HS8471) were the fifth and third largest imports in 2008–9 and 2009–10 respectively, with shares of 2.7 per cent and 3.5 per cent in total imports for the two years.[5] Other major imports during these two years at the four-digit level of HS classification were 'reception apparatus' (HS8528; sixth and seventh in 2008–9 and 2009–10 with shares of 1.8 per cent and 1.6 per cent), 'antibiotics' (HS2941; seventh and fifth in 2008–9 and 2009–10 with shares of 1.7 per cent and 1.8 per cent). 'mineral/chemical fertilisers with two or three of the fertilising elements N, P and K' (HS3105; eighth and thirty-first in 2008–9 and 2009–10 with shares of 1.7 per cent and 0.6 per cent), 'diamonds' (HS7102; ninth and fifty-sixth in 2008–9 and 2009–10 with shares of 1.5 per cent and 0.3 per cent), 'parts and accessories' (HS8473; tenth and sixth in 2008–9 and 2009–10 with shares of 1.5 per cent and 1.7 per cent) and 'electrical transformers' (HS8504; eleventh and tenth in 2008–9 and 2009–10 with shares of 1.4 per cent and 1.0 per cent).[6] Antibiotic imports include mostly penicillin and its derivatives, along with tetracycline and erythromycin and their salts. Fertilisers include di-ammonium phosphate and mono-ammonium phosphates. Diamond imports include essentially unworked non-industrial diamonds. Most of the HS8473 category imports are parts and accessories of automatic data processing machines while the leading import among electrical transformers is static converter.

Telephone apparatus and telephone sets (HS8517) have been one of India's largest imports from China. The sharp rise in imports of telephone apparatus and telephone sets from China reflects an interesting facet of the remarkable growth of the telecommunications industry in India. In 2009–10, India sourced 61.7 per cent of its HS8517 imports from China. This was far higher than similar imports from Korea (5.8 per cent), the US (4.0 per cent) and Sweden (3.7 per cent), who were the next largest sources. Interestingly, until 2006–7, the US was the biggest source of HS8517 imports for India. In 2006–7, the US accounted for 21 per cent of these imports, while China contributed 20.4 per cent, followed by Sweden with 13.9 per cent. Indeed, HS8517 did not enjoy the distinction of being the highest four-digit import category from the HS85 group till 2007–8. The position was held by a qualitatively similar category of imports – 'transmission apparatus for radio telephony etc.' (HS8525) – that includes reception apparatus, sound recording, television cameras and, most importantly, cell phones and receivers.

Table 4.2 India's imports from China (2003–4 to 2009–10)

Import	*HS code*	*2003–4*	*2004–5*	*2005–6*	*2006–7*	*2007–8*	*2008–9*	*2009–10*
		Rank						
Electrical machinery and equipment and parts thereof; sound recorders and reproducers, television image and sound recorders	85	1 (29.2)	1 (25.0)	1 (25.5)	1 (24.3)	1 (28.1)	1 (30.8)	1 (31.4)
Organic chemicals	29	2 (15.9)	4 (11.6)	3 (12.1)	3 (9.8)	3 (8.8)	3 (8.7)	3 (9.8)
Nuclear reactors, boilers, machinery and mechanical appliances; parts thereof	84	3 (12.2)	2 (14.8)	2 (19.9)	2 (18.6)	2 (17.8)	2 (17.0)	2 (20.0)
Silk	50	4 (5.5)	5 (4.3)	5 (3.5)	9 (1.9)	11 (1.4)	14 (1.1)	14 (2.2)
Mineral fuels, mineral oils and products of their distillation; bituminous substances; mineral waxes	27	5 (5.5)	3 (12.7)	4 (6.6)	4 (7.2)	5 (4.8)	5 (3.9)	13 (1.2)
Inorganic chemicals	28	6 (2.7)	7 (2.1)	7 (1.9)	10 (1.6)	9 (1.5)	11 (1.7)	9 (1.5)
Natural or cultured pearls, precious or semiprecious stones, pre. metals, clad with pre. metals and articles thereof; imitation jewellery, coin	71	7 (1.7)	6 (2.2)	14 (1.1)	28 (0.5)	12 (1.2)	9 (2.6)	17 (0.9)
Man-made filaments	54	8 (1.7)	10 (1.5)	11 (1.3)	16 (0.9)	21 (0.8)	22 (0.7)	20 (0.8)

Impregnated, coated, covered or laminated textile fabric; textile articles of a kind suitable for industrial use	59	9 (1.6)	9 (1.6)	8 (1.8)	11 (1.3)	17 (1.0)	18 (0.9)	15 (1.0)
Optical, photographic cinematographic measuring, checking precision, medical or surgical instrument and apparatus parts and accessories thereof	90	10 (1.6)	14 (1.3)	12 (1.3)	13 (1.2)	14 (1.2)	10 (1.8)	10 (1.4)
Iron and steel	72	28 (0.5)	8 (1.8)	6 (2.5)	6 (4.1)	4 (5.4)	4 (5.3)	6 (2.6)
Articles of iron and steel	73	14 (1.1)	12 (1.3)	9 (1.8)	5 (5.8)	7 (4.3)	7 (3.2)	5 (2.8)
Plastic and articles thereof	39	11 (1.4)	11 (1.4)	10 (1.7)	8 (2.2)	8 (2.3)	12 (1.6)	7 (1.7)
Project goods; some special uses	98	53 (0.1)	29 (0.4)	17 (1.0)	7 (2.9)	10 (1.5)	6 (3.7)	4 (6.8)
Fertilisers	31	36 (0.3)	61 (0.0)*	48 (0.2)	20 (0.7)	6 (4.4)	8 (2.8)	12 (1.3)
Vehicles other than railway or tramway rolling stock, and parts and accessories thereof	87	47 (0.2)	44 (0.2)	20 (0.8)	12 (1.2)	15 (1.2)	13 (1.3)	8 (1.5)

Source: Export Import Data Bank, Department of Commerce. Ministry of Commerce and Industry, Government of India; http://commerce.nic.in/eidb/default.asp.

Notes
Figures in parentheses reflect the share of the import in India's total imports from China in the particular year.
* The share is 0.04%, but is shown as 0.0% due to rounding off up to one decimal place.

The prominence of HS8517, HS8525 and HS8528 imports from China is clearly on account of the rapid growth in India's telecom industry, which is expanding in all segments, not only in terms of enlarging the fixed line and mobile subscriber bases, but also in the manufacture of telecom equipment. Indeed, India's gradual emergence as a telecom equipment manufacturing centre in addition to the unabated growth in telecom service penetration through competing technologies such as GSM (Global System Mobile) and CDMA (Code Division Multiple Access) has led to acceleration in the growth of HS8517 imports. During 2007–8 and 2008–9, India's overall total imports of HS8517 grew by 120.8 per cent and 107.9 per cent respectively. While these rates were impressive, HS8517 imports from China grew at even more remarkable rates of 348.2 per cent and 177.2 per cent respectively. More importantly, while India's overall HS8517 imports declined by 7.0 per cent in 2009–10, the imports from China grew at a positive rate of 4.1 per cent. Notably, for all other major suppliers of imports of HS8517 – the US, Korea and Sweden – growth rates of imports were negative during 2009–10, while China's HS8517 items bucked the trend.[7]

India's telecommunications industry has been experiencing a growing presence of Chinese enterprises. This is not in provision of value-added telecom services, but in supply of manufactures. The biggest examples are two of China's largest telecom equipment manufacturers – Huawei Technologies and Zhongxing Telecom (ZTE) – supplying equipment to India's largest state-owned telecom operators, Bharat Sanchar Nigam Limited (BSNL) and Mahanagar Telephone Nigam Limited (MTNL). Huawei and ZTE not only manufacture mobile phone handsets, but also produce a variety of other telecom equipment including switches, platform data cards, modems, fixed wireless terminals, wireless gateway, etc. (Greene 2006). They have been able to occupy considerable space in an Indian telecom equipment market which is growing by leaps and bounds but is largely catered by global manufacturers. Nokia, Sony Ericsson, Siemens, Motorola, Cisco, Lucent Technologies, Qualcomm and Microsoft are some of the major telecom equipment manufacturers in India, other than Huawei and ZTE. The biggest Indian presence is the state-owned Indian Telephone Industries (ITI), which has far less market share than Nokia, Sony Ericsson, Motorola or Siemens, also leading manufacturers of cell phones. Most of these firms assemble products in India or import them from their production facilities located elsewhere in the Asian region. Local Indian firms manufacturing mobile handsets (e.g. Micromax, Spice, Lemon) are also essentially assemblers relying on components imported from China. With respect to intermediate parts for further assembling as well as several final products, China is by far the biggest source of imports for India owing to geographical proximity and cheap prices. Mobile phones imported from China have become highly popular in the Indian market since they are cheaper than established brands while offering practically all features of high-end products.[8] Furthermore, most leading global manufacturers in India, like Nokia and Motorola, have production facilities in China. It is not surprising or unusual for them to import from these facilities. Finally, all telecom operators in India have to rely extensively on imports for setting up networks. Thus there is hardly any reason why Chinese imports of HS8517, HS8525 and HS8528 should not have flourished in India.

India has also been importing several items belonging to HS84, in which, as mentioned earlier, HS8471 and HS8473 are two major sub-categories at the four-digit level. Other four-digit categories such as HS8402 ('steam/other vapour generating boilers'), HS8406 ('steam turbines & other vapour turbines'), HS8414 ('air/other vacuum pumps, air/other gas compressors & fans'), HS8443 ('printing machinery including inkjet printing machines') and HS8447 ('knitting machines') have also been important imports.[9] Taken together with HS8504 and HS8507 (which between them include assorted electrical transformers, static converters, inductors and electric accumulators), these imports represent machinery and equipment required by electricity and engineering industries and computer hardware and accessories. Clearly, they have responded to the growing demand for machinery and inputs during a robust period of growth for India's manufacturing. At a further disaggregated six-digit level of HS classification, the imports from the mentioned categories include: parts of steam and vapour generating boilers, auxiliary plants used with boilers, parts of turbines, compressors, fans (table, ceiling, floor and other types), air-conditioning machines, printing machinery, knitting machines, portable digital automatic data processing units (personal computers, laptops, palmtops), storage units (hard disc drives), printers, parts and accessories for motherboards, electric transformers, converters, inductors and lead-acid and other varieties of accumulators.[10]

Like telecom, India's power sector suffers from serious deficiencies as far as availability of indigenous machinery and equipment is concerned. India has been trying hard to step up its power-generating capacities for meeting the rising demand for electricity. However, it does not produce enough equipment at home to satisfy the demand of a hungry power sector. Bharat Heavy Electricals Limited (BHEL) – the main government-owned enterprise manufacturing equipment for power plants – does not have enough capacity to match the growing demand, particularly from private power producers. For the latter, low-cost Chinese equipments are far more economic options than similar high-cost products manufactured by US and European firms (Sharma 2010). As a result, from a negligible presence in India's power equipment market until the middle of the last decade, Chinese equipment presently occupies around one-third of the total market share (Trivedi 2009). Major Chinese equipment firms such as Shanghai Electric Corporation (SEC) and Dongfang Electric Corporation (DEC) are supplying to various plants in India, particularly those being built by private producers. Demand from private indigenous power producers such as the Adani Group and Reliance Power has been a major driver of high imports of power sector equipment from China.

Chinese imports also dominate India's computer hardware industry. Personal computers from China have consistently been more than 60 per cent of India's imports of such computers (Figure 4.3). Chinese hard disc drives (HDDs) have increased their share in total imports to more than 30 per cent, while parts and accessories of motherboards manufactured in China are now almost 90 per cent of India's total import of such items (Figure 4.3). The high demand for personal computers in India has been met by low-price imports from China in spite of the presence of prominent Indian manufacturers like HCL and Zenith. Estimates indicate that while the average per unit cost of China's computer-related exports to India was US$33 in 2009, the cost of similar exports from India to China was US$274 (Workman 2010) – a reflection of the comparative price advantage enjoyed by Chinese computer hardware products. China has outpaced computer hardware imports into India from other major sources such as Singapore, Thailand, Hong Kong and Korea by a considerable distance. Though Indian manufacturers have introduced cheap computers,[11] they are still not large enough to significantly dent the market share of Chinese computers. The Chinese computer-maker Lenovo's acquisition of IBM's personal computer division in 2005 helped it greatly in gaining deeper access in the Indian market. Considerable parts of Lenovo's sales in India comprise imports from China (Greene 2006). Besides Lenovo, other leading computer manufacturers in India such as Acer and Dell also rely on imports from their production facilities in China for serving the Indian market. In addition, these manufacturers, as well as local branded manufacturers in India and the unbranded 'grey market' assemblers, rely heavily on the import of hardware parts and components (e.g. HDDs, monitors, keyboards, speakers, CD and DVD-ROMs, etc.) from China.

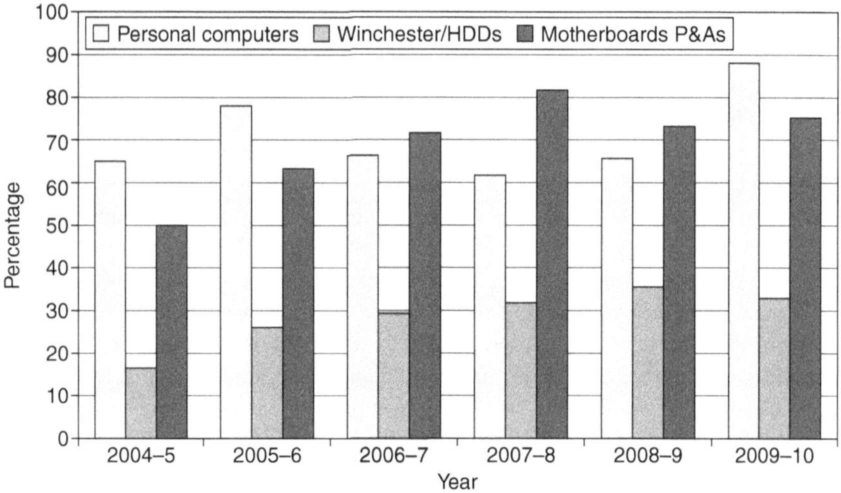

Figure 4.3 Share of China in India's imports of computer hardware (2004–5 to 2009–10) (source: 'Import: commodity-wise all countries', Export Import Data Bank, Department of Commerce, Ministry of Commerce and Industry, Government of India; http://commerce.nic.in/eidb/icomcntq.asp; note: personal computers, Winchester/HDDs (hard disc drives) and motherboards P&As (parts and accessories) represent eight-digit tariff lines HS84713010, HS84717020 and 84733020 respectively).

HS98 has emerged as another important category of India's imports from China (Table 4.2). From 2006–7 onward, these imports have figured among India's top ten imports from China (at the HS two-digit level of classification) with these becoming the fourth largest import category in 2009–10 with a share of 6.8 per cent in India's total imports from China. At a more disaggregated four-digit level, HS9801 – otherwise referred to as 'project goods' – was the second largest import by India from China in both 2008–9 and 2009–10. By their very definition, project goods represent a somewhat less-understood group of items. The Indian Trade Classification Harmonised System (ITC-HS), describing different product categories and tariff lines included in these categories, explains HS9801, or project goods, as:

> All items of machinery including prime movers, instruments, apparatus and appliances, control gear and transmission equipment, auxiliary equipment (including those required for research and development purposes, testing and quality control), as well as all components (whether finished or not) or raw materials for the manufacture of the aforesaid items and their components, required for the initial setting up of an unit, or the substantial expansion of an existing unit, of a specified: (1) Industrial plant (2) Irrigation project (3) Power project (4) Mining project (5) Project for the exploration for oil or other minerals, and (6) Such other projects as the Central Government may, having regard to the economic development of the country notify in the official Gazette in this behalf; and spare parts, other raw materials (including semi-finished material) or consumable stores not exceeding 10 per cent of the value of the goods specified above provided that such spare parts, raw materials or consumable stores are essential for the maintenance of the plant or project mentioned in (1) to (6) above.[12]

As defined above, project goods signify 'lumpy' imports – a package of different machineries, components and raw materials integral to the establishment of new industrial undertakings. At a more disaggregated description of eight-digit tariff lines, they specify such lumpy imports for particular projects such as industrial plants (HS98010011), irrigation projects (HS98010012), power plants (HS98010013), mining (HS98010014) and exploration of oil or other minerals (HS98010015). Two more tariff lines – HS98010020 and HS98010030 – pertain to components (or raw materials) and spare parts respectively for manufacturing items required in setting up different projects.

Why have project goods exports from China to India shot up in recent years? A look at the data reveals that the biggest chunks of these imports are for power plants in India. During 2008–9 and 2009–10, project imports for power plants comprised 84.0 per cent and 86.4 per cent of such imports by India from China. Imports for industrial plants and exploration of oil and other minerals followed at far distant second and third positions. Power plant project imports dominated project goods imports in 2006–7 and 2007–8 as well, and accounted for 82.5 per cent and 62.0 per cent of these imports from China.[13]

China is clearly the biggest source of project imports for power plants coming up in India, which is evident from the fact that in 2009–10 it accounted for 63.6 per cent of India's total power plant project imports. South Korea and Germany followed a long way behind in second and third spots, with 15.8 per cent and 4.8 per cent shares in total project imports. Some might argue that these shares are unrepresentative since 2009–10 was the year of the financial recession that led to severe decline in exports from various other trade partners of India, and therefore should not be taken as a benchmark year. In 2007–8 and 2008–9, China accounted for 33.1 per cent and 50.0 per cent of power plant project imports into India. Though the shares were lower than in 2009–10, in both years it was still the biggest exporter of such items into India. Germany and Korea were in second and third spots in 2007–8 and 2008–9, respectively, with shares of 21.9 per cent and 11.8 per cent in India's total power project imports. The dominance of China in project imports is clearly a reiteration of the significant role that Chinese producers are playing in India's power sector, particularly in the new projects.

As explained in Chapter 3, organic and inorganic chemical exports from China have invited several anti-dumping actions from India. Antibiotics have been one of China's major exports to India. Penicillin and its salts, 6-APA, erythromycin and its derivative salts, other antibiotics and other diloxanide fuorate, cimetidine, famotidine, etc., have been China's major antibiotic exports to India.[14] Most of these exports are driven by China's comparative advantage in production of active pharmaceutical ingredients (APIs). As Kuhrt (2009) explains, India's domestic API manufacturing suffers from technological gaps that have led to low capacities in steroid manufacturing and narcotics and have also prohibited the growth of firms strong in fermentation. However, at the upper end of the pharmaceutical value chain, several Indian firms (e.g. Dr Reddy's Laboratories, Ranbaxy) have developed strong competencies in preparing final formulations. Their products are in high demand in both domestic markets and high-income overseas markets like the US. High demand for final formulations has led to high demand for APIs, where imports from China have helped in augmenting supplies, and have created concerns among domestic manufacturers of APIs. Large flows of antibiotics from China are expected to continue until indigenous capacities in API manufacturing expand in India.

Fertilisers are another category of India's imports from China that have irked domestic producers and attracted anti-dumping duties. Both animal and vegetable fertilisers as well as chemical fertilisers are imported by India from China, with urea, mono-ammonium phosphate and di-ammonium phosphate being the main items. India meets its high domestic demand for phosphate fertilisers by importing raw materials like rock phosphate. China, one of the largest producers of rock phosphate in the world, naturally finds India an attractive market for export. In this respect again, India's home-grown capacity to supply adequate fertilisers has been affected by distortions created by inefficient subsidies. Sharma and Thaker (2009) argue that fertiliser subsidies have concentrated more states and have not experienced an equitable distribution across the country. India remains one of the largest importers in the world of all varieties of fertilisers – urea, phosphates and potash. China, on the other hand, is one of the leading exporters of urea and phosphates. The production structures clearly explain the observed flow of trade.

Finally, India's high demand for energy, primarily electricity generated by coal-fired thermal plants, has resulted in its importing large chunks of coal, which have been further necessitated by the high ash content and washing costs of Indian coal. During 2009–10, China was the source of more than 90 per cent of India's imports of HS2704. India's imports from China, though, may not be sustained as China increasingly resorts to imports itself, despite being the world's largest coal producer, on account of reasons described in Chapter 3.

There is little doubt that Chinese imports into India have been high, as they have been meeting domestic supply shortfalls in the form of capacity gaps in various key industries. These gaps are particularly conspicuous in telecommunications, power, hardware, drugs, fertilisers and coal. All these sectors have been experiencing high growths in an Indian economy that has had robust broad-based industrial expansion since 2003–4. Indigenous supplies of capital goods such as machinery and equipment have been inadequate in meeting the demand from final producers. Chinese imports have been quick to bridge the gap. They have also been the cheapest options on most occasions. Indeed, had these imports not been around then it is worth wondering whether India's key sectors, such as telecom and electricity, would have been able to sustain their fast pace of growth at a time when the Indian economy has been on an upward trajectory.

India's exports to China

Bilateral trade between China and India, as mentioned earlier, has been criticised for its imbalance. The previous section tried to identify the drivers of China's imports to India. This section examines the pattern and structure of India's exports to China. It is often argued that India's exports to China comprise raw materials and have little in the way of value-added items. It is also argued that India's major exports to other parts of the world have not been able to carve out similar niches in China. How true are these observations?

Tables 4.3 and 4.4 show India's leading exports to the world and China respectively during the same time period for the last decade, i.e. 2003–4 to 2009–10. A comparison between the two tables shows that four two-digit categories – 'articles of apparel and clothing accessories, knitted and crocheted' (HS61), 'not knitted and crocheted' (HS62), 'articles of iron and steel' (HS73) and 'vehicles other than railway and tramway rolling stock, and parts and accessories thereof' (HS87) – do not figure among India's prominent exports to China. While the rest do, there is difference in the extent by which they penetrate the Chinese market, compared to elsewhere in the world. For example, 'natural

Table 4.3 India's leading exports (2003–4 to 2009–10) and their shares (%) in total exports

Export	*HS code*	*2003–4*	*2004–5*	*2005–6*	*2006–7*	*2007–8*	*2008–9*	*2009–10*
Ores, slag and ash	26	2.0	4.5	4.3	3.8	4.3	2.9	3.7
Mineral fuels, mineral oils and products of their distillation; bituminous substances; mineral waxes	27	5.8	8.5	11.5	14.9	17.8	15.3	16.2
Organic chemicals	29	4.8	4.3	4.7	4.5	4.3	4.0	4.2
Cotton	52	3.9	2.7	2.9	3.1	3.2	1.7	2.6
Articles of apparel and clothing accessories, knitted and crocheted	61	4.2	3.2	3.1	2.9	2.6	2.7	2.6
Articles of apparel and clothing accessories, not knitted and crocheted	62	5.5	4.7	5.3	4.2	3.3	3.2	3.4
Natural or cultured pearls, precious or semi-precious stones, pre. metals, clad with pre. metals and articles thereof; imitation jewellery, coin	71	16.8	17.3	15.4	12.7	12.2	15.4	16.3
Iron and steel	72	4.1	5.0	3.7	4.4	4.0	4.1	2.5
Articles of iron and steel	73	2.4	2.8	2.7	2.7	3.2	3.1	2.3
Nuclear reactors, boilers, machinery and mechanical appliances; parts thereof	84	3.9	4.0	4.1	4.0	4.2	4.3	4.0
Electrical machinery and equipment and parts thereof; sound recorders and reproducers, television image and sound recorders	85	3.0	2.5	2.7	3.3	3.2	5.1	4.0
Vehicles other than railway and tramway rolling stock, and parts and accessories thereof	87	2.7	3.0	3.2	3.0	2.7	3.2	3.5

Source: Export Import Data Bank, Department of Commerce. Ministry of Commerce and Industry, Government of India; http://commerce.nic.in/eidb/ecomq.asp.

Table 4.4 India's leading exports to China (2003–4 to 2009–10)

Export	*HS code*	*2003–4*	*2004–5*	*2005–6*	*2006–7*	*2007–8*	*2008–9*	*2009–10*
		Rank						
Ores, slag and ash	26	1 (29.3)	1 (52.1)	1 (51.3)	1 (45.9)	1 (56.9)	1 (51.5)	1 (47.9)
Iron and steel	72	2 (20.4)	2 (11.8)	4 (6.3)	5 (5.8)	7 (2.1)	5 (3.9)	7 (2.6)
Plastic and articles thereof	39	3 (9.0)	3 (7.1)	6 (4.1)	6 (5.2)	6 (2.1)	11 (1.6)	6 (2.7)
Organic chemicals	29	4 (7.5)	4 (6.5)	3 (6.8)	4 (6.2)	3 (5.8)	3 (4.3)	4 (4.4)
Cotton	52	5 (3.6)	9 (1.6)	2 (7.6)	2 (9.1)	2 (10.1)	4 (4.2)	2 (10.9)
Inorganic chemicals	28	6 (3.4)	5 (4.0)	5 (4.9)	7 (4.2)	10 (1.4)	9 (2.3)	14 (1.0)
Salt; sulphur; earths and stone; plastic materials, lime and cement	25	7 (3.1)	6 (2.5)	7 (2.2)	8 (2.5)	8 (1.9)	6 (3.0)	9 (2.4)
Fish and crustaceans, molluscs and other aquatic invertebrates	3	8 (2.6)	8 (1.8)	9 (2.1)	11 (1.0)	11 (1.2)	17 (0.9)	11 (1.8)
Mineral fuels, mineral oils and products of their distillation; bituminous substances; mineral waxes	27	9 (2.5)	25 (0.3)	22 (0.3)	10 (1.3)	9 (1.5)	14 (1.2)	16 (0.9)
Nuclear reactors, boilers, machinery and mechanical appliances; parts thereof	84	10 (2.3)	7 (1.9)	10 (1.9)	9 (1.9)	5 (2.1)	8 (2.5)	8 (2.6)
Copper and articles thereof	74	12 (1.2)	10 (1.2)	11 (1.7)	3 (6.4)	4 (3.7)	12 (1.3)	3 (4.7)
Residues and waste from the food industry; prepared animal fodder	23	24 (0.6)	13 (0.7)	8 (2.1)	14 (0.8)	13 (0.9)	10 (1.7)	17 (0.9)
Natural or cultured pearls, precious or semi-precious stones, pre. metals, clad with pre. metals and articles thereof; imitation jewellery, coin	71	28 (0.3)	23 (0.3)	30 (0.2)	27 (0.2)	24 (0.3)	2 (7.9)	5 (3.7)
Miscellaneous goods	99	29 (0.3)	34 (0.1)	33 (0.1)	28 (0.2)	34 (0.1)	7 (2.6)	22 (0.4)
Electrical machinery and equipment and parts thereof; sound recorders and reproducers, television image and sound recorders	85	14 (1.0)	14 (0.6)	14 (0.8)	13 (0.9)	14 (0.9)	13 (1.3)	10 (2.0)

Source: Export Import Data Bank, Department of Commerce. Ministry of Commerce and Industry, Government of India; http://commerce.nic.in/eidb/default.asp.

Note
Figures in parentheses reflect the share of the import in India's total imports from China in the particular year.

or cultured pearls, precious or semi-precious stones' (HS71), which have been India's largest exports to the world with an annual average share of 15.2 per cent in total exports, had a low share in exports to China till 2007–8. Since 2008–9, however, they have become significant exports to China. Similarly, 'mineral fuels, mineral oils and products of their distillation; bituminous substances; mineral waxes' (HS27), which have emerged as India's main exports from the middle of the last decade, do not appear to have as deep a market in China.

Unlike China's exports to India, which are broad-based and comprise a variety of machinery, chemicals, parts and components, hardware and metals with use as both capital and intermediate goods, and also include consumer goods (e.g. cell phones), India's exports to China are less varied. The bulk of exports, at times more than half of total exports, are accounted for by 'ores, slag and ash' (HS26). 'Iron and steel' (HS72) and 'plastic and articles thereof' (HS39), which used to be the leading exports during 2003–4 and 2004–5, have declined in their shares in total exports to China over the years. A similar trend is noticed for 'inorganic chemicals' (HS28). 'Cotton' (HS52) and 'organic chemicals' (HS29), both India's leading exports to the rest of the world, are significant exports to China also (Table 4.4), particularly cotton, whose share in total exports has been more than 10 per cent in recent years. Exports of 'natural or cultured pearls, precious and semi-precious stones' (HS71), as mentioned earlier, have been increasing in recent years, as have been those of 'machinery and mechanical appliances' (HS84) and 'copper and copper articles' (HS74).

The domination of ores in India's exports to China is an interesting structural feature of the export basket. A closer look at these exports at the four-digit level reveals them to largely comprise iron ore and its concentrates (HS2601). A further disaggregated examination of tariff lines identifies the main exports as non-agglomerated iron ores.[15] Exports of HS2601 have shown an average annual growth rate of 51.8 per cent during the period 2003–4 to 2009–10, with such exports increasing from US$823.6 million in 2003–4 to US$5.2 billion in 2009–10 (Figure 4.4). India is one of the largest exporters of iron ore in the world along with Australia and Brazil. Heavy demand for raw materials from China's steel industry has led to soaring of these exports to China. Almost a fifth of China's iron ore imports are sourced from India. On the other hand, in 2008–9 and 2009–10, 91.7 per cent and 85.7 per cent of India's total ore exports headed to China. Both countries have been working together for expediting shipments of ore.[16] While for both iron ore producers in India and steel manufacturers in China, iron ore exports from India have implied considerable economic benefits, there have been concerns in India over diversion of iron ore to exports creating shortfalls in domestic supply of raw materials for steel producers. Strong export demand, mainly from China, has also been partly responsible for the rampant growth of ore mining, not always regulated, in some parts of India, leading to bans on exports by states like Karnataka and Orissa. Indeed, there have been specific demands from industry lobbies urging the government to ban iron ore exports or restrict them through interventionist policies. India's recent move

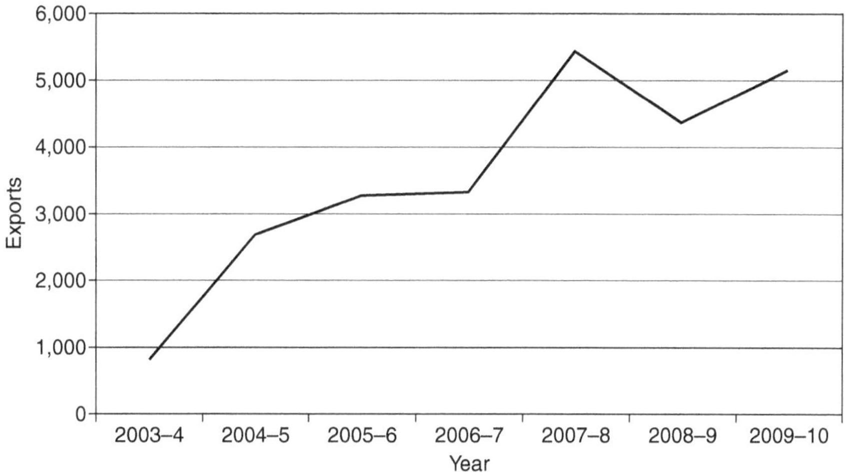

Figure 4.4 India's iron ore exports to China (2003–4 to 2009–10) (source: 'Export: commodity-wise all countries', Export Import Data Bank, Department of Commerce, Ministry of Commerce and Industry, Government of India; http://commerce.nic.in/eidb/ecntcomq.asp).

to increase export duties on iron ore fines is likely to make these exports uncompetitive in the overseas market and force them to divert to the domestic market.[17] This would also increase ore import prices for China and might depress its demand for Indian iron ore.

Along with iron ore, another export generating controversies on similar grounds is ferro-alloys (HS7202). China was the largest market for India's HS7202 exports in 2009–10 and the second largest after the Netherlands in 2008–9. It is worth noting that iron and steel (HS72) is one of India's overall leading exports (Table 4.4) and among iron and steel products, ferro-alloys and 'flat-rolled products of iron/non I alloy steel' (HS7210), are key export categories. Ferro-alloys are an example of one of India's major global exports that also enjoys strong demand in China. It is not clear, though, whether these exports to China, which are again useful for steel manufacturers, are being diverted on account of most Indian steel plants building up captive capacities for ferro-alloys, thereby depressing demand for other domestic manufacturers.

Another leading Indian export for the rest of the world, which has marked a niche in the Chinese market, is cotton. 'Cotton not carded or combed' (HS5201), and 'cotton yarn' (HS5205) are India's main cotton exports to China. Both these, like ferro-alloys, are India's main cotton exports to the rest of the world also. China was the largest global buyer of India's HS5201 exports in 2008–9 and 2009–10. India's cotton exports to China are again a reflection of peculiar domestic structural features in both countries. China, one of the world's largest cotton producers, has several scale-intensive garment manufacturing plants with almost insatiable appetites for raw cotton, which forces it to import raw cotton. On the other hand, India, despite being one of the world's largest producers of raw cotton, lacks enough scale-intensive plants that can deploy large quantities of cotton for producing final products, thereby forcing domestic manufacturers to divert production to exports. Lack of adequate scale-intensive plants compared to China is one of the main reasons behind India's apparel and clothing accessories (HS61 and HS62) exports not being able to make much impact in China – an apparel hub – while they have been successful in other markets of the world. India has replaced the US to become the largest cotton exporter to China and is expected to remain so in the foreseeable future as China's garment manufacturers keep expanding output. Indian cotton exports are also exploiting inefficiencies in the Chinese market that make indigenous cotton in China more expensive than the imported variety. However, cotton trade has evoked protectionist tendencies on both sides. Cotton-growers in China, particularly in more prolific regions like western China, are affected by imports, while rising cotton prices in India's domestic market have turned the heat on cotton exports by inviting export duties similar to those imposed on iron ore. Such protective actions are unlikely to help efforts to promote joint ventures between the two countries in cotton production.[18]

Sino-Indian bilateral trade at the broad two-digit level shows trade in certain similar commodities, the most common of which are organic chemicals (HS29). As mentioned earlier, HS29 products are India's leading exports to the world as well as to China. China has been one of the largest markets for these exports along with the US, Germany and Indonesia. Cyclic hydrocarbons (HS 2902) are common organic chemical exports from India to China, as are alcohols and their derivatives (HS2905), cyclic alcohols and their derivatives (HS2906), heterocyclic compounds (HS2933), antibiotics (HS2941) and other organic compounds (HS2942).[19] China has been the biggest market for Indian HS2905 and HS2906 exports in 2008–9 and 2009–10. As a group, while organic chemicals have been fairly prominent exports from India to China, their share in total exports has declined from 7.5 per cent in 2003–4 to 4.4 per cent in 2009–10. Nonetheless, they remain the third or fourth largest exports from India. The share of inorganic chemicals in total exports has also declined from 4.9 per cent in 2005–6 to 1.0 per cent in 2009–10, which has pushed their ranking in overall exports to fourteenth in 2009–10 from fifth in 2005–6 (Table 4.4). India's main inorganic chemical exports to China include artificial corundum and aluminium oxide (HS2818).[20] There has been some discontent on the part of Indian producers over pharmaceutical exports to China in terms of the NTBs they encounter in the Chinese market, as discussed in Chapter 3. This is a category where Indian producers have a negligible presence in the Chinese market compared to several other major markets of the world.

India's copper exports to China have slowly increased over time, with these exports becoming the third largest in 2009–10 with almost 5 per cent share in total exports (Table 4.4). The main items being exported are refined copper and copper alloys (HS7403) and copper wire (HS7408). China's copper imports have been picking up on account of demand arising from fast urbanisation as well as emphasis on production of electric or hybrid cars requiring large supplies of electrically conductive copper.[21] It has been the largest market for India's HS7403 exports in recent years. Along with copper, exports of machinery and mechanical appliances (HS84) are also increasing. These exports were the fifth largest in 2007–8 and have slipped to the eighth rank in 2009–10, though their share in total exports has increased marginally from 2.1 per cent to 2.6 per cent. 'Air/vacuum pumps, gas compressors and fans' (HS8414), 'machinery, plant and laboratory equipment' (HS8419), 'centrifuges' (HS8421), 'parts and accessories for data processing and other machines' (HS8473), 'taps, cocks, valves' (HS8481) and 'transmission shafts and cranks' (HS8483) are noted to be some of the main exports.[22] China was the largest buyer of India's HS8419 exports during 2008–9 and 2009–10 and is also gradually emerging as a major market for the other four-digit categories mentioned. Increasing HS84 exports, which again are also one of India's leading exports to the world, might mark the beginning of a structural change in India's exports to China in terms of the pattern of such exports acquiring a more capital goods (machinery and component)-oriented dimension, in place of the pronounced raw material orientation that they have had until now. This nascent trend might be reinforced by higher exports of electrical machinery and equipment (HS85), another of India's leading global exports, which now figure among India's top ten exports to China, with the share of HS85 exports increasing to 2.0 per cent of total exports in 2009–10 from 0.6 per cent in 2004–5 (Table 4.4). 'Electrical transformers, static converters and inductors' (HS8504), 'electrical apparatus for line telephony' (HS8517) and 'parts for electrical apparatus' (HS8538) are some of the main electrical machinery items being exported to China.

The slow structural shift in India's exports towards value-added items can also be discerned from the steady increase in natural or cultured pearls, precious and semi-precious stones (HS71) exports to China. From being as low as thirtieth in export rankings in 2005–6 with a share of only 0.2 per cent in total exports, HS71 exports rose to second position with 7.9 per cent share in total exports in 2008–9 (Table 4.4). As mentioned earlier, HS71 is one of India's topmost exports to the rest of the world. 'Diamonds, worked, but not mounted' (HS7102) and 'jewellery articles' (HS7113), are the main HS71 exports to China. However, the structural shift in terms of more 'finished' and value-added exports such as machinery and jewellery are unlikely to result in the immediate displacement of raw materials from India's export basket. This is evident from 'salt, sulphur; earths and stone; plastic materials, lime and cement' (HS25) exports continuing to figure among India's top ten export categories to China, despite their share reducing from 3.1 per cent to 2.4 per cent during 2003–4 to 2009–10. 'Granite, porphyry, basalt, sandstone and other building stone (HS2516), sulphur (HS2503), marble' (HS2515), and 'mica' (HS2525), are the leading HS25 exports to China. The prevalence of these construction materials in India's exports to China is indicative of the large demand for imported material in China, primarily for catering to the rapid growth in the stock of housing and infrastructure. While HS25 exports are expected to remain in demand in China's domestic market owing to sustained growth in urban infrastructure and real estate, India's main animal product exports to China – 'fish and crustaceans, molluscs and other aquatic invertebrates' (HS03) – are showing a steady decline. HS03 exports have slipped in ranking from eighth to eleventh during the period 2003–4 to 2009–10, along with a decline in their share in total exports from 2.6 per cent to 1.8 per cent. 'Frozen fish' (HS0303), 'fish fillet and fish meat' (HS0304) and 'molluscs' (HS0307) are the main HS03 exports.[23] While fish exports have declined, another category of exports derived from food products – 'residues and waste from the food industry; prepared animal fodder' (HS23) – has shown a fluctuating trend (Table 4.4) with 'oil cake and other solid residue obtained from soya bean oil extraction' (HS2304) and 'vegetable fats' (HS2306) being the main exports from this category.

The pessimism regarding India's leading exports to the rest of the world not finding their way into China possibly needs to be revisited in the light of the changing composition of the export basket. Increasing exports of HS71, HS72, HS29, HS84 and HS85 show a different trend. These exports are also more of the finished and intermediate variety, offering considerable scope for value addition in the supply chain. Having said this, raw material exports, particularly minerals, cotton and metals, continue to occupy large shares in India's export basket to China. They are expected to remain prominent in the foreseeable future because of heavy domestic demand for raw materials in the Chinese economy. However, protective moves, in terms of levy of export duties, might affect the prospects of some of these exports.

A bilateral trade deal: possible pluses

The inevitability of competition notwithstanding, collaboration between India and China on economic issues is highly feasible. Such collaboration is spreading beyond adoption of common postures on similar global concerns, discussed in the next chapter, to specific bilateral cooperation between businesses, institutions and agencies. The rapid growth in trade over the last few years underscores the benefits that both economies are reaping and can continue to reap from greater exchange of goods and services. Such exchanges can, and should, deepen and widen to take the shape of enabling institutional frameworks such as a bilateral trade pact or economic cooperation agreement.

The idea of a China–India bilateral FTA first germinated during the middle of the last decade as the countries suddenly found themselves trading vigorously with each other. Following China's entry in the WTO and the onset of robust business cycles in both countries that encouraged a rapid growth of trade and industry, a bilateral trade deal appeared a promising idea given that trade had taken off regardless of political differences. A Joint Study Group (JSG) set up in 2003 for examining ways of enhancing trade and economic cooperation between the two countries submitted its findings in March 2005. The report recommended a China–India regional trade agreement including trade in goods and services, investment, trade and investment promotion and facilitation, and also measures for promoting cooperation in different sectors.[24]

The timing of the report was perfect, with the Chinese Premier Wen Jiabao visiting India within a month of the submission of the report. The joint statement signed during the Premier's visit took explicit note of the recommendations, raising hopes of the deal coming through in the foreseeable future.[25] However, while initial signals on the initiative were encouraging, little happened thereafter. The reservations have primarily been on the Indian side. Fear of being swamped by Chinese imports in the event of a trade deal that reduced tariffs and offered greater market access to Chinese products has prevented Indian authorities from making proactive moves (Sen 2008). Thus, while bilateral trade has kept growing unabated, Sino-Indian cooperation on global issues like climate change and international financial architecture has been enhanced, and interactions between the two leaderships have become more frequent, a bilateral trade deal has been conspicuous in its absence from official statements and declarations. While the joint statement issued during Premier Wen Jiabao's visit to India in December 2010 mentions a bilateral trade target of US$100 billion by 2015, measures for promoting Indian exports to China and reducing the trade deficit, trade facilitation and even the appropriate handling of economic and trade friction, the trade agreement continues to avoid mention.[26]

Is a bilateral trade pact between China and India justified? What are the pluses from such a deal?

The JSG report's recommendation of a bilateral agreement was primarily based on the complementarities existing between the two economies. These are visible even from arguably superficial top-down impressions of China and India being manufacturing and services hubs, with the two sectors accounting for more than half of national output respectively in each country. Specialisations in manufacturing and services offer obvious complementarities that can be gainfully exploited within an institutional framework. China's pursuit of an export-oriented growth strategy relying on scale-intensive low-end manufactures has led to it developing competencies in export-oriented manufacturing. Most of the competencies emanate from the high operational productivity achieved by Chinese labour in large-scale operations. While China's undisputed comparative advantage lies in volume-based batch production, India's strengths are less in scale and more in value-based niche segments. Some of these typical niches, for example, are handicrafts and related handmade products. The Indian labour force has achieved distinction in knowledge-intensive and innovation-based production lines. The labour forces of the two countries are distinct in terms of their intrinsic attributes and offer substantive complementarities to each other. It is therefore hardly surprising that Chinese labour is found gainfully 'employable' in India's electricity and infrastructure. Similar scope exists for Indian labour in China as well. However, while producers from both sides will be keen on exploring opportunities for deploying cross-border labour, such moves will need to be tempered against the opposition likely to arise from individual country domestic work forces. Nevertheless, complementarities across a wide range of skills and activities clearly exist between the two countries, creating ample scope for efficient synergies.

The increasing fragmentation of production processes in response to location-based efficiencies is likely to result in fast growth of supply chains involving enterprises from both countries. Since the outbreak of the financial crisis in 2008 and China's conscious decision to move towards a more balanced trade relationship with the rest of the world, it is consciously introducing a structural shift in manufacturing that will result in its domestic industries producing more high value-added items in place of relatively lower-end products at present. The emphasis is also consistent with the objective outlined in the 12th Five Year Plan that outlines economic restructuring aiming to introduce a strategic shift from high reliance on external economic drivers like exports to domestic drivers like consumption and investment (Wong and Lye 2011). As Chinese manufacturing processes graduate up the value chain to more sophisticated higher-end functions, and also prepare to produce a larger range of products for domestic consumption, Indian enterprises (also those in other parts of Asia such as Vietnam, Cambodia and Bangladesh) can look forward to taking over many of the operations vacated. These will mostly be assembling operations. For several years, China has functioned as the 'assembly' centre for East Asia by importing parts and components from the region and assembling them for exports to other parts of the world (Renfeng 2007). This, however, is likely to change in the near future as China reorganises production in line with shifts in global economic circumstances and its own constraints, particularly the growing shortage of migrant labour for low-cost export-oriented activities.

Responding to each other's specific business needs in the way mentioned above and the growth of cross-border production networks should encourage intra-industry trade between China and India. Trade between manufacturers dealing with parts and components of the same industry has been a key feature of external trades of mature Asian economies like Japan, Korea, Taiwan, Hong Kong and Singapore. China has been a relatively late but remarkably successful entrant to intra-industry trade in Asia and has benefited significantly from vertical fragmentation of production, by specialising in assembling functions. Sawyer *et al.* (2009), while examining determinants of intra-industry trade for more than 20 countries in East, South, Southeast and Central Asia, find lowering of tariffs through regional trade frameworks like the Asean Free Trade Area (AFTA) one of the main factors encouraging vertical intra-industry trade in parts and components in Asia.[27] The scope for intra-industry trade between China and India is considerable and unexploited. Indian producers of iron ore, ferro-alloys and raw cotton have already become parts of the Chinese production networks as suppliers of raw material. Similarly, Chinese machinery and component manufacturers have meshed into telecom and power sector supply chains in India. But as the JSG (2005) notes, manufacturers from both countries often have different specialisations within the same industry and can combine to build effective value chains in products such as machinery and equipment, textiles, processed metals and alloys and chemicals. Such vertical specialisations and creation of new intra-industry trade involving firms from both countries will be high in volume and broad-based in nature if cross-border production networks are allowed to flourish under enabling conditions that increase market access through institutional arrangements like a bilateral trade pact.

With wages of skilled labour rising in specialised domains in both countries, greater outsourcing of production segments is inevitable in both. Such tendencies will involve each searching for complementing efficiencies vigorously in the other. Geographical proximity is expected to be a key determinant of efficiency. For two countries that are already trading goods worth almost US$50 billion (much more including services), little nudges and pushes of encouragement can serve as explosive triggers for igniting the enormous potential of intra-industry cross-border trade. Indeed, rising exports of machinery and mechanical appliances (HS84) and electrical machinery (HS85) by India to China mark the clear beginnings of new intra-industry trade patterns. These two product categories comprise China's largest exports to India. With India also beginning to export products from the same categories to China, the emergence of machinery-based intra-industry production networks between the two countries is clearly noticeable. Of particular interest in this respect is the increasing cross-trade in HS8517 products. China has been India's biggest importer of HS8517 items. But it has begun importing these products from India as well. The category probably exemplifies the growth of a dense intra-industry trade pattern, which in all probability is being promoted by multinationals having operations in both countries. Similar networks are also beginning to emerge in pharmaceuticals.

Integration of Chinese and Indian firms at different levels of cross-country production networks will be easier in the presence of a bilateral economic agreement providing the framework for speedier movement of goods, services and people between the two economic giants. It is erroneous to conceive of a bilateral trade pact that will be confined only to goods. Integrated production networks involving enterprises from both countries are unlikely to be confined to manufacturing and will extend to services. Indian expertise in software development already has a complementary support in Chinese proficiency in hardware. Similar are complementarities in telecommunications where Indian service providers' skills in building telecom networks are supplemented by Chinese expertise in manufacturing telecom equipment. In knowledge-intensive services such as software development and bio-technology research, Chinese enterprises can posit themselves at appropriate middle levels, with Indian firms managing the higher functions.

The large English-speaking work force from India can be of much use for Chinese firms if product chains are dovetailed on the basis of existing synergies. Indeed, simple but occasionally difficult-to-manage tasks, such as translation of bulk knowledge material and texts into English, can be an area where Indian expertise can be of considerable use to China. China's growth as an international business and academic conference hub requires its agencies to compile and translate large volumes of conference materials into English. India's English language skills can be of great use in this respect, particularly for technical literature. In a connected world, this does not really require the presence of workers on foreign soil, but only communication through electronic means.[28] Similarly, as the JSG (2005) had noted, China can benefit from India's large pool of accounting, auditors and consulting advisers in different vocations.

As the two countries adjust to structural shifts that impart greater services orientations to both of their economies, cooperation in services becomes a critical component of their bilateral economic engagement. A bilateral trade deal ignoring this issue will be circumscribed in scope and will create only limited trade. There are several services where both countries can trade extensively. These include energy, telecoms, health, education, transport, construction, environment, information technology, entertainment, tourism and financial services. Though cross-border investments by Chinese and Indian service providers in Indian and Chinese territories, respectively, have steadily increased, a comprehensive economic arrangement facilitating such investments can make a major difference to future trade prospects. Individual service sectors in each country are usually governed by domestic regulations that are not always accommodated within the framework of a PTA or an FTA. An Indo-China agreement, however, must take note of this issue and should be preceded by adequate reforms in domestic sectors. This has begun happening, particularly in financial services, with Chinese and Indian banks beginning to function as full-fledged commercial entities in each other's soils. Similarly, exchange of students has gone up, with China emerging as an attractive option for Indian students in medical and healthcare skills and Chinese students looking forward to India in social and management sciences. While all these developments will enhance bilateral services trade, a pact that facilitates the relatively more 'difficult' modes of service trade – 'commercial presence' (mode 3) and 'movement of natural persons' (mode 4) – between the two countries will be a major achievement. This will require the pact to ensure that service providers from both countries are able to set up commercial operations in the other's territory quickly and that professional service providers are able to migrate easily.

Lower costs are significant determinants of higher trade between two countries. Empirical research on trade costs between China and India point to a significant reduction in such costs over the last three decades. Brooks and Ferrarini (2010) find that, over the period 1980–2008, reduction in trade costs has been the major driver of bilateral trade during the last decade. Calculated as tariff equivalent, these costs have come down from 119.0 per cent in 1980 to 44.3 per cent in 2008. Trade costs comprise a variety of regulatory, distribution and transport costs including tariffs and non-tariff barriers (NTBs). For bilateral trade between China and India, aggregate trade costs reflect costs faced by exporters and importers on both sides. In this respect, reduction in aggregate costs has essentially been driven by efficiencies achieved by China. China's tariffs have come down rapidly following its entry in the WTO. Its NTBs, though, remain significant and these are difficult to quantify in empirical trade cost evaluation exercises. Indian tariffs, despite reductions, continue to remain much higher on the margin. A bilateral formal trade agreement can always facilitate the ongoing process of reduction in tariffs and other trade costs, thereby encouraging more trade.

Successful regional trade blocks such as the European Union (EU) and the Association of Southeast Asian Nations (ASEAN) have flourished by exploiting the advantage of low transport costs. Sino-Indian trade has a natural advantage in this regard. By virtue of being neighbours, the two countries can exchange goods through land posts other than sea and air routes. In the latter category, the presence of efficient trans-shipment hubs in the region such as Colombo, Singapore and Hong Kong facilitate the movement of goods. Land trade between the two countries through the Lipulekh Pass in Uttaranchal, the Shipkila Pass in Himachal Pradesh and the Nathula in Sikkim (all states in India) is still negligible in terms of commodities traded. The volume of land trade can expand much more despite constraints like hostile geographical terrain. In terms of transport costs, China is the most efficient location from an Indian perspective, compared with its other major trade partners such as the EU, the US or Japan (Palit and Palit 2009). A bilateral arrangement encouraging greater movement of goods through land routes that are currently performing far below potential can serve as another trigger for trade creation.

Panagariya (2005, 2008) highlights the strategic benefits of an India-China FTA by drawing attention to the growth of the North American Free Trade Association (NAFTA), the EU and trade deals in Latin America in the final decade of the last century, and the diversion of trade 'away' from Asia, which these have led to. He argues that an Asian response to draw back trade to the region lies in creating an Asian bloc, and an India–China FTA would be the best way of beginning such a bloc. It is true that Asia does not have an integrated trade bloc of its own, though there have been considerable discussions over possible formulations such as ASEAN+3 (China, Japan, Korea) and ASEAN+6 (China, Japan, Korea, India, Australia, New Zealand). China has already worked out goods and services deals with ASEAN. India has finished a goods trade deal with ASEAN and is negotiating on services. If the region's two largest markets and economies plan to move on a bilateral trade agreement, it will consolidate the ASEAN–China–India trade architecture and can serve as a trigger for other countries to come together for a pan-Asian trade framework.

While the consolidation of an Asian economic bloc, as Panagariya argues, has the strategic advantage of considerable trade creation, what an India–China FTA can achieve from a broader 'economics plus' perspective is also worth noting. Empirical evidence on determinants of bilateral RTAs and their impact on war and conflict examined by Martin *et al.* (2010) do indicate that pacifying relations is a major driver of the world's RTAs. The authors, however, also point out that economic gains play equally significant roles in engineering RTAs. Indeed, the economic gains flowing out of RTAs have significant peace-promoting impact. From the Sino-Indian perspective, economic gains are turning out to be significant; these are gains that both consider too precious to be whittled away through conflicts. The sense of this meaningless loss will no doubt be stronger if both countries decide to sign a bilateral pact. It can probably the best confidence-building measure (CBM) that the two countries can hope to arrive at for improving their bilateral relations. While the agreement will bolster economic gains, dividends will not be confined to economics alone. An institutional framework based on trade and investment – the strongest foundations of current bilateral ties – will convey the intentions of both countries to work closely with each other for mutual benefit. In the process, it can also be greatly instrumental in curbing the 'trust deficit' that has become nearly pervasive and is occasionally affecting pragmatic conceptualisation of the relationship between the world's largest and ancient civilisations.

5 Collaboration

The global agenda

For more than five decades after the end of the Second World War, China and India remained largely marginal in influencing global economic issues. With the Cold War becoming history from the late 1980s and the world affirming faith in market-based economic principles as the most effective means for growth and prosperity, China and India faced serious dilemmas. Both had to figure out least-resistant ways of adapting to globalisation. They had to carefully manage domestic economic reforms for integrating efficiently into a world of global commerce that was rapidly shedding controls on cross-country movements of goods, services, capital, labour and technology. At the same time, they had to ensure that such integration did not accentuate domestic vulnerabilities, which underdevelopment and uneven development had produced and perpetuated in both countries. China was the better prepared of the two for handling globalisation, as it had embarked on a selective and calibrated process of opening up its economy from the early 1980s. The cessation of the Cold War and the deepening of globalisation made it imperative for China to pursue a more exhaustive and aggressive strategy for embedding into global trade and financial systems. India, on the other hand, was forced into precipitate action on reforming its economy in an outward-oriented manner after a serious BOP crisis in the early 1990s. Unlike China, however, India had the advantage of being associated with global trade and investment negotiations more closely. Nonetheless, it had to respond to the far-reaching changes taking place in the world economy. The responses, needless to say, were often tentative owing to difficulties in aligning domestic institutions and economic systems with their evolving global counterparts, and also owing to problems in making economic reforms and globalisation politically acceptable to domestic constituencies.

From the beginning of the new millennium, both countries have gradually been assuming more significant roles in global economic issues. This is on account of their rapid economic progress and increasing weight in the global economic order. China in particular has been riding on a remarkably high growth trajectory that has been undisturbed by regional and global financial crises. India, too, has shown strong and consistent economic progress. Greater economic clout has motivated both to voice specific concerns at global economic forums forcefully. Such articulation has often been collaborative thanks to the realisation that advanced economies are unlikely to yield ground on their own agendas in matters like global trade and climate change, and that developing countries have to rally together. But from a position of primarily resisting developed country opinions, the two countries now find themselves playing leading and constructive roles in global institutions and economic governance following the financial meltdown of 2008. It is also interesting to note that their roles have been largely complementing and collaborative on issues where the concerns are similar.

This chapter examines three critical segments of global economic policies where China and India have worked together in recent years to defend common concerns. These are multilateral trade talks at the WTO, climate change negotiations under the aegis of the United Nations (UN) and the evolving global financial regulatory system and management of global financial institutions following the financial crisis. The chapter argues that convergence of interests and the unified posturing of the two countries on these interests stems from the desire to mould global economic forums and institutions in a manner that is more sympathetic to their shared concerns and also accommodative of their enhanced weights in the global economic order.

Multilateral trade talks at WTO and the Doha Development Agenda (DDA)

China was a late entrant to the WTO, unlike India, which has been a member of the multilateral trade club since its inception. China's efforts to gain admittance to the multilateral trade system began in 1986 when the Uruguay Round of negotiations was going on under the General Agreement on Tariffs and Trade (GATT). The initial progress on accession halted following the developments at Tiananmen Square in 1989. China finally entered the WTO at a time when the multilateral trade framework had begun experiencing difficulties of accommodating conflicting interests. China became member 143 of the WTO on 11 December 2001. In November 2001, the WTO had commenced discussions on the Doha Development Agenda (DDA), which has subsequently dominated multilateral trade negotiations and has split the global trade community into distinct blocks based on their respective alignments to the DDA. The most contentious issues in the DDA have been subsidies offered by developed countries on their agricultural exports, access of non-agricultural exports from developing countries in developed country markets, mobility of labour, government procurement and intellectual property rights.

Since its introduction in November 2001, the DDA has been discussed at various times including in the WTO ministerial meetings at Cancun (2003), Geneva (2004, 2006 and 2008) and Hong Kong (2005). Indeed, trade talks in the first decade of the new century have been almost entirely dominated by discussions on the implementation of the DDA or issues central to the agenda. Declared in the fourth WTO ministerial meeting at Doha in Qatar on 14 November 2001, the DDA was an attempt to impart a more 'inclusive' dimension to the multilateral trading system by allowing developing countries to play bigger roles in world trade.

> The majority of WTO members are developing countries. We seek to place their needs and interests at the heart of the Work Programme adopted in this Declaration. Recalling the Preamble to the Marrakesh Agreement, we shall continue to make positive efforts designed to ensure that developing countries, and especially the least-developed among them, secure a share in the growth of world trade commensurate with the needs of their economic development. In this context, enhanced market access, balanced rules, and well targeted, sustainably financed technical assistance and capacity-building programmes have important roles to play.[1]

Agriculture is a major component of the DDA, with the declaration's emphasis on increasing market access in world trade of agricultural commodities by phasing out export subsidies and trade-distorting domestic support. The US and the EU have traditionally provided generous subsidies to a variety of farm produce. For developing countries, particularly the least developed, many of whose key exports are primary agricultural products, and who lack resources for subsidising exports, subsidised agricultural exports from developed countries create major competitive disadvantages through their lower world prices. These lower prices affect prospects of developing country exports in the world market for farm products and also restrict their access in developed country markets. The WTO had been holding talks on agriculture since early 2000 under Article 20 of the Agreement on Agriculture (AoA) and by the time it went to Doha it had been deluged with negotiating proposals from various members. The Doha declaration committed to withdrawal of measures distorting world agricultural markets by pursuing negotiations that were to end by 1 January 2005.

Agriculture was not the only developing country concern that figured prominently in the DDA. Market access for non-agricultural products also figured prominently. This involved reducing tariffs on non-agricultural (manufactured) products by all WTO members. While tariff cuts promised greater access for developing country manufactures in developed markets, it also implied gearing up for greater competition in their own markets from developed country imports. Negotiations on tariff cuts for deciding the appropriate formula were not expected to be simple. They have indeed proved to be long and difficult and are yet to be resolved even after almost a decade.

The most striking aspect of the DDA, which in due course began exposing the deep divide between developed and developing countries in world trade, was the importance awarded to special and differential (S&D) treatment for developing countries.

> We reaffirm that provisions for special and differential treatment are an integral part of the WTO Agreements. We note the concerns expressed regarding their operation in addressing specific constraints faced by developing countries, particularly least-developed countries.... We therefore agree that all special and differential treatment provisions shall be reviewed with a view to strengthening them and making them more precise, effective and operational.[2]

The S&D provision in the WTO is an implicit recognition of the imbalance in world trade in terms of the majority of countries playing small and marginal roles in trade compared with a few playing dominant roles. The multilateral trade framework, by virtue of its vision of building a global trade family, has to necessarily adopt an accommodating posture towards developing countries, particularly small economies. Appreciating the differences in economic circumstances and the difficulties of developing countries in implementing and adjusting to changes in world trade, they were granted more time and space to adjust. The flexibilities offered included a longer time for implementing specific provisions of the WTO (e.g. customs valuation, trade-related investment measures (TRIMs), technical barriers to trade (TBT), sanitary and phytosanitary measures (SPS)) by developing countries, particularly least-developed nations. The DDA also allowed the latter to subsidise exports, something which the WTO firmly opposes otherwise, till they achieved 'export competitiveness'.[3]

China's entry into the WTO was one of the most significant developments in world trade at the beginning of the new millennium. China's formal entry to the global trade club seven years after it took off was inspired by the realisation that it had more to gain by being a part of the global trade system than by being outside it. Being left out of the WTO had certain serious implications for China's exports. Since it did not have Most Favoured Nation (MFN) status,[4] WTO members were not obliged to treat Chinese exports on a par with those of their own. They could block such exports by raising tariffs unilaterally, without worrying about the implications of such actions. Indeed, China's pre-accession years in the WTO were marked by instances of heavy anti-dumping duties imposed on its exports. Less discriminatory treatment for its exports was certainly one of the factors that prompted China to enter the WTO (Bown 2007).

China's accession to the WTO was remarkable in terms of the caution and circumspection accompanying its entry. Nothing symbolises this better than the 'Transitional Product Specific Safeguard Mechanism' in the Protocol of Accession for China in the WTO (WTO 2001). The provision enables WTO members to act against Chinese imports if the latter are suspected of threatening the prospects of domestic producers of similar products. The provision is to hold good for a period of 12 years following China's entry to the WTO. There was also a special transitional safeguard for Chinese textile exports.[5] Furthermore, with respect to anti-dumping investigations, China is to remain a 'non-market' economy till 2016. This meant that initiating action on anti-dumping measures against Chinese exports would be far easier than similar actions against other WTO members. Some WTO members (e.g. Argentina, Hungary, Mexico, Turkey, Poland, the European Community, the Slovak Republic) continued to maintain tariff and quota restrictions on Chinese products even after China's formal entry into the WTO and committed to withdrawing these restrictions only over a period in time. Thus it was evident that China's entry to the world trade club was not an entirely 'happy' development for all its members. There was apprehension that cheap Chinese exports, particularly in textiles, garments, leather goods, toys and other manufactures, would affect producers of similar items from other developing countries in both domestic and overseas markets. These concerns emanated mostly from developing country members, particularly those specialising in labour-intensive and assembling operation exports. In contrast, advanced economies appeared positively inclined to China's entry into the WTO, with the US and Europe having already concluded bilateral deals with China by the time its accession was finalised.

Despite being a developing country, China's treatment at the WTO was not as sympathetic as that normally extended to a developing country member. This is again best borne out by the temporary safeguard measures. Developing countries have access to safeguard measures for protecting their indigenous industries against sudden bursts in imports. But China's accession was unique in the sense that it was a developing country against whose exports other developing countries were empowered to resort to safeguards. Furthermore, China was also not allowed to protect its domestic agriculture as much as other developing countries. Not only did it give the commitment to reduce tariffs on agricultural imports by more than half within three years of accession (from 31.5 per cent to 14.0 per cent by 2004), it also accepted a ceiling on the domestic subsidy that it could offer to its farmers (Gertler 2002).[6] Nonetheless, China perceived major economic benefits in entering the WTO (Chow 2001) and the move enjoyed the support of China's political elites (Lim and Wang 2009). As a result, it accepted certain conditions that were somewhat unbalanced in so far as its status of being a developing country is concerned. China does not appear to regret its decision, going by Commerce Minister Chen Deming's recent assertion that the period after accession to the WTO has been one of the most successful in China's modern development history.[7]

China's official posture at the WTO, however, has consistently defended developing countries. In the first ministerial after its accession at Cancun in 2003, China expressed disappointment at the lack of progress on the DDA. It also highlighted its extensive commitments in cutting tariffs across the board and reducing export subsidies on agriculture as an example of its commitment to the multilateral trading process (WTO 2003b). This, as China reiterated, was in spite of its domestic agriculture being 'backward' with low per capita incomes. It also contended that agriculture was the central issue of the DDA and that progress could not be achieved unless developed countries cut subsidies, tariffs and domestic support on their agricultural products (WTO 2003b). The concerns were similar to those expressed by India, though with much less intensity. India took a strong position at Cancun on all concerns of developing countries. Its contention on agricultural subsidies was particularly sharp.

> It is only when the developed countries agree to take five steps forward in the removal of trade-distorting subsidies that the developing countries can take one step forward in the area of market access. The legitimate concerns of billions of farmers in developing countries, for whom agriculture means

> survival and not commercial operation, cannot be sacrificed to sub-serve agri-business profits of a few millions elsewhere sustained through $1 billion in the OECD countries.
>
> (WTO, 2003a)

At the WTO deliberations in the early years of the last decade, both China and India were noticeable in their emphasis on the iniquitous effect of agricultural subsidies on world trade. India chastised the WTO for the increasingly marginal role being played by developing countries in its decision-making process. It was clear that India had assumed leadership of a large group of developing countries for whom providing greater access to imports in domestic agriculture implied affecting livelihoods. A few months before the Cancun ministerial, India argued in favour of developing countries having recourse to protective measures for blocking imports that could affect livelihoods. Subsequently, it joined 74 other members of the WTO, including several least-developed countries, in demanding the Uruguay Round approach to tariff reductions in a common submission to the Committee on Agriculture on Special Session.[8] India, Brazil and South Africa were the emerging market economies piecing together coalitions of developing countries on common grounds of S&D treatment and safeguard mechanisms.

The main coalition of developing countries that emerged in the run-up to Cancun was a group of 20 countries that became known as the G20 group on agriculture.[9] The capacity of the group to influence trade talks increased following China's entry in the coalition. Other than large emerging market economies such as Brazil, China, India, Mexico and South Africa, the group included several developing members from South and Central America (Argentina, Bolivia, Chile, Colombia, Costa Rica, El Salvador, Guatemala, Paraguay, Peru and Venezuela) and Asia (Pakistan, the Philippines and Thailand). African countries such as Egypt and Kenya also joined the group subsequently, increasing its membership to 22. The G20 represented almost 70 per cent of the world's farmers and more than half of the world's population. It resisted the combined efforts of the US and the EU to push through an agenda proposing a particular level of reduction in export subsidies and domestic support, by demanding deeper cuts in an alternative proposal. In this respect, it represented not only a formidable grouping of emerging powers, but also demonstrated an example of proactive diplomacy on the part of these powers (Narlikar and Tussie 2004). The group took a strong position on agriculture issues and demanded the elimination of Article 6.5 of the Agreement on Agriculture (AoA),[10] which had been a bone of contention for developing countries, and also demanded duty-free access to tropical and other agricultural exports from developing countries (Government of India 2003).

Though China and India combined at the G20 to block the market access proposals of the US and EU, it is somewhat surprising that they actually did so since their policy positions in terms of degree of protection on imports were not similar. The levels of access available in domestic agricultural markets in the two countries were quite different. As mentioned earlier, China had committed to deep tariff cuts on agricultural imports as well as on domestic support to agricultural exports while annexing to the WTO. Chinese tariffs on agricultural imports were already coming down in a scheduled manner when China attended the Cancun ministerial. Indian tariffs on agriculture, on the other hand, were much higher. Thus access for the exports of other countries in Chinese and Indian agricultural markets were distinctly different, as they are even now.[11] India's interests in agriculture trade talks at Cancun were more 'defensive' than those of China. In order to maintain its defensive interests, India lobbied hard to organise several alliances of countries with similar interests in the run-up to Cancun. Its main objective at Cancun was to prevent the emergence of consensus on agriculture trade – one of the core issues of the DDA – in a manner that was against its own defensive interests. But why did China, despite having opened up its agriculture significantly, decide to join India and G20 in opposing the US and EU?

China's position at the WTO needs to be viewed in the context of its rather unique circumstances. The first of these is its paradoxical situation of being a developing country and yet one of the largest players in world trade. Indeed, China's posturing at the WTO has always varied between concerns emanating from the vantage point of a developing country and those that reflect the interests of a significant commercial player in world trade. The second is the unprecedented degree of market access it agreed to offer as a condition for joining the WTO. In view of these circumstances, China, despite heavily emphasising the 'development' component of the DDA, has generally tried to ensure that world trade talks do not become stalled, since a robust world trade meant good economic prospects for China. At Cancun, however, this was a difficult balancing act to perform. Having conceded considerable market access in order to join the WTO, it was keen on obtaining greater access elsewhere. This was probably a motivation for China for supporting the G20 in its demand for opening up developed country agriculture markets. On the other hand, it also wished to convey a signal to the developing countries of being supportive of their cause. This was necessary given that some developing countries were wary over their own market access prospects following China's entry in WTO. Besides, at the time of China's entry to the WTO there was also a perception that, despite making extensive commitments for domestic liberalisation, China might not fulfil them (Lawrence 2008). At Cancun, China emphasised the liberalisations it was implementing in line with its commitments. By highlighting the grant of access to its domestic market for the good of world trade, despite being a new member and having a relatively backward agriculture, China aimed to send a strong message to the developed world for undertaking similar liberalisations. This purpose matched well with the objectives of India and G20.

Beyond Cancun, while continuing to emphasise development and supporting developing countries in obtaining greater space in world trade, China has not taken overtly aggressive postures in defending special safeguards. Rather, on several occasions, it has advocated free trade in the context of the DDA talks, much like the US and EU (Yongnian and Kong 2009). It has been looking forward to substantive liberalisation commitments from other emerging market economies in line with the commitments that it has undertaken (Lawrence 2008; Lim and Wang 2009). In line with its own export interests, market access for manufactured products became an important priority for China in subsequent negotiations. Here again, India and other developing countries found China a convenient ally for championing their cause. While India's interests in bringing down tariffs on non-agricultural exports to developed country markets were quantitatively less than China's, both found common ground in demanding more flexibility for reducing tariffs at home (WTO 2005). China was not keen on liberalising faster, given its already large commitments; India was eager to provide a longer adjustment period to domestic producers for competing with imports. Common domestic concerns helped both in voicing similar demands in the run-up to the Hong Kong ministerial in 2005.

The Hong Kong ministerial agreed to finish Doha negotiations by 2006. However, consensus eluded the negotiations, leading to their suspension in mid-2006. Talks resumed from mid-2007 and proceeded on a promising note. The ministerial discussions at Geneva in July 2008 were expected to freeze discussions to the satisfaction of all members. However, the talks collapsed through disagreement on special safeguard mechanism for developing country members in case of surge in food and cotton imports (WTO 2008). The main difference was on determining the level of imports that would 'trigger' higher tariffs by developing countries. The level proposed by the latter was less than what the developed countries wanted and no consensus could be reached.[12]

The aftermath of the collapse found China and India being blamed by several countries for not allowing the talks to reach a consensus. The final negotiations took place among seven members who were considered key players in global trade: the US, the EU, Japan, Australia, Brazil, China and India. The joint defence by China and India took many by surprise and led them to accuse the two countries of breaking the talks.[13] On their part, however, the two countries were pictured as communicating the concerns of a large group of developing countries. India was articulating the concerns of the G33 group of developing countries as well as several other developing country imperatives. In that respect, China's support of India's position implied the two largest developing countries endorsing broader concerns of poor and low-income countries in multilateral trade talks. What was a little surprising, however, was the issue on which China and India locked horns with the rest of the major trading nations. While most would have expected export subsidies and market access for non-agricultural products to be the most contentious matters, these were not the causes for undoing the talks. Special safeguards were hardly expected to be the ground for dissent. Many, though, overlook the fact that the stalling of talks on the issue of safeguards prevented discussion on cotton subsidies, which was an even more difficult problem to resolve, and where talks might well have floundered (Jonasse 2008).

The stalemate at the WTO drew attention to several aspects of the emerging and complex dynamics within world trade and global economic architecture. The battle lines were drawn most sharply between the US and India on the special safeguard mechanism. India was uncomfortable accepting the import level for triggering the safeguard proposed by the US. The levels proposed by the US and India were unacceptable to each other and remained irreconcilable despite the US and Indian heads of states speaking to each other.[14] China, in spite of looking forward to a world trading system that would offer lower subsidies to agricultural exports and lower tariffs on manufactured products, could not strike a different chord from India on safeguards. Its domestic rural and agricultural constituencies had to be sent a politically correct signal about the government's intention to protect their interests (Zheng and Kong 2009), particularly against the backdrop of it having conceded large market access during its entry to the WTO. China would have found it politically difficult to do more. In this respect, its compulsions were similar to those of India, which had always argued for protecting its farmers. Interestingly, the safeguard issue did not find Brazil as vocal as India and China. This is because, as an agricultural exporter, Brazil was keener on developed countries reducing subsidies on their farm exports, which they had committed to do, rather than worrying about a surge of imports on domestic producers, as did India.

From a broader perspective, the collapse of talks on the DDA showed the sharp political divide in the international community. The US refusal to allow more liberal use of safeguards against imports was on account of the apprehension that it might mean arbitrary deployment of safeguards by India and China and blocking access of its own agricultural exports into these markets (South Centre 2008). For India and China, and the large number of food-importing developing countries they represented, trade could not take precedence over domestic concerns on the livelihoods of farmers. The US and the rest of the developed world had probably anticipated that offers to cut subsidies on their own exports would appease the developing world. However, such offers were expected to be reciprocated by developing countries lowering tariffs on manufacturing exports from developed countries. Indeed, this is where China's reaction to the US allegation of India and China spoiling the talks was the sharpest and made it evident that it was not willing to withdraw protection from sensitive sectors such as chemicals, electronics and machinery the way the US wanted (Lim and Wang 2009). It was clear that varying postures on the perceived trade-off between trade liberalisation and livelihood concerns had sharply split the global trade community into distinct blocks. China and India represented one end of the spectrum while the US figured in the other. It was also clear that both China and India had acquired considerable economic clout in the world economy, so much so that global trade talks could not proceed without taking their views on board. The WTO was in a hurry to get the DDA going before the impending US presidential elections in November 2008, on the assumption that political change and economic recession in the US would reinforce protectionist tendencies and obstruct further progress on the DDA

(South Centre 2008). Nonetheless, China and India refused to budge on non-negotiable issues, indicating confidence in their economic prowess that underlined the faith that they could ensure expansion of their economies through domestic growth impulses and were not overtly dependent on resurrection in world trade.

The DDA has little possibility of resumption and conclusion unless China and India play proactive roles in doing so. There is a demand from the international community on both countries, particularly China, to influence the negotiations in a manner consistent with their current 'major' status in the world economy. This implies their moving away from defensive postures to more liberal attitudes towards the overall generation and granting of market access. An emerging view in this respect is to what extent S&D measures should extend to all developing countries by considering them a homogeneous group, since between these groups economic circumstances and trading capacities differ widely (Jianfu 2010). A natural corollary of this argument would be to consider whether, given their size and status in the world economy, China and India need to emphasise on S&D as much as they have been doing in global trade talks. It might be more useful if instead of benefiting from S&D in the same measure as many other small low-income countries, which are economically almost negligible compared to the Asian giants, China and India took more proactive postures in global trade talks by ensuring their smooth and broad-based functioning.

Both China and India have individually and collectively been pressing for early conclusion of the DDA. India recently reiterated the importance of doing so by suggesting that unless the DDA concludes, the credibility of the multilateral trade framework will be at stake.[15] However, both countries, along with Brazil and South Africa, while urging for a speedy conclusion, are also taking care to drive home the point that the 'development' dimension of the package drafted in July 2008 needs to be substantially improved.[16] Their emphasis on non-acceptance of unprecedented concessions by developing countries and demand for equivalent reciprocation from the developed world suggests that neither country is yet prepared to walk the middle path.

Climate change

The ongoing multilateral talks for addressing environmental concerns arising from climate change reveal as deep a divide among the international community as do the WTO negotiations. Indeed, climate change talks have given emerging market and developing countries a further opportunity to combine and present an alternative perspective on global development that is significantly different from that advanced by the developed world. Both China and India are active in shaping the developing country response to climate change and have shown surprising willingness to collaborate on the issue.

Like the DDA in multilateral trade talks, the Kyoto Protocol on Climate Change adopted in December 1997 in the 3rd Conference of Parties (COP) of the United Nation Framework Convention on Climate Change (UNFCCC) provided a roadmap for addressing global climate change issues. The Protocol accepted that developed countries have to take the lead in fighting global warming by cutting emissions of greenhouse gases (GHGs) that contribute to global warming.[17] The onus of reducing GHGs was entirely on developed countries comprising 40 industrialised nations (including the EU), clubbed as the Annex 1 group of countries under the UNFCCC.[18] These countries were to bring down their GHG emissions by an average of 5 per cent from the 1990 levels during the period 2008–12. Developing countries were exempted from any emission commitments under the Protocol. Thus China, India, Brazil and other major emerging market and developing countries did not have any binding commitments under the Kyoto Protocol.

The Protocol has seen the global North–South divide deepening sharply in a manner similar to that created by the DDA in the WTO. Developed countries, particularly the US, have been unhappy over developing countries being completely absolved of all emission commitments under the Kyoto Protocol. The discontent has centred on big emerging market economies such as China, India, Brazil and South Africa not being dragged into the mandatory emission-cut agenda. The US, a member of the Annex 1 group, refused to ratify the Kyoto Protocol on the ground that it exempted almost 80 per cent of the world from binding commitments and was an unfair deal for addressing climate change concerns; Australia also refused to ratify the Protocol on similar grounds (Jotzo 2004).

The refusal to ratify the Protocol was expected to generate repercussions. It certainly did, with the developing countries coming together to question the commitment of the developed world in curbing global warming. The first manifestation was in the ninth conference of the UNFCCC at Delhi in 2002, where, in response to the EU's expectations of developing countries engaging in a debate over controlling future emissions, the latter indicated that they were unwilling to discuss future commitments (Jotzo 2004).

In the years that followed, a few trends emerged clearly. First, it was evident that the success of the Kyoto Protocol was going to be limited. The agreement had to be taken beyond 2012 with new modalities for cutting emissions. The results from the first phase of the emission-reducing exercise was mixed, raising doubts about the commitment of all developed country parties in tackling emissions. Barring the Commonwealth of Independent States (CIS) and East European countries, the rest of the advanced nations were actually found to have higher levels of emissions in 2005 compared to the 1990 levels, creating serious doubts about their ability to fulfil Kyoto Protocol commitments (World Bank 2008). The US and other advanced nations were unlikely to push on emission commitments because of the fear of losing industrial competitiveness (Jotzo 2004). Second, though the developed countries, particularly the EU, were investing in low-carbon projects in developing countries as part of the 'Clean Development Mechanism' (CDM), financing requirements for shifting to low-carbon technologies in developing countries were very high. This propelled the international community to operationalise the 'Adaptation Fund' at the Bali meeting of the UNFCCC in 2007.[19] Third, it was clear that developing countries, particularly large ones such as China and India, had to assume larger roles in climate change talks sooner or later. As two of the world's largest carbon emitters,[20] their views on the future course of global action in mitigating as well as adapting to climate change were becoming increasingly important. Finally, it was also clear that several developed countries, particularly the US, would not implement emission commitments unless they got clear signals that the major developing countries were also a part of the process. Indeed, in this respect, the UNFCCC's principle of 'common and differentiated responsibilities', which was the basis of the Kyoto Protocol and ordained the developed world to play a larger role in the process, was unlikely to be heeded by some from the latter.

For both China and India, responding to climate change concerns has become a new imperative. As two of the world's fastest-growing and most rapidly industrialising economies, they have become major contributors to the inventory of GHGs. Total GHG emissions of China and India were estimated at 7,480 million metric tonnes and 2,380 million metric tonnes respectively in 2005 (MNP 2007). In terms of carbon dioxide (CO_2) emissions measured in 2007, however, China has overtaken the US as the world's largest emitter by contributing 22.3 per cent of total emissions (UN 2010). By the same yardstick, India has moved up the emission ladder to occupy the third position by contributing 5.5 per cent of total emissions. In per capita terms, though, they still remain far behind their counterparts in the developed world. At the same time, both of them have begun playing increasingly influential roles in global decision-making on critical issues. The expectation of the rest of the world that both would act responsibly in addressing climate change, and perhaps show the way by setting their own houses in order, is a realisation that has dawned upon both countries. As a result, while both countries are aligning with other major emerging market economies such as Brazil and South Africa for proposing action plans that are feasible for developing countries, they are also announcing their own domestic mitigation targets. Indeed, both are probably trying to follow a policy that China has consistently employed in the WTO talks: embarrass the developed world by drawing attention to how little the former has done in improving market access compared to what China has offered. In the climate change arena, most of the industrialised Annex 1 nations from Europe, Asia-Pacific and North America hardly have much to show in terms of cutting emissions of GHG despite being signatories to the Kyoto Protocol. China and India appear keen on underscoring the lack of performance of developed countries, and their concomitant lack of responsibility to a matter of such global importance as climate change, by performing fast on their home turf.

The China–India collaboration on climate change – as part of a broader association of large developing countries – came to the fore following the G8 summit (i.e. Britain, Canada, France, Germany, Italy, Japan, Russia and the US) at Heiligendam in Germany in June 2007. The summit was convened largely to decide an alternative to the Kyoto Protocol by including developing countries such as China and India in the overall plan to cut emissions and address climate change. In this respect, the G8 meeting was a response from the industrialised nations to shift the burden of reducing emissions on to the developing world – a posture that was consistent with the US criticism of the Kyoto Protocol. Indeed, the US fear was that the principle of 'common but differentiated responsibility' will allow China and India to continue their growth with energy-inefficient technologies and contribute copiously to the GHG inventory in the atmosphere without being penalised for it (Devarakonda 2007). The G8's call for reaching a detailed pact to decide emission cuts involving China and India was expected to be rebutted by both. Not only did the two countries react adversely to the suggestion of their setting binding emission caps, they also sent out a clear signal that they thought alike and would work together on the issue.[21] They joined Brazil, Mexico and South Africa to form the G5 and appealed for continuation of differentiated responsibility in handling climate change, with particular emphasis on allowing unimpeded transfer of environment-friendly technologies from the North to the South (Devarakonda 2007). The rift continued into the next G8 summit at Hokkaido in 2008, where the US view demanding China and India to be a part of global efforts to cut emissions appeared to have unified the industrialised nations on a common agenda. The postures of the G8 clearly reflected that international climate diplomacy had reached a stage where differentiated responsibility could no longer be accepted the way it was in the Kyoto Protocol. Industrialised economies had begun feeling the heat of rising domestic protests from environment-friendly measures such as a green tax and were also wary of an impending financial recession. They could therefore hardly be enthusiastic about endorsing an action agenda that would entail them bearing the entire liability and absolve China, India and other developing nations from similar burdens (Peiser 2008).

The year 2009 was significant in climate change negotiations. The assumption of office by a new US President conveyed hopes that the US might approach the climate change agenda in a different manner. Furthermore, with the Kyoto Protocol implementation period coming to a close, the urgency of putting in place an effective action plan after 2012 was gaining momentum. The fourth assessment of the Intergovernmental Panel on Climate Change (IPCC) that struck a sombre note on the progress of global efforts by underlining the possibility of sharp increase in GHG emissions in the coming decades, the serious dangers to resources and communities arising therefrom, and the emphasis on addressing both mitigation and adaptation through international cooperation, alerted the global community to the dire need for action. In the meantime, the financial crisis had set in deeply in most parts of the world, particularly North America and Europe; this was again bound to influence the level of their commitment to new efforts.

The G8 summit at Aquila in Italy saw the G8 countries deciding to cut emissions by 80 per cent by the year 2050. However, China and India again refused to accept binding emission targets, citing their growth and development as non-negotiable issues. The G5 that met the G8 on a variety of global issues reiterated its emphasis on shared but differentiated responsibility on climate change. It was becomingly increasingly clear that, much as China, India and the G5 resisted pressure to agree to binding emission cuts, they had to outline an agenda that would indicate action even if in a different way. Given the rapid economic elevation of China and India in the global economy, not only could climate change talks not proceed without their meaningful contributions, but for the future growth prospects of the two countries as well, it was important to initiate quick action. The first step in this regard was taken in the form of a bilateral agreement on cooperation for addressing climate change signed by China and India on 21 October 2009.[22] Coming a few weeks before the eagerly awaited UNFCCC meeting at Copenhagen in December 2009, the agreement indicated that both countries were prepared to overlook outstanding differences in other aspects of their relationship to work together on common development concerns. The agreement also indicated that Copenhagen could expect to see China and India continue their agitation on common and differentiated responsibility.

In a significant development indicating China's and India's willingness to steer climate talks in a positive direction, both countries announced plans to reduce carbon-intensity[23] in production over a period in time in the run-up to the Copenhagen summit. This followed the US announcement to cut GHG emissions in 2020 by around 17 per cent from the 2005 level. China declared its decision to trim carbon-intensity by 45 per cent by 2020 (Eilperin 2009), while India announced a targeted cut of 20–25 per cent by the same year (Dhar 2009).[24] While the decisions showed the inclinations of both countries to affirmative action on climate change, they also indicated their unwillingness to commit to binding emission cuts. Bringing down carbon emissions intensity over a certain period implied shifting to cleaner and more energy efficient means of production in the long term. While blanket targets on physical reduction of GHG gases can have serious implications for industrial output that might need to be physically limited, reducing carbon-intensity as a proportion of their GDPs gives developing countries like China and India greater flexibility for introducing more efficient practices over a period of time and gradually reducing emissions. In terms of mitigation approaches, this marked a departure from the advanced country method of addressing mitigation through physical emission cuts.

The Copenhagen climate summit failed to produce specific outcomes and ended up showing the international community sharply divided on the subject. The failure was partly due to poor climate diplomacy by the European countries led by host nation Denmark, which was perceived to take the lead in circulating a draft action plan heavily tilted against the interests of developing countries. In an atmosphere underlining lack of trust between the North and South, the accord finally drafted was a political statement without any legal binding. Following strong sentiments expressed by China, India, Brazil, South Africa and other major emerging market powers on the importance of differentiated responsibility, the deal was reportedly prepared by the US and the BASIC (Brazil, India, China, South Africa) group.[25] It included demands that were raised by both developed and developing countries from time to time.

While urging developed nations (Annex 1 parties of the Kyoto Protocol) to commit to country-wide emission targets, the accord also emphasised national mitigation actions (NMAs) by non-Annex 1 parties, that is non-industrialised developing nations (UNFCCC 2009). These NMAs, however, would be 'subject to international measurement, reporting and verification in accordance with guidelines adopted by the Conference of the Parties' (UNFCCC 2009, p. 2, paragraph 5).

The international verification requirements have introduced another element of friction between the developed and developing countries post-Copenhagen. Indeed, as developing countries fear, the promise at Copenhagen by developed countries to mobilise resources for aiding mitigation and adaptation in poorer countries (UNFCCC 2009)[26] might be contingent upon satisfaction of verification needs. These concerns remain, despite the Copenhagen accord being eventually endorsed by China, India and the BASIC. The tension over availability of funds and verification requirements was evident at the UN climate meeting at Tianjin in China held in October 2010. China and India, along with Brazil and South Africa, are becoming increasingly resistant to demands of international scrutiny and are citing what they consider insufficient pledges by advanced nations for their unwillingness to be scrutinised (ICTSD 2010). For developed countries, on the other hand, financial support for climate change actions in developing countries is contingent on verification. In the run-up to the Cancun ministerial in December 2010, India proposed a flexible mechanism of international assessment of the verification actions rather than assessment by the paying country.[27] The problem, however, remained unresolved, and at Cancun the US insistence on its taking proactive measures in cutting GHG emissions and providing financial resources to developing countries being contingent on China and India committing to measurable, reportable and verifiable actions, created serious roadblocks as the latter refused to budge (IANS 2010).

It is evident that climate change talks continue to suffer from a pronounced trust deficit between developed and developing countries. Despite the Copenhagen accord and announcement of emission cuts, there are fears on each side about fulfilment of commitments by the other. China and India realise that their persistent demands for a more equitable burden-sharing among major economic powers, along with reluctance to scrutiny, can invite repercussions. The most likely reactions are imposition of tariffs on Chinese and Indian exports to US and European markets on the ground of their not conforming to climate policy norms (ICTSD 2010). There are concerns over technology transfer processes as well. Future negotiations on trade at the DDA will be intricately linked to climate change issues. The linkages will pertain to issue of climate-based tariffs, technology transfer, sustainable agriculture and movement of goods.[28] As discussions and opinions on trade and climate continue to proliferate, both China and India increasingly realise the inevitability of their choosing positions echoing identical sentiments, given the similarity of their concerns.

Global economic governance and financial architecture

Inadequate representation in the decision-making processes of multilateral institutions has always been a complaint of developing countries. The under-representation is conspicuous in Bretton Woods institutions – the International Monetary Fund (IMF) and the World Bank – where the voting powers of emerging economies such as China, India, Brazil, Indonesia and Mexico are rather limited. These countries have been aggrieved over their voices in these institutions not being commensurate with their enlarging economic size and influence. On the other hand, the ability of Bretton Woods institutions, particularly the IMF, in addressing the problems of the developing world has been increasingly questioned. The Asian financial crisis of 1997, and more currently the global financial crisis of 2008, clearly demonstrated the inability of the IMF to not only judge but also tackle the adverse outcomes of the crises.

The recognition that emerging economies were not adequately involved in core matters of global economic and financial governance led to the formation of the G20 in 1999.[29] The group represented a collection of both advanced and industrialised economies (e.g. Australia, Canada, the EU, France, Germany, Italy, Japan, Russia, Korea, the UK and the US) as well as emerging markets and developing economies (e.g. Argentina, Brazil, China, India, Indonesia, Mexico, Saudi Arabia, South Africa and Turkey). The IMF and the World Bank are also part of the G20 meetings on an ex-officio basis, ensuring the inclusion of the Bretton Woods. While it is not an all-inclusive grouping and excludes not only small and low-income countries but several middle-income countries as well, the G20 has brought greater legitimacy to global decision-making by virtue of its accounting for almost 90 per cent of global output, 80 per cent of world trade and more than 60 per cent of global population.[30] It also has members drawn from other influential global and regional groupings such as the G8 (Canada, France, Germany, Italy, Japan, Russia, the UK and the US), the WTO (all except Russia), the East Asia Summit (EAS) (Australia, China, India, Indonesia, Japan, Korea), the Organisation of Petroleum-Exporting Countries (OPEC) (Indonesia, Saudi Arabia), the Annex 1 parties of Kyoto Protocol (Australia, Canada, France, Germany, Italy, Japan, Russia, UK)[31] and the G20 on agriculture (Argentina, Brazil, China, India, Indonesia, Mexico, South Africa).

Apart from gradually emerging as the most significant entity in global economic and financial decisions during the last decade, the maturing of the G20 has had a couple of other implications. The first and most obvious is the space that it has provided to emerging market and developing economies in articulating concerns on global economic matters. The roles of these economies in global finance have become increasingly dominant since the financial crisis of 2008. The G20 has provided an enabling platform in this respect particularly in advocating far-reaching reforms in the governance structure of the IMF. The second, and probably much less recognised, implication is the opportunity that it has provided to countries such as China and India in shaping the global financial process in a collaborative and mutually beneficial manner. Absence of a forum such as the G20 would have shrunk opportunities for the Indian and Chinese leaderships to come together on issues of common concern and global significance. On such matters in the G20, both have been mature enough to rise above bilateral bickerings and address global concerns in a way that preserves both the Asian regional and developing country interests.

The financial crisis has engineered re-shaping of the global economic order in a somewhat unexpected manner. Following the outbreak of the crisis, several countries of the world particularly in Europe, have been struggling to recover their economic strengths. In this respect, China and India have been exceptions and have weathered the crisis successfully without much damage. Both have been quick to return to high growth trajectories following temporary decelerations. During 2009, the year when world output contracted by 0.6 per cent owing to the crisis, China and India grew at the exceptional rates of 9.1 per cent and 5.7 per cent respectively. They are projected to grow by 10.5 per cent and 9.7 per cent respectively in 2010 (IMF 2010b). The contrast between the post-crisis Chinese and Indian growth rates vis-à-vis those of the G7 is conspicuous given that the members of the latter are projected to grow by 1.0–3.3 per cent in 2010 (IMF 2010a, Table 1.1, page 2). At the same time, China's and India's large foreign exchange and gold reserves have provided them with deep pockets for avoiding debt crises, which have severely affected several European economies and, to some extent, the US also.[32] Indeed, China (US$50 billion) and India (US$10 billion), along with Brazil (US$10 billion), Korea (US$10 billion) and Russia (US$10 billion), contributed to the expansion of the IMF's resources at the London summit of the G20 in April 2009 that decided to mobilise more resources for supporting crisis-affected emerging economies. It must also be noted that China's control over US long-term Treasury securities, which was estimated at US$1.16 trillion at the end of December 2010 amounting to 26.1 per cent of total securities, gives it considerable influence over the future prospects of the US economy. The US, and concomitantly the G7, cannot afford to overlook Chinese views and actions on critical economic issues. India, in contrast, is a much smaller holder of US securities and holds US$40.5 billion or 0.9 per cent of these securities at the end of December 2010. Brazil (US$186.1 billion) and Russia (US$151 billion) have shares of 4.2 per cent and 3.4 per cent each.[33] Between them the BRIC (Brazil, Russia, India and China) group hold around 35 per cent of US securities making them a fairly formidable force in the larger perspective of the prospects of the US and world economy.

The demonstrated resilience of most of the major emerging market economies to the repercussions of the financial crisis, and particularly China and India, has resulted in their assuming bigger roles in global financial regulations and economic governance. The first is evident from the major global financial regulatory institutions such as the International Organisation of the Securities Committees Organisation (IOSCO), the Basel Committee on Banking Supervision (BCBS) and the Financial Stability Forum (FSF)[34] inducting China, India, Brazil and other emerging market economies into their fold after the emergency G20 meeting in November 2008 convened at Washington to address the financial crisis. It was clear that without governance reforms entailing greater participation of the larger emerging market economies, regulatory agencies such as the FSF will lack the legitimacy to frame regulatory responses to the global crisis (Helleiner and Pagliari 2009). Indeed, the post-mortem of the crisis has underlined the failure on the part of most advanced economies to regulate their financial systems in an effective and stable manner, as opposed to India and China. It was therefore obvious that these two economies, with their emphasis on expansion of the international financial regulatory system and its better supervision, will become key players in the global financial architecture (Helleiner and Pagliari 2009).

The second aspect – China and India assuming bigger roles in governance of international financial institutions – is also becoming clear from the nature of changes suggested in the governance of major global economic institutions such as the IMF. The Bretton Woods twins – the IMF and the World Bank – have traditionally influenced global economics and finances the most, through their respective agendas. While the IMF has had important roles in influencing macroeconomic policies such as exchange rates, BOP, monetary measures and fiscal policies, the World Bank has been the 'development' arm of the Bretton twins and has dominated multilateral financing of project-based development and capacity-building. Both institutions have given developing countries a limited role in their decisions. This has always irked China, India and other emerging economies. They have been particularly unhappy over their low quota shares in the IMF (Table 5.1), which has restricted their voting power and the concomitant ability to influence major decisions. The demand for having a greater role in the IMF has gained currency with China, India and the BRIC, steadily increasing their clout in the world economy over the last couple of decades. The financial crisis and subsequent deliberations among the world's major economies have underscored the importance of reforming the IMF. The first meeting of the G20 ministers and central bank governors convened right after the financial crisis at Sao Paulo in early November 2008 indicated:

> We underscored that the Bretton Woods Institutions must be comprehensively reformed so that they can more adequately reflect changing economic weights in the world economy and be more responsive to future challenges. Emerging and developing economies should have greater voice and representation in these institutions. We welcome the progress made this year in reforming the IMF. We also noted the first step in the ongoing process of reform of the World Bank Group, which is to be followed by a wider share realignment. We emphasized our commitment to further reform the Bretton Woods Institutions in order to increase their legitimacy and effectiveness. Such reforms should also take into account the interests of the poorest countries and reflect their distinct mandates.
>
> (G20 2008a, p. 4, paragraph 12)

The above sentiments were reiterated in the declaration of the G20 summit in Washington that took place soon after and also in the G20 Leaders' meeting in London in April 2009 (G20 2008b, 2009a). The London meeting urged the IMF to quickly conclude its ongoing process of quota reviews that was expected to yield larger quota shares for China, India and other emerging market economies. The Pittsburgh Leaders' meeting in September 2009 committed to a shift of the IMF quota towards emerging markets and developing countries by ensuring a redistribution in quotas of at least 5 per cent from over-represented to under-represented countries (G20 2009b). In a further follow-up meeting at St Andrews in November 2009 to assess progress on various decisions taken by the G20 for addressing the financial crisis, the conclusion of the quota review by January 2011 was again emphasised (G20 2009c). The review was to consider not only the increase in the size of the quotas, but also possible changes in the composition of the IMF Executive Board. On 5 November 2010, the IMF announced the much-awaited quota reforms entailing a shift of more than 6 per cent of the existing quota shares from the advanced to the emerging market and developing economies. Along with these changes in quota shares, the Executive Board is also expected to become more representative by reducing the representation of advanced countries and having all its members elected, as opposed to the current practice of having some directors appointed (IMF 2010a).

The reforms at the IMF are expected to be followed by similar changes in the World Bank Group, also over a period in time. The joint Development Committee of the IMF and the World Bank in its annual spring meeting in April 2010 has endorsed a larger shift of the voting power in the International Bank for

Table 5.1 IMF and World Bank quota and vote shares (current and proposed)

	IMF quota and vote – current		*IMF quota and vote – proposed*		*World bank vote – current*	
	Quota (%)	*Vote (%)*	*Quota (%)*	*Vote (%)*	*IBRD (%)*	*IDA (%)*
G7 (Canada, France, Germany, Italy, Japan, UK and US)	45.2	44.4	43.4	41.2	42.9	42.7
BRIC (Brazil, Russia, India and China)	9.8	9.6	14.2	13.5	10.4	6.9
G20[1]	65.8	64.7	68.3	64.8	63.2	58.1

Source: IMF (2010b) www.imf.org/external/np/sec/pr/2010/pdfs/pr10418_table.pdf (accessed on 14 November 2010); Kawai and Petri (2010). G20 and BRIC shares are computed from these two sources.

Notes

1 The EU has one seat in the G20. The calculations here are for the remaining 19 members. They include all the G7 members that are part of the EU, such as France, Germany, Italy and Turkey.

2 IBRD and IDA are two of the five organisations comprising the World Bank Group. The other three are the International Finance Corporation (IFC), the Multilateral Investment Guarantee Agency (MIGA) and the International Centre for Settlement of Investment Disputes (ICSID). IBRD and IDA are the two agencies that provide loans and grants to members.

3 The shares of BRIC and G20 are the authors' calculations.

Reconstruction and Development (IBRD) to developing country members. This is expected to increase the voting power of developing countries and transition economies to 47.19 per cent from the existing 44.06 per cent (World Bank 2010). An increase in basic votes has also been proposed at the International Finance Corporation (IFC) that should result in the share of developing and transition economies increasing by more than 6 per cent to a total of 39.48 per cent (World Bank 2010).

The current gap between the G7 and the BRIC – the combine representing the four largest and most influential emerging market economies in the world – is rather conspicuous in both the IMF and the World Bank (Table 5.1). The BRIC has only 21.6 per cent of the G7's total quota in the IMF, and its corresponding votes are also 21.6 per cent of those of the G7. In the World Bank group, at the IBRD and IDA, the vote shares of the BRIC are 24.2 per cent and 16.2 per cent of the G7 respectively. China with 81,151 votes has 3.6 per cent of the IMF's total votes. This is lower than the total votes and vote shares of the US (371,743 votes; 16.7 per cent share), Japan (133,378 votes, 6.0 per cent share), Germany (130,332 votes; 5.9 per cent share), France and United Kingdom (107,635 votes, 4.8 per cent shares). Only Canada (63,942 votes; 2.9 per cent share) among the G7 has a smaller number of votes and a lower vote share than China. This distribution of votes is certainly inconsistent if looked at in terms of current economic size, with China having emerged as the second largest economy in the world. On the other hand, India, with 41,832 votes, has 1.9 per cent share of total votes. Other than the G7 and China, India has fewer votes and lower vote shares than Belgium (46,302 votes, 2.1 per cent), the Netherlands (51,874 votes; 2.3 per cent), Saudi Arabia (70,105 votes; 3.2 per cent) and Russia (59,704 votes; 2.7 per cent). Whether it is in terms of nominal GDP measured at current market prices, or in PPP terms, India's economic size is greater than at least Belgium, Netherlands, Russia and Saudi Arabia.[35] China and India have also been irked by the fact that the IMF's executive board has five appointed (non-elected) directors from among the G7, who hold 38.7 per cent of total votes. Elected directors represent the remaining 61.3 per cent of the IMF's votes, out of which China and India account for only 14.5 per cent.[36]

Even after the proposed reforms, which are a result of the fast-changing economic landscape following the financial crisis in which China, India and other major emerging markets are playing much bigger roles, the balance of power in the IMF will remain with the G7 and developed countries (Table 5.1). From an administrative sense as well, the IMF Executive Board, which is now dominated by the G7 and Europe, is unlikely to undergo major changes immediately. It would also be irrational to expect that the Board, which is now heavily dominated by the G7, will give way to one with greater representation of emerging economic powers. China and India will have to accept the reality that reforming the IMF governance in a manner of their choice will require more effort and time. However, they can certainly be happy over the fact that the G20 has emerged as the most powerful decision-making body on global economic matters and has been dictating the way in which the IMF should function (Palit 2010b).

The G20 has been firmly emphasising not only a more 'balanced' IMF for reflecting the right weights of countries in the world economy, but also the importance of achieving sustainable development. The latest G20 summit in Seoul in November 2010 has articulated a 'Development Consensus' urging co-ordinated action for reducing poverty, improving food security and progressing on Millennium Development Goals (MDGs) (G20 2010). The G20's emphasis on development, balanced global institutions and effective financial regulations reflects the increasing influence of emerging markets and developing countries, particularly India and China, in shaping its views. From a larger geo-political sense, China and India, along with Brazil, Mexico, Russia and South Africa have been successful in ensuring that the G20 is not dominated by the interests of the G7. The financial crisis has been an unexpected help in this respect and has turned the tide firmly in favour of emerging market economies. While the IMF will take more time to become 'balanced', its increasing subordination to the G20, and the rising influence of China and India in the latter, signals the success they have begun to achieve in collaborating on transforming international institutions.

6 The economics–politics dynamics, competition and collaboration

It is well known that the economic engagement between the two Asian giants has been accompanied by a turbulent political relationship. Though there are examples of countries having good economic ties along with uneasy political relations (e.g. China and Taiwan), the dichotomy always creates anxiety over whether political problems will affect economic engagement and make it unsustainable in the longer term. Healthy political ties are considered conducive to bilateral economic engagement. Bilateral trade, investment and commercial transactions are expected to profit and multiply with improvement in mutual political ties. The reverse posturing underlines the possibility of bad political ties disrupting good economic relationships. Both underpin a positive association between political and economic ties with improvement (deterioration) in political ties similarly influencing economic ties. Like other bilateral relationships that possess these contrasting features, the India–China ties too cannot be outside the domain of this association, though until now the relationship has appeared to be progressing irrespective of the contrasts. Nonetheless, whether political tensions will affect the good economic relations between the two countries is a question that agitates not only the observers of the relationship, but also the different economic actors involved in the China–India bilateral economics.

From a macro-perspective, the Sino-Indian relationship can be clearly distinguished into healthy (economic) and unhealthy (political) components. While this macro-perspective helps in distinguishing between the economic and non-economic components of the relationship in terms of their quality, the economic component can be further distinguished into competition and collaboration (or cooperation). This implies that the Sino-Indian economic relationship is not only somewhat exclusive of politics, but is also heterogeneous by itself, comprising contradictory traits. Indeed, this is where one would be tempted to argue that political estrangement can occasionally reinforce the competitive aspect of economic ties by increasing trade friction and race for global natural resources. As the earlier chapters have discussed, Sino-Indian economic relations include a visible competitive strand, with the two racing to acquire energy assets in different parts of the world, trying to gain access to new markets through regional and preferential trade agreements and building partnerships with smaller economies by disbursing innovative development assistance. Though these responses can be partly explained as supply-side measures for meeting rising demands from large populations and fast-expanding domestic economies, strategic motives driven by geo-political considerations are equally, if not more, important. Unfortunately, if economic decisions such as buying overseas energy assets or entering into trade agreements with other countries are driven less by non-economic considerations and more by political factors, they end up entailing fairly large costs. For China and India, such costs involve trying to outbid each other in purchasing energy assets in different parts of the world, or striking trade deals with countries with whom the other has already done so, leading to unnecessary trade diversion. A legitimate concern with respect to the future outlook for the China–India economic relationship is that political difficulties might increase bilateral trade friction or force both to compete unnecessarily with each other.

How real is the fear that bad politics can affect good economics between China and India? This chapter attempts to examine this concern by taking a close look at other bilateral relationships that have contextual similarities with the Sino-Indian case for assessing whether divergent political and economic trajectories between two countries are sustainable over time. However, it must be admitted at the outset that obtaining close parallels of the Sino-Indian contemporary relationship is difficult, since the relationship is rather unique. This is because, in addition to the political mistrust and competition over resources and markets, China and India have a strong and positive collaborative component to their economic ties, as discussed in the earlier chapters. This is evident from robust growth in bilateral trade, increasing cross-border investments, more and more business and commercial exchanges and consistent cooperation at global forums on issues of mutual concern (such as climate change and world trade). The co-existence of competition and collaboration in the Sino-Indian relationship is probably what makes it unique in a globalised world and makes it essential to study how the two countries manage the two conspicuous 'C's. The key objective of this chapter is to examine whether politics has the possibility of interrupting or reversing economics between China and India at any point in time, either exogenously or by influencing counterproductive competition.

The Sino-Indian context: searching parallels

Each bilateral relationship between pairs of countries is unique by itself. It is difficult to generalise these relationships and draw parallels with others. However, comparison of similar traits between relationships can help in identifying those relations that are contextually similar. This, again, can at best be a broad sweep for clubbing some relationships in a common group or category.

As mentioned earlier, finding parallels with the Sino-Indian relationship is not easy, because it has distinct competitive and collaborative traits. Beyond these qualitative aspects, the Sino-Indian relationship has several other distinct features that make it unique and difficult to locate parallels. It actually has far more distinct features than other contemporary bilateral relationships because of the ancient histories and civilisations of both countries. They share common boundaries and are the world's largest and most populous countries, with records of commercial and cultural exchanges dating back to centuries. Both have been victims of colonial oppression and have embarked on new courses after the end of the Second World War after nearly two centuries of economic and cultural suppression. The history of the last five decades shows both of them passing through periods of prolonged economic stagnation before breaking free from the shackles of low growth to figure among the world's fastest-growing economies in the current century. Both have large militaries and nuclear capabilities. They enjoy considerable strategic influence in the modern world, particularly after the financial crisis of 2008, which has seen the advanced economies in the West struggling to recover but China and India bouncing back fast. They now trade vigorously with each other and are also becoming prominent investors in each other's countries. But they speak different languages and have different political systems, rule of law and institutions. Finally, they have outstanding territorial disputes that have remained unresolved for decades. And, in an overarching sense, they are somewhat circumspect of each other's presence, rise and growth, and are therefore not fully willing to trust each other.

There would hardly be relationships that have as many diverse common features as the complex China–India relationship. In terms of drawing insights from other bilateral relationships on whether politics can ruin the economics between China–India, it is probably sensible to look for parallels among relationships that have similar contrasting trajectories; bad – or, more precisely, not so good – political ties along with strong economic ties.[1] Within the broad choice set of such relationships, it is also probably logical to select those that involve either China or India: in other words, examine bilateral partnerships involving China or India where there is co-existence of political tension and economic bonhomie.

There could be two starting points for this examination: to begin with countries with whom China and India have good economic relations and then analyse whether such relations are accompanied with difficult political ties, or the reverse – that is, commence from difficult political relations and search the nature of economic quality in them. Given that both countries are large emerging markets in a globalised world where the majority of commercial transactions take place between big economies, the density of China's and India's economic engagements are greater with other large economies and big markets. This narrows down the choice of sets for examination to bigger economic partners of both economies, which would arguably be major world economies by themselves. In this respect, a simple way of proceeding with the empirical analysis is to identify the top trade partners of both countries, with trade being the best proxy of economic engagement, and investigating the quality of political relations that China and India have with these countries.

There is, though, a certain methodological shortcoming in employing this analysis. China's and India's major trade partners may not, in their own bilateral relations with China or India, reflect most of the features of the Sino-Indian relationship. This is more so for India. China is India's only neighbour who is one of its largest trade partners as well as one with whom India has territorial disputes and serious political differences. None of India's other neighbours – Bangladesh, Sri Lanka or Pakistan – are among its major trade partners, though with all these countries India's political relations have experienced fairly turbulent phases. On the other hand, none of its other large trade partners, such as the US, Japan, Saudi Arabia, Europe or the United Arab Emirates (UAE), are its neighbours in terms of sharing common boundaries (though Saudi Arabia and the UAE are in considerably close geographical proximity) nor does India have territorial disputes with them. From an Indian perspective, therefore, its relation with China is unique in the sense of it reflecting engagement with a neighbour with whom commercial relations are robust but political ties are lukewarm. China, on the other hand, has relatively closer parallels vis-à-vis its relations with India. Taiwan, South Korea and Japan are three of its major trade partners, who are not only in its neighbourhood but with whom it has had territorial skirmishes and volatile political exchanges. Thus, while the good economics–bad politics dynamics has more scope for empirical application in China's relations, the flexibility is less in India's case. Nonetheless, for both countries, parallels are chosen that reflect as much of their mutual contexts as possible. For China, the examination in the remaining part of this chapter will focus on Taiwan (or Chinese Taipei), South Korea (Republic of Korea) and Japan. For India, a similar exercise will include Japan, Saudi Arabia and the UAE. Finally, for both, the US and EU will also be examined, given their significance as China and India's economic partners.

It is common knowledge that bilateral data reflecting trade between countries varies widely among national source agencies. This can be a problem in proceeding with the analysis proposed and can produce empirical inconsistencies. In order to avoid the problem, the chapter sticks to two main data sources for studying trends in trade. China's bilateral trades are studied on the basis of statistics provided by the Direction of Trade Statistics (DOTS) database of the International Monetary Fund (IMF). On the other hand, India's bilateral trades with the countries studied in this chapter are reported on the basis of statistics obtained from the Reserve Bank of India (RBI)'s *Handbook of Statistics on the Indian Economy*.

China–Taiwan

China's trade relations with Taiwan have not only been robust, but have also been scaling new heights with both countries enmeshing deeply in each other's production networks through extensive intra-industry trade in a variety of manufactures. Table 6.1 shows the trend in China–Taiwan trade from 2002, since the time China joined the WTO. During this period, the trade increased six-fold, rising from US$18.5 billion in 2002 to US$112.9 billion in 2010. Excluding re-exports and re-imports, bilateral trade has increased from US$17.9 billion to US$108.3 billion, representing an identical six-fold increase. This indicates that China–Taiwan trade is not driven by mere transfer of products from one customs territory to another – as re-exports and re-imports are – but is driven more by exchanges involving value addition on each other's soil. From a production network perspective, China–Taiwan trade is a key example of the informal ethnic business networks that have flourished in East Asia for decades and have been the key drivers for sustaining economic activity in the region.

The depth and intensity of China and Taiwan's trade engagement can be gauged from the fact that during the period 2002–10, China has been Taiwan's largest trade partner. Taiwan's total trade during this period is estimated at US$3.5 trillion, out of which trade with China is US$598.7 billion, accounting for 17.3 per cent of Taiwan's total trade.[2] China has been Taiwan's largest export market, absorbing 22.4 per cent of its total exports during 2002–10, and the second largest source of imports during this period with 11.9 per cent of total imports. China runs a trade deficit with Taiwan, which is reflective of the fact that it has been importing several manufactures from Taiwan, mostly parts and components, and assembling the same for re-export to other markets. This is largely consistent with the trade pattern followed by China with the rest of the East Asian region (Zhao 2007).

Political relations between China and Taiwan – or more precisely between the People's Republic of China (PRC) and the Republic of China (ROC) – have been particularly adverse since 1949, when the two countries on the western and eastern sides of the Taiwan Strait (i.e. Mainland China and Taiwan) became domains of different governments representing different political ideologies at the end of the Chinese Civil War. While both have staked claims for custodianship of 'all China' and have frequently run into conflicts over control of islands in the neighbourhood, relations have become more complicated with Taiwan showing signs of shifting from the 'One China'[3] policy and articulating demands of independence and separate political identity. The interesting aspect of the relationship, however, is the almost complete lack of influence that strained political ties have had on economic relations. As mentioned earlier, in the years that followed China's entry in the WTO, i.e. 2002–10, it has been the largest trade partner of Taiwan. The remarkable increase in bilateral trade during this period has taken place notwithstanding a

Table 6.1 China–Taiwan bilateral trade (2002–10)

Year	*Trade (US$ billion) including re-exports and re-imports*	*Trade (US$ billion) excluding re-exports and re-imports*
2002	18.5	17.9
2003	33.9	32.4
2004	53.1	50.7
2005	63.7	60.8
2006	76.6	72.9
2007	90.4	86.3
2008	98.3	94.3
2009	78.7	75.2
2010	112.9	108.3

Source: Trade Statistics, Bureau of Foreign Trade, Government of Taiwan; http://cus93.trade.gov.tw/ENGLISH/FSCE/.

souring of political ties subsequent to Taiwan's intentions of pursuing democracy. On the contrary, the maintenance of robust trade and economic ties has led to certain marked improvement of relations as far as the establishment of deeper territorial linkages is concerned, through full resumption of direct shipping, air and postal services from December 2008 after a hiatus of nearly six decades.[4]

The astonishing part of China–Taiwan trade is the growth and intensity it has experienced despite trade-discouraging barriers imposed on political grounds. A key part of these barriers was the lack of transportation links between the two economies. Lack of direct air and sea connections between Mainland China and Taiwan heavily increased the cost of exchange of goods. All shipping between China and Taiwan had to be routed through the Okinawa islands, resulting in large shipping costs on both sides. Similarly, flights between the two countries had to be routed through Hong Kong, which resulted in unnecessary costs. While these costs will substantially reduce, the notable feature is that they probably would have remained unchanged had both countries not realised that it is important to maintain the robust bilateral economic activity and taken steps for facilitating it. The facilitation has not remained confined to the establishment of transport and trade links; it has extended to the signing of an Economic Cooperation Framework Agreement (ECFA) between Taiwan and China on 12 September 2010. Though there are some concerns in Taiwan over the impact of the Agreement on the domestic labour market arising from the influx of workers from Mainland China, the ECFA has been signed and executed.

China–Taiwan relations clearly indicate that bad politics could not act as a dampener on good economics. Indeed, good economics overcame the opportunity costs inflicted by bad politics to encourage a significant confidence-building measure (CBM) such as the ECFA. This is not to suggest, though, that the ECFA does not have other motivations. As Rosen and Wang (2010) argue, Taiwan's motivations behind the ECFA could have been competing regional agreements such as the China–ASEAN agreement, which might have influenced Taiwan into thinking that strategic economic costs of not having an economic agreement with China might be high, given that the region's core economies are already pursuing such agreements. The authors further suggest that Beijing's hopes from the ECFA, besides economic gains, are longer-term expectations of cross-straits relations gradually normalising. Both Taiwan and China are conscious of the deep integration between their economies and realise that lack of formal close relations might entail significant economic losses. This is probably the main reason that has helped the China–Taiwan economic relationship to overcome negative political interference.

China–South Korea

China's diplomatic ties with South Korea, or more precisely the Republic of Korea (ROK), were established only after the end of the Cold War in 1992. Four decades of diplomatic vacuum and political estrangement did not prove to be detrimental to economic ties. From a paltry US$5 billion in 1992, bilateral trade increased to US$186.1 billion in 2008, exhibiting an annual average growth of almost 30 per cent during 1992–2008 (Zhou 2010). The last decade, which captures bilateral trade trends after China's entry into the WTO (Table 6.2), shows an annual increase of 21.5 per cent, which of course has been influenced by the negative growth in trade in the year 2009, when the financial crisis took its toll on bilateral trade.

The pattern of China's trade with the ROK is similar to its trade with Taiwan, with the balance of trade being in the ROK's favour. China's imports from Korea outweigh its exports and the trade gap between the two countries has widened over time. With bilateral trade with China being more than 20 per cent of the ROK's total trade, China has been the ROK's key destination for exports and source of imports. Over time, the structure of bilateral trade has shifted more towards capital- and technology-intensive products, with South Korean firms in China playing a major role in influencing the structure of trade and giving it a more pronounced horizontal intra-industry dimension (Zhou 2010).

While statistics do indicate that bilateral trade is high and both countries are key trade partners of each other, annual growth trends point to a deceleration in the rate of growth in bilateral trade. From a high rate of 43.4 per cent in 2003, growth in trade has dropped to 16.2 per cent in 2008. The lower growth has been induced largely by a steady decline in China's imports from Korea, which have reduced from a peak annual growth of 50.9 per cent in 2003 to only 7.8 per cent in 2008. China's exports to Korea, however, do not exhibit a declining growth rate and have grown in the range of 38.4 per cent – 26.0 per cent during the period.

It could purely be a coincidence that the declining trend in bilateral trade has set in from a time when China–ROK political relations entered a difficult phase after being stable and positive for more than a decade. The ROK's political ties with China since resumption of diplomatic relations have been based largely on economic engagement since China has never distanced itself politically from North Korea. But China's commencement of the 'Northeast Asian History

Table 6.2 China–South Korea bilateral trade (2002–9)

	Exports (US$ billion)	*Imports (US$ billion)*	*Trade (US$ billion)*
2002	15.5	28.6	44.1
2003	20.1	43.1	63.2
2004	27.8	62.2	90.0
2005	35.1	76.8	112.0
2006	44.6	89.8	134.4
2007	56.1	104.1	160.2
2008	73.9	112.2	186.1
2009	53.6	102.5	156.1

Source: IMF, Direction of Trade Statistics (DOTS).

Note

Export+Import and Export–Import may not always produce the reflected trade and trade balance numbers because of rounding off of decimals.

Project' and the backlash in the ROK following China's decision to eliminate historical references to Korea in connection to the Goguryeo kingdom was the first major bilateral political dispute since normalisation of relations in 1992 (Snyder 2004). The incident led to a considerable shift in public opinion in Korea against China. Gries (2005) argues that China's claim of Goguryeo as its vassal state aroused suspicion among Koreans about their neighbour. The political jolt over Goguryeo was followed by trade disputes over *kimchi* in 2005[5] that led to tightening of food safety and inspection norms in both countries. More political irritation was created by the territorial dispute over a submerged rock between Korea's Mara Island and China's Tongdao Island which both claim to be part of their own exclusive economic zones (Zhou 2010).

While political tensions could have influenced hardening of positions on trade issues and contributed indirectly to deterioration in trade and business prospects, the deceleration in trade growth can be explained more directly by a steady erosion in competitiveness of Korean manufactures compared to their Chinese counterparts. Lower competitiveness explains a steady reduction in the growth rate of the ROK's exports to China and the corresponding decline in overall bilateral trade. Zhou (2010) and Snyder (2007) refer to surveys by Korean agencies that clearly indicate loss of competitiveness of Korean manufactures vis-à-vis those of China, particularly in technology. Chinese products are not only penetrating deeper into Korea's domestic market, they are also eating into spaces occupied by Korean firms in third-country markets. Mounting worries of Korean producers over loss of competitiveness are aggravated by concerns over potential adverse impacts of a bilateral FTA offering greater tariff concessions and deeper market access to Chinese products.

On the whole, bilateral economic relations between the two economic giants of East Asia over the last few years have experienced a few rough patches, primarily due to narrowing of the competitive gap that Korean products had over China. While at the macro-level economic relations remain strong, with both countries being key trade partners of each other and cross-border investments and economic agreements continuing to occur, the loss of comparative advantage of Korean producers may influence the quality of future economic engagement. Anxieties of further losses in market share can generate protective tendencies. Such tendencies strengthen in situations of ebbing political goodwill, leading to protective actions like anti-dumping and the imposition of rigid technical standards on exports, creating more trade friction. Indeed, South Korean industry's apprehensions about a bilateral trade deal with China are qualitatively similar to those of the Indian industries. Both are worried about Chinese exports driving domestic producers out of business. The worries are accentuated by the political 'trust deficit' that both the ROK and India have with respect to China.

China–Japan

The relationship between Northeast Asia's two major powers, which are also the world's second and third largest economies at present, has been one of the more complex bilateral relationships of contemporary times. The two countries – among the world's ancient civilisations and geographically separated by only a short stretch of water – have had a history of military skirmishes in the nineteenth and twentieth centuries, followed by a period of tense co-existence during the Cold War years. Yet Japan was one of the earliest to scout out deeper economic ties with China following the latter's opening up and adoption of economic reforms from 1978. It was quick to realise the potential of the Chinese economy and was keen on playing an active role in China's economic modernisation. It did so through official development assistance (ODA) and investments by Japanese firms. The latter were among the first to open factories in a reforming China. Indeed, Chinese Premier Deng Xiaoping reportedly requested Akio Morita, head of Sony, a few weeks after China's introduction of economic reforms, to invest in China.[6] Japanese firms have been one of the largest sources of foreign direct investment (FDI), for China with a significant part of the FDI being of the export-oriented variety, i.e. producing in China with the objective of exporting to third-country markets.

Bilateral trade in 2001, just before China entered the WTO, was US$87.9 billion. During the years that followed, trade increased at a rapid pace (Table 6.3). The bilateral trade pattern shows a similarity with the patterns of trade that China has with Taiwan and South Korea, reflecting its dependence on imports from Japan for assembling and eventual export to other markets. Japanese firms, like South Korean and Taiwanese firms based in China, have been instrumental in engineering this vertical intra-industry trade. Xing (2008) estimates share of intra-industry trade in total bilateral trade to have increased from 37 per cent to 72 per cent during 1990–2007, making intra-industry trade the main driver of bilateral trade.

Sino-Japanese bilateral trade of US$228.9 billion in 2009 was larger than both Sino-ROK and Sino-Taiwan trade for the year (Tables 6.2 and 6.1), underlining the significance of China and Japan's bilateral economic exchanges for

Table 6.3 China–Japan bilateral trade (2002–9)

	Exports (US$ billion)	*Imports (US$ billion)*	*Trade (US$ billion)*
2002	48.5	53.5	102.0
2003	59.4	74.2	133.6
2004	73.5	94.4	167.9
2005	84.1	100.5	184.6
2006	91.8	115.8	207.6
2007	102.2	133.9	236.1
2008	116.2	150.8	267.0
2009	98.0	130.9	228.9

Source: IMF, Direction of Trade Statistics (DOTS).

Note
Export+Import and Export–Import may not always produce the reflected trade and trade balance numbers because of rounding off of decimals.

the Asia-Pacific region. The interesting point to note is that the growth in trade has occurred notwithstanding the surfacing of political tensions during Japanese Prime Minister Koizumi's administration. The middle years of the last decade particularly were marked by a low exchange of high-level visits and protests in both countries against each other. Nonetheless, as Xing (2008) notes, growth in trade and investment remained indifferent to political tensions experienced otherwise, particularly the Prime Minister's visit to the Yasukuni shrine.[7] What is also noteworthy is that fast growth of trade and deeper economic integration with China was one of the major reasons behind Japan's quick recovery from the prolonged economic stagnation that it suffered from during the 1990s.

Armstrong (2010) argues that the volatile China–Japan political relationship over the last three or four decades never really upset the economic relationship despite apprehensions that it might do so. He explains the stability and steady growth in bilateral economic ties, despite political irritants to the complementary economic structures and the fact that both are part of the multilateral trade framework run by the WTO. Japan, a long supporter of multilateral trade as well as a keen contributor to China's economic modernisation, drew considerable confidence from China's decision to join the WTO, which signalled the latter's commitment to a rules-based trade regime. Complementarities in economic structures and featuring in the WTO are traits common to China and India as well. An interesting exception in the India–China case, though, is India's apprehensions over China's domination of its domestic market and the frequent application of anti-dumping actions. Japan–China trade relations have had much less friction arising from protective tendencies on either side.

In more recent months, political turbulence in the Sino-Japan relationship reached a new high in September 2010 with Japan's detention of a Chinese fishing boat captain close to the Senkaku Islands northeast of Taiwan. The islands are the subject of territorial dispute between the two countries. The incident led to widespread protests in China and also retaliatory actions in economic, cultural and diplomatic fields (Mulgan 2010). More incidents like these, symbolising political lows, can generate disruptive costs for trade and business. The possibility of disruption needs to be viewed in the context of some fundamental changes occurring in the bilateral relationship. The rapid narrowing of the economic gap between China and Japan has forced the latter to visualise China as at least an equivalent, if not a superior, economic entity. This is a far cry from the days when Japan played a key role in building capacities of the Chinese economy. Not only has China's dependence on Japanese aid become marginal, its shift to high value-added exports is making several of its products technologically as competitive as those of Japan. This is a trend observed in the Sino-ROK relationship as well. Japan's own economic difficulties, which would be aggravated by the catastrophic earthquake and tsunami in March 2011, coupled with increasing isolation on multilateral issues such as climate change, have led to both economic and strategic frustration for the country. Japan's dominance of the Asia-Pacific has clearly made way for China, as is evident from the region's acquiring an increasingly

'China-centric' character since the Asian financial crisis of 1997 and more so after the global financial crisis of 2008. These geo-economic rebalancings contain triggers that can provoke fairly strong nationalist responses from both sides – a Japan feeling increasingly marginal and a China more confident and secure in its progress. Whether commercial relations between two of Asia's and the world's giant economies will remain immune to the latest hardening of political tensions, as they mostly have in the past, will be revealed only over time. But the facts that they are Asia's largest markets and complementary to each other in economic and production structures may well help them in rising above political skirmishes for economic benefits.

China–European Union (EU)

The EU and the US, as discussed later in this chapter, are two relationships that are qualitatively distinct from a Chinese perspective from those discussed earlier. Taiwan, the ROK and Japan are not only China's close neighbours in Northeast Asia, they are also countries with whom China has had, or continues to have, territorial disputes. All three and China are major economies of the Asia-Pacific with fairly close integration of production and business networks. None of these features are present in the China–EU or China–US relationships. Nonetheless, these relationships are being analysed from the point of view of examining the association between politics and economics for China's major economic partners. Though China does not have territorial disputes with the EU or the US simply because geography does not permit such possibilities, its political ties with both have experienced rough patches. From the larger 'politics–economics' nexus therefore, the two are interesting partners of China to look at.

The China–EU bilateral trade is one of the largest bilateral trade relationships in the world. The trade was US$281.9 billion in 2009, which was lower than the US$330.5 billion recorded in 2008. The decline was on account of the global financial crisis that resulted in a sharp deceleration of global and bilateral trade between the world's two largest trade entities. Barring this exceptional year, however, China's entry in the multilateral trade system of the world has been followed by sustained growth in bilateral trade with trade experiencing an almost five-fold increase during 2002–8. Chinese exports to the EU have been expanding rapidly showing an average growth of 31.7 per cent during 2002–8, while imports show a corresponding annual average growth of 21.3 per cent. The burgeoning trade has resulted in the EU becoming China's largest trade partner and China becoming the EU's second largest trade partner.[8] This has happened despite the EU not granting China market economy status under the WTO, while it has recognised the same for Russia.

Traditionally, the EU and China have belonged to different cultures, traditions, systems and ideologies. Though today the EU is a homogeneous group of 27 countries, before it assumed a collective identity, during the Cold War period, China's relations with most of Europe were cold on account of irreconcilable political and ideological differences. After the end of the Cold War, the

Table 6.4 China–EU bilateral trade (2002–9)

	Exports (US$ billion)	*Imports (US$ billion)*	*Trade (US$ billion)*
2002	38.9	33.1	72.0
2003	59.1	46.2	105.3
2004	82.0	59.4	141.4
2005	111.8	62.3	174.1
2006	139.9	76.9	216.8
2007	184.0	93.6	277.5
2008	219.3	111.2	330.5
2009	174.4	107.5	281.9

Source: IMF, Direction of Trade Statistics (DOTS).

Note
Export+Import and Export–Import may not always produce the reflected trade and trade balance numbers because of rounding off of decimals.

formation of the EU and the emergence of the WTO, Europe and China have been at opposite ends of the spectrums of most issues. These include some of the contentious issues in the Doha round of multilateral trade negotiations, particularly agricultural subsidies and government procurement. Climate change is another area where the positions have been very different, with China emphasising 'common, but differentiated responsibilities' along with India, Brazil and other countries and urging for more burden-sharing by Kyoto Protocol countries, whereas the EU has taken a markedly different position. Europe has periodically expressed its reservations over lack of political freedom in China, and particularly human rights, and has been uncomfortable with the lack of democratic foundations and institutions. Its stance on Tibet and Taiwan has also been uncomfortable for China.

The potential source of disruptions in trade and commerce has arisen from Europe's unhappiness over the deep intrusion of Chinese exports into its domestic market, affecting the interests of local producers. The biggest occasion for friction arose after Chinese textile exports flooded European markets following the abolition of international garment quotas in the erstwhile Multi-Fibre Agreement (MFA) from 1 January 2005. There have also been several occasions of anti-dumping actions against China. An important factor that continues to remain a political irritant is the European embargo on arms sales to China that was imposed after the Tiananmen Square incident of 1989. The EU's tendency to link the lifting of the embargo to the human rights record in China and other associated reforms probably means it will not be lifted immediately. In more recent times, a somewhat conspicuous political confrontation was noticed during November 2008, when China refused to proceed with the EU–China summit on account of President Sarkozy's meeting with the Dalai Lama.

Barring intrinsic differences between the two sides over their political, legal, business and economic systems, which do create difficulties in trade and investment on non-tariff barriers (e.g. labelling and certification standards) in China and high agricultural subsidies and technical barriers in the EU, there have not been abrupt political flare-ups threatening the economic relationship. This is, in fact, a major difference with respect to China's relations with its Asian neighbours discussed here, with whom sudden tensions over disputed territories or on other outstanding issues have tended to mar political relations, with attendant anxieties of the tensions spilling over into the economic arena. China and EU appear to have recognised their differences well and are keen on doing business while maintaining a clear political distance. Fox and Godement (2011), commenting on the EU's strategy towards China, emphasises that for the EU engagement with China is positive in itself, since Europe holds the view that an increase in China's interface with the continent will change China in a manner preferred by Europe. China, on the other hand, has been conscious of Europe's internal divisions (which probably prevent it from adopting a strong and focused China policy) and has been keen to exploit the continent's economic size through meaningful commercial ties.

As of now, economic ties show little possibility of succumbing to political differences. But the future outlook for bilateral commerce will depend on shapes assumed by a few emerging issues. One of these is how much European and Chinese views contradict and conflict with each other in African countries and other 'imperfect' states of the world with respect to the relationship between human rights records and receipt of development assistance. The second and more powerful downside could be the rapid economic deterioration of the EU after the global financial crisis and its own debt mismanagement. China has assured the EU of its support by pledging to buy debts of precariously placed EU members such as Spain, Greece and Portugal (Dreyer 2011). The revival of its largest trade partner's domestic economy is important to China for maintaining its export and economic growth. However, greater purchase of debt denominated in euros can influence the exchange rates of the yuan vis-à-vis both euro and dollar, which may not be in China's best economic interests. China's economic strategy towards Europe, therefore, will need to carefully balance various priorities. Such balancing might generate occasional political tensions, though these are not expected to affect economic ties, which depend more on the global and bilateral economic outlooks.

China–US

In terms of bilateral economic relationships, the China–US pairing is among the largest, if not the largest, of such relationships. They are not only the world's largest and second largest economies, but also two of the most populated countries, with the world's largest militaries and biggest energy consumers and carbon emitters. Despite having contrasting systems and institutions – political, social and economic – the China–US economic relationship has grown from strength to strength, notwithstanding numerous differences between the two countries on political issues.

Following almost three decades of diplomatic estrangement after the Second World War, China–US diplomatic relations commenced from 1979. Bilateral trade picked up immediately, as did US business interests in China until the developments in Tiananmen Square in 1989 halted the robust growth. The decade of 1990s was a relatively lukewarm period in both diplomatic and economic ties. However, the first decade of the current century saw both political and economic relations taking off on a strong footing. With both economies growing strongly and responding positively to each other's strengths, bilateral trade increased almost four-fold, from US$97.3 billion in 2002 to US$334.5 billion in 2008. After a brief deceleration due to the financial crisis, bilateral trade was projected to grow to US$459 billion in 2010 (Morrison 2011).[9] The US is currently China's largest trade partner, while China is the US's second largest trade partner after Canada.

The two countries have different positions on a range of issues including Taiwan, Tibet, North Korea, human rights issues, climate change and market access matters in the WTO. Though these differences have not affected the robust growth of trade and investment, there have been several occasions when diplomatic spats have become conspicuous. In more recent months, particularly after the financial crisis, relations have become more stressed, with the US pressurising China to freely float the yuan. The US holds the policy of pegging the yuan artificially to the dollar for making Chinese exports more competitive as the main reason behind its high trade deficit with China. Prasad (2010) points out that a lot of the irritants in the bilateral relationship can be attributed to the rising deficit, which was about 1.6 per cent of the US GDP in 2009. The issue has overshadowed most other aspects of the bilateral relationship and is an example of how an economic issue can grow into a political obstacle between two countries in a globalised world.

With both countries conscious of each other's economic strengths, the strategic implications of their large economic sizes in global geo-politics, and the almost organic dependence that they have developed with each other's

Table 6.5 China–US bilateral trade (2002–9)

	Exports (US$ billion)	*Imports (US$ billion)*	*Trade (US$ billion)*	*Trade balance (US$ billion)*
2002	70.1	27.3	97.3	42.8
2003	92.6	33.9	126.6	58.7
2004	125.2	44.8	169.9	80.4
2005	163.3	48.9	212.3	114.4
2006	204.0	59.3	263.2	144.6
2007	233.2	70.0	303.2	163.2
2008	252.8	81.7	334.5	171.1
2009	221.4	77.8	299.2	143.6

Source: IMF, Direction of Trade Statistics (DOTS).

Note
Export+Import and Export−Import may not always produce the reflected trade and trade balance numbers because of rounding off of decimals.

economies, China and the US have tried hard to balance difficulties in an otherwise successful economic relationship. The regular strategic and economic dialogues between the two countries reflect their desire to resolve issues through dialogue. However, in spite of these efforts there have been plenty of trade disputes between the two countries. The China–US relationship, particularly after China's entry in the WTO, has had several episodes of intense trade disputes. Most of these arise from the US's dissatisfaction over various systems of subsidies, export incentives and government procurement operations in China. The US argues that these imperfections discriminate against US companies in the Chinese domestic market and also gives Chinese exporters unfair advantage in the US market. Morrison (2011) mentions that as of December 2010, the US had initiated 11 dispute resolutions cases against China at the WTO. These include litigations brought on grounds of discriminatory export subsidies, improper enforcement of intellectual property rights (IPR) and restriction on import of films and their distribution by foreign companies. While China has been the victim of several trade actions initiated by the US, it has also retaliated on occasions. Warm water shrimps are a case in point. China's warm water shrimp exports have been targets of US anti-dumping action for several years. Citing unfair imposition and prolongation of such duties, China has recently dragged the US to the WTO on the grounds that these duties have been calculated by unfair methods.[10]

In the years ahead, as China and the US try to adjust to the new economic dynamics emerging after the financial crisis, they face a situation where economic issues, ironically, can trigger political differences. The first of these issues is the exchange rate. The US will continue to exert pressure on China to make its currency more 'free' and market-determined as it tries to reverse the trade imbalance and make its own products more competitive in the world market. US lawmakers have introduced several bills to Congress over the currency issue that propose retaliatory action in the event of China not changing its policy. The second issue with significant political ramifications is the Chinese holding of US debt. Prasad (2010) estimates China to hold around 17 per cent of the US's net outstanding public debt. There are concerns over implications on the US and the global economy of a sudden decision by China to liquidate these holdings. Finally, as the US tries hard to recover from its own domestic difficulties and supports some protectionist measures, it may adopt a hard position towards China on trade issues that have traditionally invited its ire, such as subsidies, intellectual property and safety standards. The US has had the tendency to use WTO litigation as an instrument for launching trade offensives against China. China has also been retaliative. The worrying aspect in this regard is the possibility of trade actions and litigation blowing up into a trade conflict and affecting political and security relations between the two countries (Malawer 2007). Exchange rate and trade friction dominated the backdrop of Chinese President Hu Jintao's visit to the US in January 2011. They are expected to do so in a relationship where the economic and strategic gap between the two partners is rapidly narrowing.

India–Saudi Arabia

On account of their geographical co-ordinates, China and India have had closer linkages and connections with distinct parts of Asia. While for China these links pertain more to Northeast and Southeast Asia, India has had greater interactions with its neighbours in the West, particularly the Middle East. Among the Middle East countries, its economic linkages are strongest with Saudi Arabia and the UAE, both of which figure among its largest trade partners.

Though India does not have a contiguous border with Saudi Arabia, its western coast is easily connectable to Saudi through the Arabian Sea and Gulf of Oman. This is the route that saw considerable movement of commerce in ancient times. Now it serves as the main route for trade between India and Saudi Arabia. Energy trade, particularly in crude oil, has been the main driver of bilateral trade between the two countries. A large part of India's crude oil requirements are met by Saudi Arabia and the UAE. They supply 18 per cent and 8 per cent of India's crude oil imports respectively (EIA 2010a). India's economic engagement with Saudi Arabia has increased substantially over the last decade. According to statistics provided by the Ministry of Commerce, Government of India, the size of bilateral trade expanded from US$1.4 billion in 2000–1 to US$24.5 billion in 2008–9.[11] A considerable part of the increase in trade has been contributed by the volume as well as the value of oil trade between the two countries. This trade, while comprising crude oil exports from Saudi to India, also includes refined petroleum product exports from India to Saudi. The latter accounted for 3.4 per cent (almost US$1 billion) of India's refined petroleum product exports in the year 2009–10. It also accounted for the largest share (30.3 per cent) of India's total exports of basmati rice during the year. Saudi was India's tenth largest export market in 2009–10 catering for 2.2 per cent of its total exports, and was the third largest source of India's imports, accounting for 5.9 per cent of total imports for the year. Thanks to heavy crude oil imports, the balance of trade is in Saudi's favour.

India and Saudi Arabia have had to be careful in managing a relationship that has a few sensitive spots. The two states are markedly different in terms of the nature of their political and governance systems, with India being a multi-party secular democracy and Saudi an autocratic monarchy. Bilateral relations have faced particular difficulties over Saudi's close ties with Pakistan, with whom India has often had an estranged relationship. Saudi's support of Pakistan on the Kashmir conflict, as well as India's non-condemnation of the Soviet invasion of Afghanistan in 1979, and maintaining a neutral posture during the Gulf War of 1991, variously affected sentiments on both sides (Pandita 2010). The end of the Cold War and Saudi's conscious practice of oil diplomacy in Asia, particularly in view of the energy needs of India and China, have produced results with India also responding positively. Indeed, India's import of crude oil from Saudi has increased sharply since the visit of Saudi King Abdullah in 2006, with Saudi replacing the UAE as India's largest source of crude oil (Pandita 2010). On the other hand, Indian investments to the Saudi kingdom have increased sharply, as has the number of expatriate Indians. The high tide of commerce reflects a positive response to Saudi's 'Look East' policy by India's 'Look West' policy focusing beyond Pakistan (Kapila 2010).

There is little doubt that positive political overtures have made a major difference to the volume of trade between the two countries. From US$2.7 billion in 2004–5, bilateral trade has increased to US$24.5 billion in 2008–9. The size of trade is likely to increase further with India's demand for crude oil growing in the years to come. The relationship reflects good economic results obtained through sensible and positive diplomacy. However, from India's perspective, a trade relationship that is essentially resource-driven (energy on this occasion) and with a country located in a geo-strategically sensitive location may provide the possibilities of regional developments disrupting oil supplies and bilateral trade. The recent political upheavals in Egypt and Libya have already begun creating anxieties in this respect. Regional factors apart, India will always be somewhat wary of Saudi's long and deep links with Pakistan. The fairly robust economic relationship being witnessed now is essentially out of necessity. Both Saudi and India will attempt to reduce their dependence on oil in the long run – Saudi for greater economic diversification and India for self-sufficiency. Till then, however, the economic relationship is expected to continue smoothly. But the possibility of disruptions in trade and business arising from political developments outside the sphere of bilateral ties, like those in the region or with respect to Pakistan and Kashmir, cannot be entirely ruled out.

India–United Arab Emirates (UAE)

Unlike Saudi, with whom India has had occasional political friction, the record has been almost untarnished with respect to the UAE. Over the last four decades, since the time the UAE came together as a federation in the Gulf in 1971, the relationship between the Emirates and India has been strong and secure. Commercial ties have been robust, with the UAE becoming India's largest trade partner with a bilateral trade of US$43.4 billion in 2009–10, which was 9.3 per cent of India's total trade during the year (Diwan 2010).[12] The UAE was India's largest export market in 2009–10, while being its second largest source of imports. Oil forms a significant part of total trade although, over the years, bilateral trade has diversified considerably to include non-oil products. The Emirates provide the biggest export market for Indian gems and jewellery and also account for the largest chunk of India's refined petroleum product exports. Like Saudi, the Emirates also account for a significant part of India's basmati rice exports. Trade in precious metals has become an important part of the non-oil trade between India and the Emirates, with the latter being India's biggest sources of gold and pearls and semi-precious stone imports. As Diwan (2010) points out, Dubai in the UAE performs as a major trans-shipment hub for India. The trans-shipment role of Dubai is particularly visible in the gold and refined petroleum trade between the two countries. Indian gold jewellery and articles, as well as refined petroleum products, flow out from the Dubai port to various countries in South Asia, the Gulf and Africa. In this respect, Dubai and the Emirates perform for India a vital commercial function similar to the one Singapore performs for it in the East.

Migrant workers have been one of the ticklish issues in an otherwise stable relationship. The Emirates have one of the largest segments of expatriate Indian workers. These workers are not only in high value-added technical and professional services, but also in more modest and low-skilled professions. Violation of human rights and the abuse of workers' rights have been common complaints of Indian workers. Construction workers, manual labourers and domestic workers have faced the brunt of human rights abuses. Human rights agencies have been pressing for more effective labour protection for these workers.[13] With Indian labour continuing to move to jobs in the Gulf, particularly from states on India's western coast like Kerala, workers' rights will remain an issue between the two countries. At this time, this appears to be the only potential source of friction between the two countries. Both appear to have overcome tensions experienced in the past over extradition. India's unhappiness over the UAE's ineffectiveness in handing over criminals despite a bilateral extradition treaty has resulted in acrimonious exchanges between the two governments.[14] An extradition treaty is also high on India's diplomatic agenda with respect to Saudi Arabia (Tiwari and Jacob 2010).

India has fairly high stakes in ensuring that political differences do not upset its economic relationship with either Saudi Arabia or the UAE. Both countries are members of the Organisation of Petroleum Exporting Countries (OPEC). India's dependence on imported crude, which is expected to increase as its economy grows further and modernises faster, makes it reliant on oil supplies from both these Arab countries. The two are geographically closest to India among its various sources of imported crude, entailing low shipping costs and accounting for more than a quarter of the crude oil imported by India (EIA 2010a). Disturbance of crude oil supplies implies high economic costs for India. Both countries are also members of the Gulf Coordination Council (GCC) and are important strategic variables in determining the policies of the Arab world with respect to the rest of the world. Saudi Arabia and India are also members of the G20. The countries hold high economic and strategic values for India. Similarly, India is also a critical partner for both in terms of being the largest fast-growing emerging market in their immediate neighbourhood. Both economies are keen on diversifying their economic capacities on non-resource-based areas and find India to be a major market in this regard. Thus economic and strategic stakes are high on both sides and political gaps are unlikely to damage the economic bonhomie. However, unexpected exogenous developments in the Arab world can complicate matters in an unforeseen manner.

India–Japan ties

Japan's role in India's economic development begun, rather unusually, at a time, when Cold War dynamics had compelled both countries to follow different global political courses and align with ideologically distinct blocks. Notwithstanding Cold War compulsions, Japan emerged as India's largest bilateral overseas development assistance (ODA) provider, a position it continues to hold even now. The end of the Cold War and liberalisation of the Indian economy provided a strong fillip to bilateral economic ties. The Japanese automobile manufacturer Suzuki moved into India well before India was anywhere close to becoming an automobile hub and when it was still a much-controlled economy. The Indo-Japan economic relationship has grown stronger over the years, though Indo-Japan bilateral trade has fallen well short of Indo-China trade. Indo-Japan trade was US$10.8 billion in 2008–9, which was about a quarter of the Indo-China trade of US$41.3 billion in the same year. Indeed, during the period 2000–1 to 2008–9, Indo-Japan trade grew from US$3.6 billion to US$10.8 billion, a three-fold increase, whereas Indo-China trade grew from US$2.3 billion to US$41.3 billion, an almost 18-fold increase. India's trade with Japan during the last decade has grown at a slower pace compared to its trade with other Asian countries such as China and the UAE, and also ASEAN. This is, of course, not to suggest that Japan's role has become marginal in India's economic development. Indeed, Japanese resources and expertise continue to play a critical role in the development of physical infrastructure in India. India's ambitious infrastructure project – the upcoming Delhi Mumbai Industrial Corridor (DMIC)[15] – marks Japan's continuing and deepening involvement in the Indian economy. Furthermore, leading Japanese manufacturers – Sony, Toyota, Mitsubishi, Honda, Docomo, JFE Steel – have established production facilities in India.

History has been a positive driver of Indo-Japan ties, beginning from the political association and exchange that started from the Meiji era. Cultural ties have also resulted in extensive people-to-people contacts and positive perceptions about each other. The warmth in political ties, which probably was subdued during the Cold War, has begun reviving over the last couple of decades. As Asia's two major democracies, both countries should ideally be natural allies. However, the political relationship has not been as robust as one would have expected it to be, given Japan's extensive involvement in India's economic progress. Rajamohan *et al.* (2008) argue that economics has not yielded as much political capital as it could have on account of relatively low interfaces between different communities in the two countries. Other than specific business-based and official government-to-government interactions, socio-cultural 'engagement' between the two countries has not been particularly high in modern times. As a result, there have been gaps in understanding and responding to each other.

The biggest strain in Indo-Japan political ties occurred in 1998, when Japan imposed economic sanctions following India's nuclear detonations at Pokhran. Relations have vastly improved since then, with the top political leadership from both countries – Yoshiro Mori, Junichiro Koizumi and Shinzo Abe from Japan and Atal Behari Vajpayee and Manmohan Singh from India – striking a good personal rapport and making institutional efforts for improving relations. The

Indo-Japan bilateral comprehensive economic partnership agreement (CEPA) marks the investment of political efforts and goodwill in formalising the trade and economic relationship between the two countries. India's nuclear energy market is also a major business opportunity for Japanese firms as India strives to build more nuclear reactors for satiating its power-hungry economy. Japan's defence and security cooperation with India signifies its deepening strategic links with the country that are expected to consolidate the economic links. However, its presence in India's nuclear energy market is unlikely until the passage of the Nuclear Liability Bill in India's Parliament.[16] While the passage of the legislation is what Japanese nuclear supplier firms have been waiting for, the catastrophe on 11 March 2011 in Sendai which led to damage in the Fukushima nuclear plant has raised serious questions in India and other countries about the safety issues involved in pursuing a nuclear energy programme. While this is not a bilateral political issue and is not expected to damage the fundamentals of the economic relationship in any way, it might hold back closer integration of the relationship from a strategic sense.

India–European Union (EU)

India's economic ties have traditionally been strong with most of the OECD members of Europe, particularly Belgium, France, Germany, Italy, Netherlands and the United Kingdom. Currently the EU (27 members) is India's single largest trade partner with India's bilateral trade with the EU being US$82 billion in 2008–9. This amounted to almost 17 per cent of India's trade with the rest of the world. Germany, France and the UK continue to remain India's largest trade partners on a country basis. Other than trade, European investments into India have also been assuming substantive proportions.

From a broader geo-political perspective, India's relations with the EU are qualitatively similar to those between China and the EU. For both China and India, the EU is the largest trade partner. However, beyond economics, there has not been much else to the relationships in terms of strategic content, particularly political. As in the case of China, the EU has occasionally been critical of India's human rights record. The EU has also been disappointed over India's refusal to sign the nuclear non-proliferation treaty (NPT). On the other hand, India has been critical about the lack of internal consensus within the EU on issues that are important for it, such as the permanent membership of the UN Security Council (Sandhu 2009). Indeed, India has shown a greater tendency to bilaterally engage and discuss with larger members of the EU than with the Union as a whole. This clearly shows that, like China, India has also been conscious of the internal divisions within the EU on several issues. Thus, while it has been keen on strengthening commercial ties with Europe and has been negotiating a bilateral trade agreement for formalising the ties, it has not visualised the region as a major variable in the multipolar world (Sandhu 2009).

India remains a much smaller player in Europe's external trade compared with the prominence that Europe has in India's trade. The EU is conscious of

India's large market potential and has often expressed its frustration at not only the high tariffs but also non-tariff barriers, such as quantitative restrictions and licensing requirements.[17] Similarly, India has also expressed its unhappiness over lack of access to the EU's domestic market for both agricultural and manufacturing products, through barriers like subsidies to agricultural producers and technical standards for exports. While politically there have not been any flashpoints, the two countries have had sharply different positions on multilateral trade negotiations at the WTO. They have also been pursuing alternative paths at global talks on climate change.[18] In these respects, again, India has been differing with the EU on subjects where Europe finds itself differing with China. The major exception, though, is Europe's greater comfort with India's democratic systems and institutions compared to the lack of such systems in China. Moreover after the 11 September 2001 terrorist attacks in New York and the 7 July 2005 bombings in London, Europe and India have become close allies in fighting global terrorism.

As a 'strategic partner' of India and as focused in its Country Strategy Paper for India,[19] the EU will continue to play an active role in helping India to meet its Millennium Development Goal (MDG) targets. India needs external development resources and would be looking forward to the EU's support in this respect. However, the financial difficulties of the smaller countries in Europe might encourage India to confine its EU focus even more strongly towards the larger economies like Germany. Most of India's relations with the EU are being dominated by its interfaces with the larger European economies and are expected to be influenced similarly in future. In the post-Cold War globalised world, there are hardly any striking political differences that can dent bilateral ties between India and the EU, just as between China and the EU. But changes in the global economic order and the steady erosion of EU's economic clout might generate more friction on trade and economic issues in future.

India–US

The world's largest democracies trod different paths after the Second World War and had a cold, if not acrimonious, relationship for almost four decades. India's leadership of the non-aligned movement (NAM), pursuit of the 'mixed economy' model of development, and strategic partnership with the Soviet Union, and the US's strong links with Pakistan created considerable distance between the two countries. The end of the Cold War and the collapse of the Soviet Union began changing the political dynamics between the two countries from the early 1990s. In addition, India's economic reforms and rapid economic growth favourably influenced the US view of the Indian economy and facilitated the growth of robust ties. The bilateral relationship lifted to a remarkably high trajectory during the last decade after the signing of a civilian nuclear deal between the two countries at the end of 2008. The two countries now also have defence and security partnerships and annual strategic dialogues. High-level visits between the two countries have become common, as have extensive people-to-people contacts.

Mutual concerns over China in terms of India's fears of being 'encircled' in South Asia by China's deep engagement of its neighbours (e.g. Pakistan, Bangladesh, Nepal), and US apprehensions over China becoming the dominant power in the region, have encouraged strategic communities on both sides to cultivate each other aggressively.

While the US has been one of India's largest trade partners, India is yet to become as large for the US, which is similar to its economic positioning with respect to the EU. Merchandise trade between the two countries increased more than three-fold from US$12.4 billion in 2000–1 to US$39.4 billion in 2008–9. The US is a country with which India's bilateral services trade relations are also strong. Bilateral service trade between the two countries was US$22.7 billion in 2008, with most of the trade taking place in financial services, business, professional and technical services, including information technology (IT) (Kronstadt *et al.* 2010). The US has also been a major investor in India, with major American firms such as General Electric (GE), Microsoft, IBM, Dell, Oracle and Ford operating out of India.

Though there has been a marked improvement in Indo-US bilateral ties in the current century, there are doubts over the fundamentals of the relationship. The current geo-political circumstances have brought the countries close to each other on common grounds such as terrorism. But there are several issues on which the two do not see eye to eye. Trade and economic matters comprise the bulk of these. The US government's discomfort with the outsourcing of functions by US companies to Indian firms and the steep hike in H-1B visa[20] fees for Indian professionals moving to the US are protectionist measures that have been agitating India's IT industry.[21] Arising from US efforts to assuage sentiments of a domestic work force affected by lack of adequate opportunities due to recessionary conditions, India has expressed its disappointment over the US move and has contemplated raising the issue at the WTO.[22] Both countries have been critical over access limitations to each other's domestic markets for their respective exports. The US complaints have focused on India's sanitary and phyto-sanitary (SPS) barriers on its exports, and also on India's refusal to open up its key services to foreign service providers. India, on the other hand, has been critical about the US subsidising its farmers, which makes India's agricultural exports uncompetitive in the US market, and also restrictions imposed on movements of Indian professionals to the US through H-1B visa quotas. In addition to bilateral disputes, the two countries have clashed frequently at the WTO and have held radically different positions in negotiations on the Doha round issues. Climate change has been another contentious area between the two countries. The US has steadfastly refused to sign the Kyoto Protocol, which puts a larger burden on developed countries for curbing emissions. India, along with China and other emerging markets, has always argued for greater burden-sharing by developed countries and has therefore been at loggerheads with the US. It is also important to note that though the much-discussed Indo-US civilian nuclear deal has been signed, its results are yet to become manifest. As mentioned earlier, the supplier liability legislation is pending in the Indian Parliament, making it difficult for US nuclear companies to enter India.

Strategic compulsions have encouraged both countries to upgrade their bilateral ties through formal institutional frameworks. However, fundamental differences remain, since the domestic concerns of both are radically different, as might be expected between the world's largest economy and a fast-growing emerging market with several development challenges. However, strong business synergies between the two countries, particularly in modern value-added economic sectors such as finance and IT, are likely to ensure that economic ties remain robust. These economic complementarities, along with strategic compulsions, should protect economic ties from getting strained. This is, of course, not to suggest that potential sources of friction are entirely missing.

The analysis of China's and India's relationships with their major trade partners reveals that political differences, up to now, have not dominated economic relationships. The association between politics and economics does not appear strong, particularly in China's case. Had politics and economics had a positive association, then China's economic ties with its neighbours such as Taiwan and Japan would have remained stunted. These are countries with which China has had acrimonious relationships and yet has been successful in enhancing economic engagement. China's economic relations with the US have also expanded over time despite the two countries having irreconcilable political differences over several issues. China's relationships clearly demonstrate the separation of politics from economics, with the poor quality of the former hardly affecting the latter except on a few short-lived occasions. Indeed, one might be tempted to argue that the depth and quality of China's economic ties with countries with which it has political tensions have improved so much that they have not allowed political differences to play spoilsport. Economics has probably been a major deterrent to the escalation of political estrangement. This is borne out by China's relations not only with its biggest trade partners, but also with Russia and relatively smaller partners such as Vietnam, the Philippines and Indonesia. Notwithstanding major political differences, China's trade and economic ties with all these countries have been sharply improving over the years.

For India, a similar lack of association between politics and economics is more difficult to establish. Unlike China, India's political ties with its major partners have never been so hostile so as to apprehend disruptions in economic engagement. While it has had its own differences with Saudi or the US on various issues, these have hardly reached flashpoints at any stage. But countries with which it has had serious political differences or conflicts are those that are in its immediate neighbourhood. It has major territorial disputes with Pakistan and China and relatively minor ones with Bangladesh, Nepal and the Maldives. Except for China, none of the other countries is a major trade partner of India. While the size of bilateral trade with Bangladesh, Pakistan, Sri Lanka (with whom India does not have major territorial disputes but has had serious problems over Tamil insurgents) and Nepal has increased, the shares of these countries in India's trade have either remained stagnant or decreased over time. During the period 2000–1 to 2008–9, the share of India's trade with Pakistan in its total external trade increased from only 0.3 per cent to 0.4 per cent, while those of trade with Bangladesh and Sri Lanka declined from 1.1 per cent to 0.6 per cent and 0.7 per cent to 0.6 per cent respectively, and that with Nepal remained unchanged at 0.4 per cent.[23] India's trade with its neighbours with whom it has strained ties has not shown any signs of increasing (proportionally), while its overall trade has increased fairly rapidly. India's neighbours themselves have had mostly moderate rates of economic growth and integration with the world economy, largely on account of domestic difficulties. Unlike China, whose neighbours are fast-growing outward-oriented economies themselves, India's neighbours are economically smaller and subdued. India's growth in external trade has drawn greater inspiration from outside its neighbourhood where its political ties have also been better.

India's bilateral trade with China, however, has been an exception to this trend. The share of India's trade with China in its total external trade increased from 2.5 per cent in 2000–1 to 8.5 per cent in 2008–9. For India, China is a clear outlier, or an exception, to the general observation that its economic engagement is subdued with neighbours and countries with which it has bad political relations.

There are surely factors specific to China and India's history, culture, geography and pattern of engagements with various countries that explain why the lack of association between politics and economics in bilateral ties is stronger in the case of China compared with India. China clearly has a more extensive record of managing relationships that have good economics with bad politics than does India. For India, its relations with China are probably the first where it has had to handle the dichotomy. How successfully it manages the relations will be revealed over time. One impression, though, that comes out of the analysis of bilateral relationships and that can partly explain India's exceptional relationship with China is the importance of economic size. China's neighbours, who are its major trade partners and with whom it also has political differences, are all large economies, exerting considerable influence in regional and global economic activity. But India's neighbours are hardly so. For a large economy like China, the benefits of engaging with other large economies are considerable in terms of the scale and complementarities which such engagement offers. It has done so and is expected to do so with India, another large economy in its neighbourhood. For India, China is the only large economy in the neighbourhood. As a large economy itself, it is realising the benefits of engaging with the largest regional economy, China. Economic size clearly has been an important determinant of India's robust economic ties with China and partly explains why, unlike its other neighbours with whom it has poor political and economic ties, it has good economics with China despite bad politics.

7 Gazing into the crystal ball

The China–India bilateral economic relationship, up to now, would probably be considered small in terms of the monetised value of exchanges it signifies, as compared to several other similar relationships elsewhere in the world. But it would be erroneous to judge the capacity of the relationship purely in terms of what trade statistics indicate. Bilateral trade is expected to exceed US$100 billion in the near future. That would make the trade equivalent to the economic sizes of Iraq and Morocco and not too far behind those of Vietnam and Bangladesh. Nonetheless, as a proportion of world trade, China–India trade would still remain small compared with trade between the US, the EU and China. But the economic relationship between the world's second and eleventh largest economies, which are also among Asia's largest and the most populous countries of the world, is not only confined to statistical details of cross-border flows of goods, services and capital. There are several qualitative aspects of the relationship in terms of how the two economies visualise their configurations in the region and the world, how they respond to challenges, many of which are common, and how in the process of such visualisation and responses they interact with each other. Both countries, undoubtedly, have their own spaces to grow and expand; but their sizes and high growth trajectories in a world that is becoming increasingly dominated by the actions and ambitions of the two economies, create numerous occasions where economic interests clash or converge. An analysis of the bilateral relationship can hardly forego these occasions where the two will compete or collaborate.

The preceding chapters in this volume have tried to analyse the different facets of the China–India economic relationship in terms of the common challenges to development they encounter and how such challenges can be potential drivers for collaboration; systemic and attitudinal roadblocks to collaboration; spheres where both economies are competing and the nature of trade frictions; the bilateral trade relationship and its nuances and the potential gains from a bilateral trade deal; instances of mutual collaboration on global issues and the reasons fashioning such collaborations; and finally the gnawing worry lurking in the background of the euphoria on robust trade growth: will bad politics overcome good economics at some stage? This chapter aims to serve two main objectives. Apart from summarising the emerging thoughts from the analysis so far, it attempts to pin down the thoughts from a futuristic perspective. In other words, it tries to anticipate what the nature of the bilateral relationship is expected to be in the foreseeable future in the distinct spheres of common challenges, competition, global collaboration, a trade agreement and the larger dynamics between politics and economics.

Managing common challenges

People can be both assets and liabilities for economies, depending upon how they are reared, harnessed and utilised. As the world's most populous countries, China and India have the daunting task of ensuring that their people remain assets and contribute productively to economic growth. While this entails providing populations with access to basic needs and equipping them with right skills, large populations, by themselves, produce serious challenges for sustainable development. Both countries are experiencing these challenges as they try to cope with differing trajectories of demographic transitions.

Managing cities and urban habitats is becoming an increasingly complicated process, with both trying to accommodate more people in cities as efficiently as possible. The process is unlikely to get easier in future, given the rapid urbanisation in both countries. China's concerns in this respect are more with managing migrant populations. Distinguishing migrants from permanent residents is important in cities such as Beijing and Shanghai for determining the quality of social benefits for each group (Palit 2010a). Unlike China, which has a long history of household registration beginning from imperial times that enabled it to keep rural and urban populations distinct, India has not had any policies, restrictive or otherwise, for regulating internal migration. Nonetheless, the effects of rapid urbanisation, whether induced by migration or natural increase, are similar in both countries as they are to those in most other parts of the developing world. Given the scale of their problems, though, which are larger than those of counterpart emerging markets such as Brazil, Russia or South Africa, China and India require early innovative solutions for ensuring that transport and housing woes in their cities do not assume gigantic proportions.

Energy security concerns have driven both to institutional cooperation, as highlighted by the agreement signed for enhancing cooperation on oil and natural gas in January 2006 (Zhao 2009; Mills 2010). Both countries have also taken to prior consultations for preserving mutual interests in acquisition of energy assets. Sinopec's assurance of not contending OVL's acquisition of Imperial Energy, reciprocated subsequently by Indian firms refraining from contesting Sinopec's bid for Tanganyika Oil in Syria (Mills 2010), is an encouraging example. Such collaborations need to be increased from case-by-case instances to institutionalised processes for minimising adversities likely to be faced by both countries from fluctuations in global energy prices. The recent political turmoil in the Arab world is a pertinent example, where global energy prices, as it is northward-bound due to supply concerns, might inflate more if China and India rattle the world oil market with large uncoordinated purchases. The benefits from coordinating responses in occasions like these can be significant.

It is also important to ensure that both countries manage the downsides of high energy demand by minimising the loss of human and material resources. Illegal mining operations have shot up in both countries, as have mining accidents. Neither country can afford to perpetuate these trends as they have significant socio-economic and political implications. China has been closing down several illegal mines in Henan, Shanxi and other provinces that sprung up in response to high demand and rising coal prices. India, on the other hand, has been trying to ensure a balance between the growth of mining and the protection of forest resources and the occupational rights of tribal populations. Multinational mining activities by Vedanta and Posco in India's mineral-rich states have stirred considerable political and economic unrest. There are also incidences of mining operations growing without obtaining environmental and other necessary clearances. These demand-side downsides of the inexhaustible craving for energy in the two countries can manifest themselves in serious consequences. Both countries have their work cut out in this respect and must handle carefully the repercussions of high energy import prices and mushrooming energy operations produced by rapid growth in population, industry and urbanisation.

Since the middle of the last decade, domestic commodity prices in both countries have been rising at uncomfortably high rates. The extents of rises revealed by price indices in both countries understate the actual rise. Consumer price indices in China are reportedly based on a consumption basket that does not reflect changing habits of consumers and also excludes variations in high price assets such as owner-occupied housing (Bradsher 2011b). India, on the other hand, does not have a composite consumer price index. Its wholesale price index does not capture many services that are susceptible to sharp price changes. It is indeed worrying to perceive how much the actual inflation rates in both countries would be if the shortcomings of the indices are corrected. While that is something that each would require to take up individually, collectively China and India are vulnerable to high prices arising from high demand, large circulation of cash in the domestic economies, stiff global commodity and natural resource prices particularly oil, a steadily declining US dollar, and fluctuations in global outputs of agricultural products which they import due to diversion of cultivable acreage to bio-fuels and speculation in commodity markets. All these commonalities in domestic and external objective conditions create considerable grounds for conceiving common responses through mutual consultations. These consultations are also important for tackling price rises arising from unanticipated supply shortages such as the recent prolonged drought in northern China and similar seasonal aberrations in India.

Much attention has been focused on China and India's collaboration at global climate change negotiations. The two countries are also collaborating bilaterally for addressing climate change. As the world's largest and third largest carbon emitters, both need to take up the issue on a priority basis. Their individual national action plans indicate their realisation of the imperatives. However, long-term actions on climate change must also be accompanied by efforts to bring down water and air pollution. In this respect, given the negative externalities being suffered by both countries from health damage inflicted by air and water pollution, it is necessary to focus on effective regulations. Limiting movement of cars in Beijing during the 2008 Olympic Games significantly reduced air pollution in the city (Wu 2009). It is important for both China and India to think of similar measures that can make major differences to pollution. Effective regulations and their sincere enforcement can reduce pollution quicker than complicated policies. India, particularly, needs to pay heed to this aspect given its poor record on enforcement. For both countries, heavy pollution is threatening lives and livelihoods and there is hardly any room for complacency.

Both countries have shown welcome urgencies in responding to climate change concerns by pursuing the development of clean technologies and managing natural resources. What, though, will be a critical concern for both is the extent by which climate change and its downsides are capturing public imagination. Unlike inflation, which affects the purchasing power of households and is a trigger for corrective measures by authorities (even if ad hoc), climate change is yet to become a visible concern for the common person in both countries. It hardly figures in discussions beyond academic and intellectual spaces. While food prices win or lose elections in India, climate change does not even remotely feature in election agendas and political campaigns. Even in China, notwithstanding much less scope for venting discontent against the establishment, public unhappiness over inflation is noticeable. But climate change, again, is not a 'public' issue despite China being the largest global emitter of carbon. Low public sensitivity to dangers of climate change is a handicap for both countries in implementing effective climate policies. Though catastrophes such as the latest drought in northern China – the most severe in centuries – drive home dangers of drastic changes in weather patterns, they are not enough to galvanise people and communities into long-term preventive action. Climate change is yet to dawn upon people of both countries as a serious threat to lives and livelihoods. Large majorities of Chinese and Indian people hardly comprehend that climate change can entail loss of human security, particularly through deleterious impacts like forced migration of populations from unsustainable lands and habitats, food shortages, malnutrition and vulnerability to diseases (Elliott 2011).

Has the exercise of eminent domain – the power of the state to acquire property – assumed counterproductive proportions in China and India where the downsides of industrialisation, population growth and urbanisation are manifesting in growing land scarcity, high land prices, real estate speculation and corruption? The literature on China and India and their respective development trajectories has hardly focused on land or its growing paucity as an emerging policy challenge, or a limiting factor on economic growth. It is probably reflective of the unusual phenomenon of the two countries being the fastest-growing economies and yet developing countries, and the heterogeneous economic structures and institutions which they have for justifying the paradox that land markets in both are hardly as efficient as some of their other factor markets. Indeed, state control over land supplies, entirely in China and significantly in India, and the power vested in the government by law to take over land in 'public interest', prevents the growth of efficient land markets in either country. The state and its arms continue to be the biggest entities in land markets in both. Given the overarching dominance of the state, it is difficult to conceive of well-functioning markets where prices are strictly determined by forces of demand and supply. Sooner or later, both China and India will need to think hard about their land markets (or lack of such markets), since efficient supplies of a geographically limited factor like land are hardly conceivable without its effective markets.

Competition: high negative externalities?

Both China and India need to reconcile themselves to the imperatives of accessing and managing resources and markets in a world where they are the largest competitors for each other, given their upward trajectories of rapid growth. The priorities of maintaining sustained rapid growth for improving living standards of large sections of the population entail accessing resources and markets beyond domestic domains. The incentives for competition are well defined for both, as are the spheres for such competition.

Competition for new energy resources has resulted in two outcomes. First, both China and India are reaching out to 'pariah' states. These include Myanmar and Sudan. The trend began with China and has been picked up by India. Negotiating with imperfect states that have governments and political systems largely unacceptable to the international community involves the costs of justifying the moves to allies and partners. On the other hand, both countries are deploying strategies entailing 'oil-for-infrastructure' arrangements. In the short run, these have benefited recipient countries and have also given China and India access to new resources. Over time, however, both might show a greater shift towards the acquisition of existing assets rather than entering into oil–infrastructure trade-offs. The latter, of course, has a strategic connotation and is likely to earn both China and India new dividends as they are perceived as sympathetic and stable patrons of the recipients. Nonetheless, infrastructure projects involve several problems, such as long gestation periods and delayed recovery of costs. For both countries, these might become onerous over time and encourage them to shift to simpler acquisition models.

Water is clearly an issue over which China and India will have to tread carefully. Scholars and experts agree on water having the potential for brewing inter-state conflicts (Dinar 2002; Economy 2008). Water is not a 'tradable' commodity in the sense of it being physically transportable from one geographical point to another, like oil. The source of water has to be reasonably close to its consumption. As a result, both countries have to watch out for their respective major sources of water, which are located in their neighbourhood. Energy, fortunately, has not witnessed intense Sino-Indian competition in the neighbourhood except in Myanmar and partly Central Asia. The demand–supply imbalance driving competition in energy will do so in water as well. The territorial domain for competition, however, is expected to be different, with water occupying attention much closer to home. The fact that Tibet is the source of major rivers for both will introduce further complexities, given the prolonged estrangement between the two countries on Tibet.

Increasing market access in a globalised yet unbalanced economic world will remain a key priority for both countries. Globalisation has ensured that external sectors in both countries emerge as key sectors for growth and future economic prospects. In their race to narrow the gap with the advanced world, both realise the importance of enlarging trade by accessing new markets and deepening footholds in these markets. Most of the targeted markets will be developing countries in Asia, Africa and Latin America, since several of these economies not only possess trade structures complementary to China and India, but also have market segments that are largely untapped. As of now, the multilateral trade framework shows little possibility of these markets opening up to China and India in a generic manner. Both will therefore persuade bilateral efforts to consolidate access.

An important implication of simultaneous bilateral efforts for obtaining incremental market access is devotion of greater time and energy to negotiations with partners. The knowledge on the part of Indian (Chinese) negotiators that China (India) is also negotiating with the same partner can influence ongoing negotiations in an inefficient manner, with both trying to pre-empt and negate the other's perceived gains from the trade deals. While eventual gains will depend upon the quality of negotiations, as well as other factors such as diplomatic relations, an approach emphasising limiting the other's potential gains will be counterproductive and can squeeze gains for both. This is a possibility on occasions where FTA initiatives on the part of China (India) are primarily 'retaliatory' responses to similar initiatives by India (China). Indeed, rushing into FTAs without assessing economic feasibilities and purely as a strategic response is likely to yield inefficient outcomes. From a broader perspective, these inefficiencies can manifest themselves in a larger and more exhaustive manner, as the proliferation of FTAs can lead to complex and overlapping rules and higher cost of trade (Jiangyu 2010).

Panagariya (2007) reacts sharply to the FTA pursuits by China and India from the perspective of such deals fragmenting the trading system and lacking economic substance. Citing India's deals with Chile, Mauritius, the SAARC and Sri Lanka as agreements peppered with long lists of products excluded from tariff cuts and also fairly stringent rules of origin, he argues that these deals aim to protect inefficient domestic producers. China's agreements with Chile and Pakistan are also criticised by Panagariya on account of being partial in coverage. Indeed, India in particular, but also China, needs to be careful about entering into bilateral trade deals that search for selected preferences for certain groups of items and producers and do not aim at across-the-board gains from trade liberalisation. These deals that are secondary and selective in economic gains are probably aimed at securing more non-economic strategic gains. A China–India race for such deals is not in the best interests of global and regional trading systems, nor is it beneficial for their individual national economic interests in view of the fresh complications and negative externalities creates such races. Rather than competing for small chunks of market access and ambiguous strategic dividends, both economic and non-economic gains can multiply if China and India work towards a bilateral trade framework. As Panagariya (2008) explains, instead of diverting trade to smaller countries through piecemeal tariff liberalisations in 'political' FTAs, both China and India stand to gain by adding to their existing bilateral trade through new trade 'creation', which such a framework can produce.

Inefficiencies can also arise in the gradually intensifying race for courting other developing countries through 'generous' development assistance. There are two critical issues in this regard. The first is: can both countries afford to sustain aid over a period of time despite their economic ascent? Poverty is still pervasive in both countries, more so in India than in China. Does it make sense for China and India to extend development assistance to other countries when the resources can be deployed for making lives better for the poor at home? The question will loom large before both countries as they expand their aid programmes. Again, this is a dilemma they face because of their unprecedented situation of becoming strategically influential players on the world stage in spite of being developing economies. It is difficult to convince domestic audiences, particularly in a country like India where government actions are subject to greater scrutiny and debate compared to China, that higher foreign aid and resultant diplomatic gains yield more benefits than those that could have accrued from deploying the same resources at home. The opportunity costs of becoming aid donors, irrespective of convincing reasons, can be high. Both countries will need to be mindful of this as long as they remain developing countries with substantive economically marginal populations.

China and India's emergence as aid donors is a critical geo-political development in the sense that it challenges the dominance of OECD countries as sources of development assistance for low-income countries. This is unlikely to go unchallenged. With both countries deploying aid in manners distinct from OECD practices in several respect (e.g. classification, conditionalities), the global aid basket is likely to get divided between the traditional OECD classified ODA and the China–India 'emerging market' variety aid. Growth of this new variety of aid has attracted criticism on the grounds of being opaque and overlooking issues such as human rights and good governance records on the part of recipients. China has borne the brunt of this criticism up to now (Kilby 2010). Multilateral institutions have maligned Chinese aid to Africa for abetting corruption and encouraging human rights abuses (Wang and Lim 2007). India, up to now, has escaped such criticism as its aid is smaller and less conspicuous compared to China's, and also because the emphasis has been more on training-based capacity development through the ITEC. This, however, might change over time. The new 'emerging market' variety of aid promoted by both countries is shaping as a key instrument for South–South cooperation with far-reaching strategic implications. Both countries should be prepared to encounter more criticism in this respect as they encroach upon a turf that has been the traditional bastion of the developed North.

Collaboration: the road ahead

The first decade of the new millennium has been significant in terms of the rapport witnessed between China and India on approaching global economic issues of common concern. The collaboration on these issues in global forums has proceeded unimpeded, despite the two countries clashing occasionally on other aspects of their bilateral relationship, particularly in strategic and political matters. This reflects the overarching desire of the two countries to collaborate in order to achieve common global economic objectives notwithstanding irreconcilable differences elsewhere. But why have both shown collaborative urges that are unexpected between neighbours highly circumspect of each other?

The answer probably lies in the realisation that achieving common goals is much easier working together than working individually. The most important objective that both countries have wanted to achieve in this respect is re-shaping international institutions and economic systems in a way that serves their interests. In their effort to do so, they have not only sided with each other but have also figured in broader coalitions involving other emerging market economies and developing countries. In the process, they have contributed to the shaping of a new order in the global political economy: it is not merely an order where the developed North and the developing South are pitted against each other, as outlined briefly earlier in the context of development assistance. It is also an order where the balance of economic power is showing clear signs of shifting towards certain segments of the South.

China is a unique developing country that is also one of the largest players in global trade. Over time, it has realised that major global international institutions such as the WTO, the IMF or the UNFCCC are overtly dominated by views of the G7 and other advanced economies. Indeed, global institutions hardly reflect the interests and sentiments of developing countries that are maturing into strong economic powers. These are not run in a manner in which China would prefer them to be run – a view shared by India, Brazil and other economies that also qualify as developing countries graduating into significant economic presences. In organisations such as the WTO, frustrations over institutional insensitivities to specific concerns have forced China and India to join forces. Indeed, in the WTO as well as the UNFCCC, where developed and developing country interests are markedly different and decisions require consensus, progress on contentious issues are unlikely till the major emerging markets and the G7 arrive at mutually acceptable solutions. In this respect, the importance of the G20 is expected to increase even more, since China, India, Brazil, Russia and other emerging economic powers can influence G20 decisions in manners suiting their interests (Whalley and Agarwal 2010). As the balance of power in the world economy shifts towards emerging markets, China and India are expected to collaborate more at the G20 for reforming other institutions in enabling manners.

As both countries work together to reform global institutions, they need to be aware of a couple of downsides. Till now, they have enjoyed the support of non-emerging market, low- and lower-middle-income countries. The latter have been happy to allow China and India to represent them and articulate their concerns. However, as the economic gap widens between China and India and these countries, country-specific interests may begin diverging. China has already encountered this dilemma, where it has had to manage its interests from a developing country perspective with those from the vantage point of a major player in global trade. India may also find its interests' changing as it assumes greater significance in world trade. Both countries need to manage their relationship with the rest of the developing world carefully in this respect. They have already shown signs of doing so by interacting intensively with small island countries on mutually acceptable patterns of emission cuts and climate policies. Ensuring collective growth involving all countries, particularly the low-income ones, is a process that will benefit both China and India given their abilities to serve as both producers and consumers for the rest of the world.

There is also a need on the part of both countries to revisit their negotiating postures at the WTO and the UNFCCC. As the world's largest, most populous and fastest-growing economies, they need to approach global issues involving delivery of global public goods in a more responsible and far-sighted fashion. India in particular has consistently played a defensive and obstructive role in the WTO. Both India and China must align their postures in the global trade and climate talks in a way that is commensurate with their economic status. Both must begin to take pride in not blocking talks, but in steering them towards a constructive direction. This is what the rest of the developing world expects from them.

The bilateral trade deal: illusion or reality?

The spate of collaborations, particularly prospective ones like those between Chinese and Indian drug-makers, marks a tentative beginning towards what greater economic engagement through trade needs to overcome: anxieties of indigenous producers over competition from cheap imports. Domestic market sentiments in India are not favourably inclined towards Chinese products. Drugs and chemical exports from China particularly have been the targets of anti-dumping actions. On the other hand, Indian drug exports to China have been affected by NTBs. Cooperation in drug development and marketing exploiting China and India's respective strengths in production of active pharmaceutical ingredients (APIs) and formulations can generate great benefits for both in the global market. Such cooperation can also set examples for thwarting protective mindsets. Examples like these vindicate formalisation of trade ties through institutional bilateral arrangements.

From a larger perspective, Chinese exports have been inviting retaliatory actions from almost all their markets. They have raised the hackles of domestic producers of similar items in most emerging markets of Asia and Latin America. Indian manufacturers, like their counterparts in these markets, have been aggrieved over Chinese domination of their domestic niches. The discontent has led to a large incidence of anti-dumping actions against China. Possibilities of generating more trade through a bilateral pact will not materialise unless Indian industry stops feeling threatened by Chinese imports. Unfortunately, the recent history of India's trade negotiations does not offer much scope for optimism in this respect. India's interests in market access for manufactured products have often been conspicuously defensive, whether it is at the WTO's DDA or at trade negotiations with a regional block like ASEAN.

Hyped concerns over cheap Chinese imports overlook reasons behind such imports dominating Indian markets. Disaggregated product-wise analysis of different imports from China in Chapter 4 clearly underlines how they have helped in bridging indigenous capacity gaps arising from existing market imperfections. As long as these imperfections remain, industrial and manufacturing growth will force domestic producers of final products in India to rely on Chinese imports. One of the biggest imperfections is the pronounced difference in rates of growth in demand and expansion of indigenous capacity in strategic industries such as telecommunications, power and computer hardware. Explosive growth in the demand for telecom services has not been accompanied by similar growth of a domestic industry that can supply equipment at competitive rates. The situation is fairly identical in electricity generation. In both telecom and power – hitherto state-controlled activities – new private producers have been hamstrung by lack of adequate domestic supplies. Neither ITI in telecom equipment, nor BHEL and Larsen & Toubro (L&T) in power plant equipment, have enough capacity for meeting the rising demands. Chinese imports have been filling the supply gaps well. They would not have been as successful in securing market access had the expansion in India's communication and energy services been commensurate with expansions in domestic manufacturing capacities. For similar reasons, Huawei and ZTE have continued to command considerable market space in India's telecom industry in spite of them being put under the scanner for espionage fears (Aiyar 2008). There is not much evidence of indigenous capacity in telecommunications expanding rapidly in the medium term. As far as electricity is concerned, although BHEL plans to double production and upcoming joint ventures such as those between Alstom of France and India's Bharat Forge are in the pipeline (Sharma 2010), they may not be adequate for meeting the exponential growth in demand for electricity. Given that the supply gaps are unlikely to be filled up in near future, for sustaining expansion of the industry, it makes greater sense to facilitate imports, probably through more facilitating frameworks such as an FTA.

India's tariffs on most imports are still higher than those maintained by other emerging market economies. On non-agricultural products, India's average final bound tariff is 34.4 per cent. This is not only much higher than China's 9.2 per cent, but also higher than Brazil's (30.4 per cent), Russia's (10.1 per cent) and South Africa's (15.8 per cent). For agricultural products, India remains one of the most protected countries in the world with an average tariff of 113.1 per cent. With respect to its bilateral trade with China, it is the protection offered to non-agricultural or manufactured products which becomes a significant issue, since India's import basket from China comprises mostly non-agricultural products. India's tendency of protecting domestic industries by erecting tariff walls remains strong despite its figuring in the multilateral trade framework for several years. Such protection has affected the ability of Indian industries to compete with more efficient products. Vocal industry lobbies have succeeded in extracting additional protection through anti-dumping actions. Though Chinese imports have been at the receiving end of these actions, this is not a 'China'-specific phenomenon; imports from Thailand and Southeast Asia have also been targeted for anti-dumping actions in the past.

Other than suffering from high tariff walls, Indian industry continues to encounter adverse outcomes of past policies that restrict it from competing efficiently with imports. One of the vital impediments is lack of scale-intensive production. Large-scale capacities in Indian manufacturing are mostly absent because of the policy of reserving several items of manufacture exclusively for small industries. Though the policy has been significantly reversed over the last couple of decades, Indian industries in several key segments of manufacturing, particularly machinery, equipment and also consumer goods, do not have the ability to produce on such a large scale as Chinese firms. As discussed in Chapter 4, capacity constraints handicap the ability of Indian producers of capital and intermediate goods to respond to higher demand from infrastructure and manufacturing industries, thereby necessitating imports. Capacity bottlenecks also restrict supply responses elsewhere, leading to high imports of antibiotics and coking coal. Indeed, it is ironic that while capacity constraints in domestic production of capital goods force Indian manufacturers to rely more on Chinese imports (including composite 'lumpy' project good imports for power plants), large installed capacities and their high utilisation rates in China's manufacturing sectors create demand for imported raw materials from India – iron ore, cotton, steel fines and copper – items that India has been exporting regularly to China.

Apart from systemic imperfections that make Indian producers uncompetitive against Chinese imports on their own domestic turf, further disadvantages are planted by unfavourable tax and duty structures. Chinese manufacturers benefit from a range of input subsidies at home; in addition, Indian manufacturers like BHEL complain that while Indian firms have to pay excise duties on supply of equipment to mega power projects, their Chinese counterparts don't have to (Pannu 2010). Indian companies are also burdened by other taxes like octroi (imposed on inter-state movement of goods) and state value-added tax (VAT). These grievances are justified on grounds of distorting parity. However, impositions of customs or anti-dumping duties on imports are not solutions for correcting these cost distortions. These can end up creating more inefficiency as higher duties – on either domestic products or imports – eventually result in increasing the final cost of production. While admitting that duties are essential for mobilising state revenues, it is important to align their structure in a manner that they do not become decisive in determining competitiveness.

India's trade negotiations, at either multilateral or regional forums, have tended to be 'defensive', particularly in goods. This is because of the high tariff walls it has vis-à-vis its trade partners. A comparative analysis clearly explains the difference in this respect. On the basis of MFN applied tariffs for the year 2009, 77.6 per cent of agricultural goods imported into India invited tariffs of more than 25 per cent. For China, the comparable proportion is 9.8 per cent. Brazil does not apply 25 per cent plus tariffs for any agricultural imports, while for Mexico such imports comprise around 10 per cent of tariff lines. India has been most sensitive on the issue of agricultural imports, which, as explained in Chapter 5, has resulted in its repeated emphasis on safeguards. In non-agricultural products, the tariff walls are less high; on the basis of applied tariff rates only 5 per cent of tariff lines invite duties beyond 25 per cent. But on the basis of bound rates (upper ceilings of tariffs), the proportion is as much as 51.3 per cent. This indicates that India has the flexibility to increase tariff rates much above the applied rates as long as it is within the bound rates. For China, only 1.0 per cent of non-agricultural tariff lines invite duties of more than 25 per cent on applied rates and 1.4 per cent does so on the basis of final bound rates. With respect to non-agricultural goods, India's tariff levels on non-agricultural products are, however, comparable to those of Brazil and Mexico, which have 14 per cent and 6.9 per cent of tariff lines inviting duties of more than 25 per cent on applied rates, and much higher percentages on bound rates. With respect to China in particular, India's tariff barriers appear conspicuous, since China made unprecedented concessions while entering the WTO. Indeed, China's tariffs also appear much less than other emerging markets such as Brazil and Mexico. With respect to China again, tariff comparisons across product groups reveal interesting differences between the two countries. In non-electrical and electrical machinery respectively, India's average applied and bound rates are 7.3 per cent and 28.2 per cent, and 7.2 per cent and 27.0 per cent, respectively. Similar average applied and bound rates for China on the two product categories are 7.8 per cent and 8.5 per cent, and 8.0 and 9.0 per cent respectively. In cotton and fruit and vegetables, China's average applied and bound rates are 15.2 per cent and 22.0 per cent, and 14.8 per cent and 14.9 per cent, respectively. For the same categories, similar rates for India are 12.0 per cent and 110.0 per cent, and 30.4 per cent and 99.3 per cent respectively. Clearly, the main differences between the tariff walls of the two countries are with respect to the gaps they have between applied and bound rates, which are much more in India's case.

The tariff structures have important implications for the prospects of a bilateral trade deal between China and India. Rationalisation of tariffs is an important component of bilateral trade negotiations. India faces a disadvantage in this respect, as it did in several other negotiations, particularly those with ASEAN, where tariffs of negotiating partners are much lower than India's. Since China's tariffs are already much lower than India's, India will have to give up more in tariff concessions, particularly in terms of cutting the room between applied and bound tariffs. For ensuring parity in tariff rates between the two countries, India will have to cut its duties much more than China, thereby offering more market access gains to Chinese exporters compared with Indian exporters. This, surely, is unacceptable to Indian industry, which is already agitated over Chinese imports. Thus, on tariff grounds, there are strong possibilities of bilateral trade talks remaining a non-starter. China, no doubt, will be keen on pushing an agreement as it envisages more market access gains. However, until Indian tariffs come down autonomously and align themselves more closely to the prevailing Chinese ones, India is unlikely to push ahead. A positive development in this respect is India's goods agreement with ASEAN, where tariffs are being reduced in a phased manner over a large range of tariff lines. These tariffs, rather than the tariffs maintained in the WTO framework, might become the eventual benchmarks for negotiations between the two countries, if and when they eventually decide to pursue the deal.

While tariffs are one tricky component of the negotiations, the bilateral deal might get stuck on other grounds as well. One of these involves the NTBs in the Chinese market. China's generous tariff concessions at the time of acceding to the WTO and the substantive market access it granted to foreign country exporters as a result have forced it to occasionally protect domestic producers through specific NTBs. For Indian producers, as mentioned in Chapter 3, these NTBs affect prospects of key exports like fruits and vegetables, bovine meat, basmati rice and pharmaceuticals. In addition, the Chinese practice of offering generous capital subsidies to its domestic industries and also the preference given to domestic producers in government procurement create considerable difficulties for exporters and foreign producers in China. These are imperfections in systems and practices that are expected to be sorted out by the time China is awarded market economy status under the WTO. But the prevalence of these NTBs – already sore points with India for several products – might be another obstacle to the movement on a bilateral agreement. While India needs to rationalise tariffs before proceeding to negotiations on the FTA, China needs to address the problem of proliferation of domestic NTBs.

India's main interests in trade negotiations in all forums have been in services. However, in services too its interests have been selectively offensive. China, on the other hand, has always been keen on obtaining greater market access in goods given its thrust on low-cost export-intensive manufacturing. However, with the steady increase in share of services in national output, trade in services has become a priority for China and is taking up considerable space in its negotiations with other partners. The most relevant example in this respect is the Economic Integration Agreement in services that it has entered into with ASEAN. Thus services will feature prominently in all negotiations that India and China hold with respect to a prospective bilateral trade deal. The biggest problem in such negotiations will be the domestic policy rigidities that still remain in vital services for both countries and that are likely to influence the quality of negotiations. Telecommunication services provide an interesting example in this respect. For mobile voice and data services in China, according to its submitted commitments in the WTO, foreign service providers in joint ventures with local partners cannot have equity holdings of more than 49 per cent. India too does not allow majority foreign equity holding in joint ventures in telecommunication services and mandates provision of services only after obtaining a licence from the regulatory authorities. There are several other services where considerable ambiguities exist in terms of domestic policy regulations, and neither country has made any open commitments at the multilateral forum, thereby leaving considerable discretionary space. These include key services such as education and health, where trade interests will be quite high. But much progress will depend on the extent by which both countries are willing to revisit their extant domestic regulations.

Politics and economics: remaining exclusive

A study of China's and India's bilateral relationships reveals fairly different insights about the qualitative nature of such ties. China has strong economic links with several of its neighbours, with whom, at the same time, it nurses political differences on significant issues. Japan, Taiwan and South Korea are three important examples. With all three countries, China has strong political differences and also territorial skirmishes that occasionally surface, leading to political tensions. But politics, until now, has not overpowered economics to disrupt the flow of goods, services and people between China and these countries in a permanent manner. One of the reasons behind economics not succumbing to political downsides is the strong integration of production networks in Northeast Asia. Chinese manufacturers and producers figure in densely knit inter-connected supply chains that include producers from several parts of Northeast and Southeast Asia, particularly from Taiwan, Hong Kong, Japan, Korea and Singapore. The informal integration of production processes across the region that intensified after China's economic reforms and modernisation from the late 1970s has proved to be a more powerful force for promoting trade and commerce than formal integration arrangements in Asia and other parts of the world. The close integration of China's production systems with those of its neighbours and the economic benefits flowing from such integration ensure that China and its neighbours do not allow political differences to affect economic exchanges.

From the Chinese vantage point, China has followed, and benefited from, a policy of not allowing political differences to clash with economic interests. This is obviously an approach aiming to maximise national interests overriding impediments of ideological differences and territorial disputes. China's eagerness to consolidate economic ties with the US, despite the two nations belonging to entirely opposite ends of the political spectrum, underlines the pragmatism that characterises its foreign policy. Satisfying the demands of realpolitik by aligning with the capitalist West and also an ideologically dissimilar neighbourhood underscores China's emphasis on optimising national interests arising from large-scale economic benefits. In this respect, China's approach finds resonance with what Morgenthau (1967) would espouse as the central component of national foreign policies – pursuit of national interests. India, however, appears to have been guided less by realpolitik, and more by ideological postures. Future policies determining India's engagements with various global and regional partners might show a more pragmatic trend as India slowly becomes reconciled to its status as a large economy with considerable strategic influence in the region and the world. Shades of such pragmatism are surfacing in its enunciation of a more nuanced 'middle' path in global climate change negotiations. But in bilateral ties, particularly with the neighbourhood, it still does not appear emphatic in following policies that would encourage economic gains for reducing negative externalities flowing from bad politics. It appears to be influenced by the notion that its GDP and trade can grow and expand irrespective of the neighbourhood. The neighbourhood for India essentially symbolises hostile countries (including China) with which deep economic engagement is hardly feasible. While China has shown exceptional political will in building strong ties with a hostile neighbourhood in order to garner economic benefits, India has hardly done so. And because China is also a part of India's neighbourhood and therefore a 'hostile' entity, and yet one of its largest trade partners, China has become a policy enigma for India.

Arguments suggesting that, unlike China, India can possibly afford to overlook its South Asian neighbourhood in its economic quest, stem from assumptions that India's neighbourhood is different from China's in its internal political volatility and economic development. Unlike China, which despite its large size was much more economically backward than most of Northeast Asia and parts of Southeast Asia when it embarked on economic reforms, India's economy was well ahead of its neighbours' when it began reforming. Its economic distance from its neighbours has remained more or less unchanged during the last couple of decades. Unlike China, it does not have Taiwan, Japan or Korea, all high-income mature economies, as its neighbours. It is the most dominant economic entity in its neighbourhood of South Asia. This is quite different from the economic constellation in East Asia, where, in spite of its large size, China has close neighbours, some of whom have higher per capita incomes and better economic indicators. Japan (US$42,325), Hong Kong (US$31,799), South Korea (US$20,165) and Taiwan (US$18,303) all have higher per capita incomes than China (US$4,520) and also higher human development indices. Indeed, despite being the world's second largest economy, China is the only economy among those mentioned which has a per capita income lower than the world average. For both China and its economically developed neighbours, maintaining good economic links with each other makes imminent sense because of the complementarities that China and its neighbours have in terms of economic structures and embedded production networks. In South Asia, India's per capita income (US$1,176) is lower than Sri Lanka's (US$2,364), but higher than Pakistan's (US$1,049) and Bangladesh's (US$640). None of these countries have per capita incomes higher than the world average. Nor do they have incomes close to that of China. India's sheer economic size of US$1.3 trillion makes it a significant economic force globally and regionally. But unlike China, it belongs to a much more economically underdeveloped region. The region has hardly any intra-industry trade linkages and production networks like those of Northeast Asia. Given the lack of such links, there are views that India might be better off focusing on economic engagement with other economically vibrant parts of Asia rather than its immediate neighbourhood.

China's economic growth has been an organic part of the economic progress of its neighbourhood, while India's growth has hardly been so. Thus, for China, the imperatives of maintaining strong economic ties with neighbours are high. Realpolitik would encourage consolidation of such ties for maximising the national interest. For India, its neighbours other than China are relatively small players in global trade and also not its major bilateral trade partners. On paper, therefore, unlike China, India does not have strong imperatives for consolidating economic ties with neighbours with whom it has delicate political ties. With respect to China, it faces a piquant situation for the first time in its history. Its economic engagement with China has advanced to an extent where disruptions can entail major economic losses. China is not only India's largest source of imports, but also a major export market. Beyond the sphere of trade-based exchanges, Chinese investments in India have begun picking up, particularly in vital segments like electricity and telecommunications. Obstructing these processes implies significant loss of economic welfare. The 'economics' in the relationship with China needs to be managed carefully in spite of political tensions. This is a new situation and a major challenge for India. It is more familiar terrain and much less a challenge for China, which has been accustomed to managing political and economic contradictions in its neighbourhood. China, therefore, appears more comfortable in handling the economic and political aspects of its ties with India in a mutually exclusive fashion. For India, though, implementing a mutually exclusive policy towards China with distinct political and economic arms may be more difficult.

This is probably where India needs to take stock of the emerging regional and global circumstances in a pragmatic manner for deciding an appropriate 'China' policy. Such a policy should grow out of an altered perception of its neighbourhood and can take a leaf out of China's book. Negative externalities of poor relations with neighbours can impose large costs on economic growth. Political differences cannot be resolved overnight. Strengthening of economic relations can help in alleviating the costs of politics to an extent. Over time, deeper economic ties can become a major deterrent to political hostilities. The empirical literature on trade provides evidence in favour of bilateral trade dependency reducing the possibility of bilateral conflicts (Martin *et al.* 2010). China's relationships also provide evidence in this respect where bilateral trade has been instrumental in ameliorating political concerns. India needs to look at trade with its neighbourhood more realistically, not only as just an economic activity, but also as an instrument for securing political stability. A similar approach with respect to China will also help. There is little doubt that Sino-Indian political ties could have been much worse than they are had good economics not acted as a deterrent. Approaching China with a more pragmatic perspective of optimising national interests by securing greater economic gains through more trade and investment is what realpolitik calls for.

The bilateral economic relationship in the medium term is expected to see mutual exclusion of political and economic components from both sides: convincingly from China and somewhat awkwardly, at least initially, from India. India is expected to broadly adhere to economic pragmatism with respect to China, through support for such pragmatism from two key quarters. The first is the government. Despite strong pressures from some domestic constituencies, particularly the security and strategic community and several major industrial producers, the Indian government has not allowed cross-border trade and investment to be affected by negative sentiments. This is not to suggest that it has been indifferent to domestic apprehensions. Democratically constituted governments in India can hardly afford to do so, particularly when they have to satisfy compulsions of coalition politics. Such compulsions on the part of the government have been reflected in regular anti-dumping actions on Chinese exports and also periodic restrictions on the supply of imported telecom equipment and the issue of work permits to Chinese workers. While these developments have had some adverse short-term impact on bilateral economic activities, they have not snowballed to inflict serious reverses. The government is appearing to play a carefully balanced role by assuaging domestic protectionist and security concerns on one hand while leaving the bilateral economic momentum undisturbed on the other. Given the fairly negative perceptions on China in large sections of India's strategic circle, industry and media, it is difficult for the government to adopt an effusive posture. The fact that it has shown commitment to a regular process of consultation and dialogue, and has been encouraging Chinese investments in India while trying to ensure greater market access for Indian exports in China, reflects its sincerity in protecting the robust economic relationship, albeit in a more balanced manner. In this regard, it is also important to note that occasional assertive actions by China in the form of discriminatory visa treatment for residents from certain parts of India as opposed to others have also been contained by the Chinese government and not allowed to mature into major skirmishes. The governments on both sides, up to now, have shown consistency in being pragmatic in their relationship.

The second factor positively influencing economic pragmatism from the Indian side is the spirited outlook of several Indian companies towards doing business with China. While large segments of Indian producers are wary of competing with China, quite a few others are heavily bullish about the prospects of doing business in the Chinese market. There can hardly be a better example than NIIT. In just over a decade since it began operating in China in 1997, NIIT has been recognised as the most influential IT training brand in China by the Chinese Ministry of Education.[1] Khanna (2007) mentions the growing business collaboration and synergies shaping between China and India. This is reflected in the prowess and initiatives of Indian firms operating successfully in China, such as Tata Consultancy Services (TCS), Wipro, Mahindra & Mahindra, Sundaram Fasteners, Bharat Forge and Suzlon Industries, to name only a few. For these firms, as well as Indian businesses such as the Adani Group and Reliance Power that are making full use of Chinese expertise in electricity generation, China implies a highly gainful and stable business prospect. Similar views about China are no doubt held by India's several electronic device designers, whose designed products are being manufactured in large numbers by Chinese vendors.[2] The design capabilities of Indian professionals blend well with Chinese scales of operation, and the results are immensely beneficial on both sides. There are several such examples where Indian firms are conscious of the benefits that can be obtained from operating in the Chinese market and collaborating with Chinese firms. Their confidence has no doubt been boosted by assurances from the Chinese government about providing greater market access to Indian goods and services.[3] Indeed, an encouraging initiative underlining the nascent willingness of Indian manufacturers and agencies to collaborate with China for maximising benefits is evident from Indian drug-makers exploring such options.[4]

The tendency of both governments to avoid confrontation and stay focused on pragmatic postures has much to do with the equation between the top leaderships. In particular, the personal rapport between Manmohan Singh and Wen Jiabao may have ensured that both governments work carefully to avoid potential flashpoints and ensure that economic exchanges function smoothly. Not only have the leaders been meeting each other frequently at different bilateral and multilateral forums, they have also been issuing statements that are positive on bilateral ties and accommodative of each other's growth and expansion in the regional and global domain. Personal chemistry between leaders is a major factor behind constructive bilateral ties, and history is replete with numerous such examples. But this is where concerns remain about the posturing of the leaderships once the current dispensation gives way to new incumbents. One would hope that future Premiers and top leadership of both countries would be able to retain the bonhomie that has characterised their predecessors. Pragmatism has much to do with personalities, as the current China–India relationship clearly demonstrates.

Notes

1 China–India economics: contour and context

1 *Sino Indian Joint Press Communiqué*, Beijing, 23 December 1988; Ministry of Foreign Affairs of the People's Republic of China; www.fmprc.gov.cn/eng/wjdt/2649/t15800.htm (accessed on 1 May 2011).
2 *Joint Communiqué of the Republic of India and the People's Republic of China*, 16 December 2010, Ministry of External Affairs, India; http://meaindia.nic.in/mystart.php?id=530516879 (accessed on 1 May 2011).
3 The two main disputed territories are Aksai Chin and Arunachal Pradesh
4 *Arthashastra*, written by Kautilya (better known as Chanakya, the Prime Minister of the ancient Indian empire headed by Chandragupta Maurya), is a celebrated treatise on statecraft with elaborate discussions on economic management and defence strategies.
5 For both electricity consumption and carbon dioxide emissions, per capital levels for China and India are much less than their developed counterparts such as the US and Europe, though in absolute terms both consumption and emissions have shot up rapidly.
6 China and India produced 451,633,000 tonnes and 77,243,000 tonnes of vegetables, 3,830,000 tonnes and 770,000 tonnes of sheep and goat meat, 5,849,000 tonnes and 1,282,000 tonnes of cattle meat, and 1,183,502 tonnes and 949,220 tonnes of tea in the year 2007 (FAO 2009). They were the largest and second largest producers of vegetables, sheep and goat meat and tea. They were the third and ninth largest producers of cattle meat.
7 *The World Factbook*, Central Intelligence Agency (CIA); https://www.cia.gov/library/publications/the-world-factbook/rankorder/2095rank.html#top (accessed on 23 April 2011).
8 Maddison's estimates of world, regional and country GDPs on PPP basis, despite providing illuminating insights into historical contributions to global output and the relative strength of different economies, are best taken as illustrative rather than definitive estimates, since statistical systems in earlier centuries hardly had methods of measuring GDP that are similar to those in modern times.
9 These are based on economic sizes estimated on the basis of GDPs calculated at nominal market prices. These indicate China and India as the second and eleventh largest economies in the world respectively. India figures among the top ten economies on PPP GDP estimates.
10 Emerging market economies typically imply economies that figure between developed and developing countries. They have high growth and are rapidly industrialising, offering investors good rates of return. Brazil, Russia, India, China and South Africa comprise the BRICS group of emerging market economies.

11 The Non-Aligned Movement (NAM) was a move on the part of several countries of the world to forge a distinct international identity by staying away from the two major power blocs led by the US and the erstwhile Soviet Union respectively during the Cold War. Founded in 1961, the NAM, which was formed to thwart the Cold War, has become largely irrelevant since the end of the Cold War.

12 The movement is named after the village of Naxalbari, located in the northern part of the state of West Bengal in India, where the first uprising declaring the intention to follow armed struggle for establishing the rights of the landless took place in 1967. Its leadership was inspired by the doctrines of Mao Zedong, which provided the ideological foundations for the movement. It petered out over the next decade. In more recent years, Maoist insurgency has resurfaced as one of the biggest internal security threats for India. However, with China having moved away from its earlier practice of rigid socialism and having embraced 'market-based' socialism, the latest movement does not find resonance with modern China's political principles.

13 See Gao Xu, 'State owned enterprises in China: how big are they?' 19 January 2010, blogs.worldbank.org. The estimate is on the basis of the Second National Economic Census conducted in 2008. See http://blogs.worldbank.org/eastasiapacific/state-owned-enterprises-in-china-how-big-are-they (accessed on 30 April 2011).

14 'Public sector enterprises in India – catalyst for growth', Indian Chamber of Commerce; www.indianchamber.org/policy_forms/3.pdf (accessed on 30 April 2011). The share of SOEs in total industrial output will be larger if state government-owned enterprises are included.

15 'Chinese workers fuel India's staggering infrastructure boom', *The Washington Post*, 24 October 2010; www.washingtonpost.com/wp-dyn/content/article/2010/10/23/AR2010102303956.html (accessed on 3 May 2011).

16 'JV model is the way to go in the Chinese market', *The Economic Times*, 4 April 2010; http://articles.economictimes.indiatimes.com/2010–04–04/news/28471818_1_jadebird-joint-venture-aptech (accessed on 8 September 2011).

17 'Renewable energy – China and India's next best bet', 4 May 2011; http://inchin-closer.com/2011/05/04/renewable-energy-china-and-indias-next-best-bet/ (accessed on 7 May 2011).

18 The Tianjin University of Finance and Economics in China has been collaborating with the Honeybee Network of India for patenting grassroot innovations. The Honeybee Network has been active in India for several years. The author's field interviews indicate that patenting grassroot innovations in China was unknown until the collaboration with Honeybee and reproduction of the model that Honeybee is following in India.

2 Common challenges and prospects for collaboration

1 The draft 12th Five Year Plan introduced at the 11th National People's Congress in March 2011 indicates that population will be controlled below 1.39 billion; *China Daily*, 4 March 2011. See www.chinadaily.com.cn/china/2011npc/2011–03/05/content_12120198.htm (accessed on 4 March 2011).

2 China and India are expected to have 1,453.1 million and 1,431.3 million people in 2025. As proportions of a projected world population of 8,011,533 million in the same year, both are expected to account for 1.8 per cent. By 2030, however, India is expected to have more people than China with its estimated population at 1,484.6 million as against China's population of 1,462.5 million. Statistically, both countries would still account for 1.8 per cent of the world population (8,308,895 million). From 2030 onward, China's population growth is expected to turn negative, culminating in its share in world population reducing to 1.7 per cent by 2035.

3 Chien (2007) points out that these estimates could be on the low side since the household registration system relaxations have been rather recent and the impact of the migration induced by such changes is yet to be captured fully. The latest census has tried to capture this aspect.
4 See www.world-gazetteer.com/wg.php?x=&men=gcis&lng=en&dat=32&geo=-104&srt=npan&col=aohdq&pt=c&va=&srt=pnan (accessed on 8 January 2011) for details of Indian cities and their populations.
5 Author's computations based on urban population estimates provided by UNFPA (2010).
6 The UN defines slums as 'contiguous settlements where inhabitants are characterized with inadequate housing and basic services. Slums are often unrecognized and unaddressed by public authorities as integral or equal parts of the city' (Arimah 2010).
7 The United Nations Populations Division defines populations in urban agglomeration as people residing in cities or towns plus those in suburban areas that are outside, but adjacent to, city boundaries. See http://esa.un.org/unpd/wup/unup/index.asp?panel=6 (accessed on 9 January 2011) for more details.
8 The figures in parentheses refer to the rank of the agglomeration in size (as determined by number of people in the agglomeration) followed by estimated population in 2008. The data is obtained from www.geohive.com/earth/cy_aggmillion2.aspx (accessed on 9 January 2011) and is estimated for the year 2010.
9 Author's computations from data reported in www.geohive.com/earth/cy_aggmillion2.aspx (accessed on 9 January 2011).
10 'Rajiv Awas Yojana: 7,900 flats ready for allocation', *Indian Express*, 4 February 2010; www.indianexpress.com/news/rajiv-awas-yojana-7-900-flats-ready-for-all/575269/ (accessed on 10 January 2011).
11 The statistics are provided in IMF's *World Economic Outlook*, April 2005 and re-obtained from ADB (2008).
12 These are according to the reference scenarios for China and India in IEA (2007). There are other alternative scenarios for both countries under different consumptions, showing different rates of growth in demand for coal.
13 Over the period in question, demand for oil in world energy is expected to decline from 35 per cent to 32 per cent. The decline is expected to be fully matched by the increase in demand for coal (IEA 2007).
14 'China, India driving global oil demand: Obama', *The Times of India*, 12 March 2011; www.samachar.com/China-India-driving-global-oil-demand-Obama-ldmhTlbjecc.html?source=recommended_news (accessed on 12 March 2011).
15 Output gap is the ratio of actual GDP to the trend GDP.
16 'Graft, inflation threaten growth', *The Financial Express*, New Delhi, 5 February 2011; http://www.financialexpress.com/news/graft-inflation-threaten-growth-pm/746344/ (accessed on 8 September 2011).
17 'Agreement on Cooperation on Addressing Climate Change Between the Government of the Republic of India and the Government of the People's Republic of China'; Ministry of Environment and Forests, Government of India; http://moef.nic.in/downloads/public-information/India-China%20Agreement%20on%20Climate%20Change.pdf (accessed on 30 January 2011).
18 Ibid.
19 The Doing Business database is annually compiled by the International Finance Corporation (IFC) and the World Bank. It is available at http://doingbusiness.org.
20 The survey was done in the middle of 2010 by Landesa (a rural development institute in the US), Michigan State University and Renmin University. See Wang Jingqiong (2011) for more details.
21 'Indian media damaging India–China ties: Chinese Premier Wen Jiabao', *India Today*, http://indiatoday.intoday.in/site/Story/123676/chinese-pms-india-visit/indian-media-damaging-indo-china-ties-chinese-premier-wen-jiabao.html (accessed on 11 February 2011).

3 Competition: present and future

1 The US, China, Russia and India consumed 2,182 mtoe, 2,177 mtoe, 635 mtoe and 470 mtoe respectively in 2009. Japan was the fifth largest consumer at 463 mtoe. See BP (2010, pp. 40–1) for more details on energy consumption of major economies.
2 Consumption estimates include inland demand, international aviation, marine bunkers, refinery fuel, fuel ethanol and biodiesel (BP 2010).
3 The ratio of current reserves to current production showing the number of years it will take for the reserves to be depleted if production remains at the current level.
4 '000mt denotes thousand million tonnes.
5 China's SPRs, which were 178 million barrels at the end of 2010, are expected to reach 274 million barrels by 2012. See 'Fuel reserve project moves into new phase'; www.cdeclips.com/en/business/Fuel_reserve_project_moves_into_new_phase/fullstory_59545.html (accessed on 28 January 2011).
6 tcm represents trillion cubic metres.
7 In January 2009, OVL acquired the Imperial Energy Corporation in western Siberia at a cost of US$2.1 billion. See www.ongcvidesh.com/Assets.aspx?tab=0 (accessed on 30 November 2010) for more details.
8 Sinopec and IOC – China and India's leading oil refiners – have been buying oil from Africa, particularly countries like Nigeria, through forward contracts or occasional spot purchases.
9 China has picked up a stake in South Africa's Standard Bank for funding infrastructure investments throughout the continent (Ahmad 2008).
10 This is an impression attributable to Arne Walther, former Secretary General of the International Energy Forum, shared at the 16th Annual Energy Conference of the Emirates Centre for Strategic Studies and Research (ECSSR). See http://timesofindia.indiatimes.com/business/international-business/India-China-make-competition-for-oil-intenseIndia-China-make-competition-for-oil-intense/articleshow/6906449.cms (accessed on 24 November 2010).
11 India has supported railway rehabilitation in Angola and has also extended several credit lines amounting to around US$75 million during 2004–7. But these have been dwarfed by China's US$2 billion support to various programmes during the period. Similarly, during the bid by ONGC in 2004, its offer of US$310 million was far exceeded by the Sinopec consortium's US$710 million (Vines *et al.* 2009).
12 China and India held these summits in 2006 and 2008 respectively.
13 For more details on other stakeholders in the field see www.ongcvidesh.com/Assets.aspx?tab=0 (accessed on 30 November 2010).
14 China's Yanzhou Coal Mining Company and India's Aditya Birla Group have been shortlisted in a bid to acquire Australia's Whitehaven coal mine. See 'China and India compete for Australian coal', http://inchincloser.com (accessed on 25 March 2011).
15 Competition for water has resulted in conflicts in the Middle East. Some of the major water conflicts are those witnessed in the Gaza Strip, over the Nile and the Jordan, and elsewhere in the world over the Danube and the Cauvery (in India).
16 Computed from projected water requirements in 2030 WRG (2009, ch. 2, p. 45, Exhibit 5).
17 According to SFG (2010), the share of the agriculture sector in total water consumption will reduce from the current level of 65 per cent to 55 per cent in 2030, but it will still be the major consumer.
18 Over-extraction is particularly critical in northern China and north and western India. See Bardhan (2010).
19 'India violating Indus Water Treaty says US report', *Samachar.com* 25 February 2011; www.samachar.com/India-violating-Indus-Water-treaty-says-US-report-ldbxNufhbhg.html?source=recommended_news (accessed on 2 March 2011).

20 Excluding intra-EU trade, India's rank in global export and import of commercial services was sixth in 2009.

21 The 'domino effect' in the context of regionalism illustrates how a particular development stimulating deeper economic integration can encourage others to become a part of the ongoing integration. Baldwin's original arguments on the 'domino effect' were with respect to American and European regionalism initiatives in the late 1980s. For a more detailed analysis see Baldwin (1993).

22 Section 15 of China's Accession Protocol to the WTO allows other WTO members to treat China as a 'non-market' economy, which makes China vulnerable to anti-dumping actions. This is discussed further in Chapter 5. The bilateral and regional agreements have enabled China to address this imbalance, with almost 80 countries granting it market economy status (Gao 2009).

23 The FTA includes all ASEAN exports under Chapters 1–8 of the Harmonised System (HS) of international trade classification (ITC) for preferential tariff treatment from China. However, similar reciprocation from ASEAN does not extend to all items under Chapters 1–8 (Jiangyu 2010).

24 Japan and South Korea are ranked fifth and nineteenth largest foreign aid donors in the world; www.nationmaster.com/graph/eco_eco_aid_don-economy-economic-aid-donor (accessed on 20 December 2010).

25 Computed from data provided in Chanana (2009, p. 12, Table 1) at an exchange rate of 1 US$=45 INR.

26 See Lum *et al.* (2009) and Lancaster (2007) for the OECD's conceptualisation of ODA. As Lancaster (2007), points out, 'development' largely covers humanitarian relief, debt relief and interventions resulting in improvement of human conditions'.

27 See Lum *et al.* (2009) for details on Chinese investments in Africa, Southeast Asia and South Asia.

28 The eligible list of countries includes 40 HIPCs, 22 low-income countries and LDCs, and 66 middle-income countries. See Exim Bank of India (2009a, p. 6).

29 The lines are updated till 13 December 2010. Computed from Exim Bank of India (2009b).

30 The ITEC programme began in 1964. The programme now covers 158 countries in Asia, East Europe, Central Asia, Latin America, Africa, the Caribbean and the Pacific and Small Island countries. More details are available at www.itec.mea.gov.in/ (accessed on 22 December 2010).

31 In the India–Africa Forum Summit held in April 2008, India pledged US$500 million as concessional credit to several African countries in addition to US$5.4 billion of credit lines. Similarly, in Afghanistan in South Asia, India has become one of the largest donors by pledging more than US$1 billion. See Ramachandran (2010) and Kragelund (2010).

32 This is a rough estimate as in quite a few cases the anti-dumping database gives tariff lines at four-digit or six-digit levels of commodity classification. The four- or six-digit classifications can include multiple eight-digit lines, which are the lowest level of tariffs. The figure of 200 can be more if all the eight-digit lines were available.

33 The anti-dumping actions are computed from the Global Anti-Dumping Database (GAD) of the World Bank. The database is part of the Temporary Trade Barriers Database (TTBD). See http://econ.worldbank.org/WBSITE/EXTERNAL/EXTDEC/EXTRESEARCH/0,,contentMDK:22574930~pagePK:64214825~piPK:64214943~theSitePK:469382,00.html for more details.

34 Antibiotics are one of the rare Indian exports that have invited anti-dumping duties in China. Sulfamethoxazole is the antibiotic whose exports were reportedly causing injury to domestic producers in China. See 'China imposes anti-dumping duty on antibiotic from India', *The Economic Times*, 16 June 2007; http://articles.economictimes.indiatimes.com/2007–06–16/news/28493063_1_anti-dumping-duty-anti-dumping-investigation-cheap-imports (accessed on 27 June 2011).

35 'C&IM visits China for the 8th India–China Joint Economic Group Meeting', Press Release, 19 January 2010, Embassy of India, Beijing; www.indianembassy.org.cn/NewsDetails.aspx?NewsId=6 (accessed on 27 January 2011); *Joint Communique of the Republic of India and the People's Republic of China*, 16 December 2010; http://meaindia.nic.in/mystart.php?id=530516879 (accessed on 27 January 2011).

36 *Joint Communique of the Republic of India and the People's Republic of China*, 16 December 2010; http://meaindia.nic.in/mystart.php?id=530516879 (accessed on 27 January 2011).

4 Trade: engine of bilateral collaboration

1 See 'China India to build strategic partnership', Xinhua News Agency, 12 April 2005; www.china.org.cn/english/2005/Apr/125627.htm (accessed on 25 March 2011); *China India Joint Declaration*, Embassy of the People's Republic of China in India, 30 November 2006; http://in.china-embassy.org/eng/sgxw/2006en/t282045.htm (accessed on 25 March 2011); *Joint Communiqué of the Republic of India and the People's Republic of China*, 16 December 2010; http://meaindia.nic.in/mystart.php?id=530516879 (accessed on 25 March 2011).

2 'Trade salute', Indrajit Basu, *China Daily* Asia Weekly, 10–16 December 2010, pp. 1, 3. www.cdeclips.com/files/asiapdf/20101210/cdasiaweekly20101210p03.pdf (accessed on 5 September 2011).

3 The Index of Industrial Production (IIP) measures the growth in industrial output by aggregating growth in manufacturing, electricity and mining. These three sectors have 79.36 per cent, 10.17 per cent and 10.47 per cent weight respectively in IIP. The index is compiled by Central Statistical Organisation (CSO) India. For a detailed time series of IIP growth rates see Reserve Bank of India, *Handbook of Statistics on Indian Economy 2009–10* (15 September 2010), p. 411, Table 225; available at http://rbidocs.rbi.org.in/rdocs/Publications/PDFs/225T_HBSE200910.pdf.

4 'SMEs hit hard by Chinese imports', *Silicon India News*; 15 June 2009; www.siliconindia.com/shownews/SMEs_hit_hard_by_cheap_Chinese_imports_FICCI-nid-58100.html (accessed on 15 February 2011).

5 An even closer look at the eight-digit level of HS tariff lines reveals personal computers (palmtop, laptop) (HS84713010) as the largest import items under HS8471 for both 2008–9 and 2009–10. The other significant imports were Winchester/hard disc drives (HS84717020), parts and accessories of motherboards (HS84733020) and other digital automatic data processing machines with keyboard and display consisting of central processing machines (HS84713090). See http://commerce.nic.in/eidb/default.asp for more details.

6 Some of the four-digit categories have been mentioned in their shorter versions. HS8528 is 'Reception apparatus incorporating radio broadcast receivers/sound/video recording reproducing apparatus, video monitors etc.'; HS3105 is 'mineral/chemical fertilisers with two/three of the fertilising elements N, P and K; other fertilisers/similar goods in tablets/like form in packet of weight less than or equal to 10 kg'; HS7102 is 'diamonds worked but not mounted/set'; HS8473 is 'parts & accessories (excluding covers, carrying cases, etc.) used with machines of heading numbers HS8469 to HS8472'; and HS8504 is 'electrical transformers, static converters (for example rectifiers) and inductors'.

7 All computations for growth rates and shares of HS8517 and HS8525 are done by the author on the basis of information from Export Import Data Bank, Department of Commerce, Ministry of Commerce and Industry, Government of India; http://commerce.nic.in/eidb/Icomcnt.asp.

8 Mobile phones manufactured in China are popular in various parts of India. The more widely selling ones include ZTC T58 and ZT6191; these are dual SIM phones having features of other highly priced branded phones. Some market reports show the

Chinese mobile phone manufacturer G'Five at third place in terms of the share of the market after Nokia and Samsung. See 'India is world's fastest growing mobile phone market: IDC Report', 30 September 2010; www.starbytecomputers.com/blog/2010/09/india-fastest-growing-mobile-market-idc-market/1471/ (accessed on 20 February 2011).

9 Some of the categories have again been briefly described. HS8402 is 'Steam/other vapour generating boilers (excluding central heating hot water boilers capable of producing low pressure steam); super-heated water boilers'; HS8414 is 'Air/vacuum pumps. air/other gas compressors & fans; ventilating/recycling hoods incorporating a fan with filters'; HS8443 is 'Printing machinery, including inkjet printing machines excluding Heading no 8471; machines for uses ancillary to printing'; HS8447 is 'Knitting machines, stitch-binding machines, & machines for making yarn, tulle, lace, embroidery, trimming, braid/net and machines for tufting'.

10 Documented on the basis of information available from Export Import Data Bank, Department of Commerce, Ministry of Commerce and Industry, Government of India; http://commerce.nic.in/eidb/Icntcom.asp.

11 'HCL launches cheapest laptop @ Rs13,990', *Business Standard*, 16 January 2008; www.business-standard.com/india/news/hcl-launches-cheapest-laptop-@-rs-13990/310806/ (accessed on 21 February 2011).

12 'Project imports; laboratory chemicals; passenger's baggage, personal importations by air or post; ship stores'; Indian Trade Classification (Harmonised System), Chapter 98, p. 1013; Section XXI; Directorate General of Commercial Intelligence and Statistics (DGCI&S), Ministry of Commerce and Industry, Government of India; www.dgciskol.nic.in/.

13 Author's computations from source as indicated in note 7.

14 The eight-digit tariff lines are HS29411010, HS29411050, HS29415000, HS29419090 and HS29420090.

15 Tariff lines represented by HS26011130 and HS26011140, indicating iron ore fines.

16 'Iron ore exports to be streamlined', *The Economic Times*, 22 November 2006; http://articles.economictimes.indiatimes.com/2006–11–22/news/27426939_1_iron-ore-ore-exports-iron-content (accessed on 1 March 2011).

17 'RPT-Update-3 India ups iron ore export duty China hardest hit', Reuters, 28 February 2011; www.reuters.com/article/2011/03/01/india-ironore-idUSSGE72001120110301 (accessed on 1 March 2011).

18 'India becomes China's largest cotton exporter, New Delhi imposes duty on cotton exports', *Inchincloser*, 15 April 2010; http://inchincloser.com/2010/04/15/india-becomes-chinas-largest-cotton-exporter-new-delhi-imposes-duty-on-cotton-exports/ (accessed on 1 March 2011).

19 Some of the major eight-digit tariff lines of export from these categories during 2008–9 and 2009–10 were oxylene (HS29024100), pyridine and its salts (HS29333100), menthol (HS29061100), ethylene glycol (HS29053310), other diloxanide furoate, cimetidine, famotidine (HS29420090) and other antibiotics (HS29419090).

20 The main eight-digit export tariff line is alumina calcined (HS28182010).

21 For more details see 'Copper: demand and supply analysis', at http://seekingalpha.com/instablog/638554-miguel-herschberg/70320-copper-demand-and-supply-analysis (accessed on 23 March 2011).

22 Leading exports at disaggregated eight-digit tariff line include gas compressors used in air-conditioning (HS84148011).

23 The main eight-digit export tariff lines are ribbon fish (HS03037930), croaker, grouper, hounder (HS03037980), cuttle fish (HS03074110) and whole squid frozen (HS03074920).

24 'Report of the India–China Joint Study Group on Comprehensive Trade and Economic Cooperation', ch. 6, p. 74, paragraph 6.13; www.hinduonnet.com/thehindu/nic/0041/report.pdf (accessed on 27 February 2011).

25 'The Prime Ministers agreed to appoint a Joint Task Force to study in detail the feasibility of, and the benefits that may derive from, the India–China Regional Trading Arrangement and give recommendations regarding its content.' See 'Joint Statement of the Republic of India and the People's Republic of China', *The Hindu*, 11 April 2005; www.hinduonnet.com/thehindu/nic/0041/jointstatement.htm (accessed on 27 February 2011).
26 'Joint Communiqué of the Republic of India and the Republic of China', Ministry of External Affairs, Government of India, 16 December; http://meaindia.nic.in/mystart.php?id=530516879 (accessed on 27 February 2011).
27 Ando (2006) highlights the growth of intra-industry trade in East Asia including China as a result of vertical specialisation and fragmentation of production in the region. For more details of the literature on intra-industry trade in Asia see Sawyer *et al.* (2009).
28 This particular activity was specifically mentioned as an example of Chinese and Indian businesses benefiting from each other during the author's meetings with entrepreneurs and experts at Tianjin in September 2010.

5 Collaboration: the global agenda

1 Doha WTO Ministerial 2001: Ministerial Declaration; WT/MIN(01)/DEC/1 20 November 2001; Ministerial Declaration adopted on 14 November 2001; paragraph 2; www.wto.org/english/thewto_e/minist_e/min01_e/mindecl_e.htm (accessed on 14 October 2010).
2 Ibid., paragraph 44.
3 Article 27.6 of WTO defines 'export competitiveness' as achieving a 3.25 per cent share of world trade in a particular product; www.wto.org/english/tratop_e/dda_e/implem_explained_e.htm#crosscutting (accessed on 21 October 2010).
4 WTO members do not discriminate between their partners and treat all of them equally or as Most Favoured Nations (MFNs).
5 Though the international quota regime on textile exports was to end by 2004 for Chinese products, WTO members could resort to safeguards for a longer period, that is, till the end of 2008.
6 The cap of 8.5 per cent was less than that normally available for developing countries under WTO (Gertler 2002).
7 'China prospers with world after WTO accession', *China Daily*, 28 January 2011; www.chinadaily.com.cn/bizchina/2011–01/28/content_11935664.htm (accessed on 28 January 2011).
8 The countries included Chinese Taipei and Japan, but not China. See http://commerce.nic.in/trade/international_trade_papers_nextDetail.asp?id=7 (accessed on 24 October 2010).
9 The G20 on Agriculture at WTO is different from the other global grouping, the G20, which was formed in 1999 by a group of developed and emerging market economies to address global macroeconomic and financial issues and includes finance ministers and central bank governors from the latter.
10 Article 6.5 of AoA refers to 'blue box' subsidies. These are the ones that are given to farmers for limiting production. While these can be challenged by other members, the imposing countries do not have any obligations to remove them.
11 The average rate of tariffs applied by China on agricultural and non-agricultural exports are 15.6 per cent and 8.7 per cent respectively. For India, the similar rates are 31.8 per cent and 10.1 per cent. India, however, has bound rates 113.1 per cent and 34.1 per cent on agriculture and non-agriculture imports, meaning it can raise tariffs to these levels within WTO norms. For China, these bound rates are at the much lower levels of 15.7 per cent and 9.2 per cent respectively.
12 The US proposed a 150 per cent increase in the volume of imports for setting off the trigger. India, representing the developing countries, proposed 110 per cent. The US

later 'compromised' by agreeing to a 140 per cent increase proposed by the Director-General of the WTO. However, it refused to budge any further, as did the developing countries (Jonasse 2008).

13 The US and EU were particularly sharp in their criticism of the two countries, as was Japan.

14 'Bush calls Manmohan on WTO talk', *The Economic Times*, 24 July.

15 See 'Doha deal must be done this year', www.samachar.com/Doha-deal-must-be-done-this-year-India-ldtcKGgiahj.html (accessed on 19 March 2011).

16 'Call for early conclusion of Doha round talks', *The Hindu*, 28 January 2011; www.thehindu.com/business/Economy/article1134451.ece?service=mobile (accessed on 19 March 2011).

17 The gases identified for action are carbon dioxide, nitrous oxide, methane and sulphur hexafluoride. Hydro fluorocarbons and per fluorocarbons are also identified as contributors to global warming.

18 Annex 1 countries include Australia, Austria, Belarus, Belgium, Bulgaria, Canada, Croatia, Czech Republic, Denmark, Estonia, Finland, France, Germany, Greece, Hungary, Iceland, Ireland, Italy, Japan, Latvia, Liechtenstein, Lithuania, Luxembourg, Monaco, Netherlands, New Zealand, Norway, Poland, Portugal, Romania, Russia, Slovakia, Slovenia, Spain, Sweden, Switzerland, Turkey, Ukraine, United Kingdom, United States of America.

19 World Bank and Oxfam estimates put costs of adaptation between US$4 billion and 37 billion/annum. The UNDP estimates are even higher after taking into account the progress towards Millennium Development Goals (MDGs). The Adaptation Fund was estimated at between US$80 and one billion by 2012 to be financed by mainly by 2 per cent levies imposed on revenues from CDM projects (World Bank 2008).

20 According to GHG emission estimates in 2005, China, Indonesia, India, Brazil and Mexico were the first, fourth, fifth, seventh and tenth largest GHG emitters, accounting for 17 per cent, 6 per cent, 5 per cent, 4 per cent and 2 per cent of total global GHG emissions respectively. However, on a per capita basis, they were ranked much lower than the US and Canada (MNP 2007).

21 Chinese media opined that the Indian Prime Minister Manmohan Singh and the Chinese President Hu Jintao have similar views on the subject. These were that, given the historical responsibility and current capabilities, developed countries had to take the lead role in cutting emissions and helping developing countries to adapt to environment-friendly technologies. See Spencer and Foster (2007).

22 'Agreement on Cooperation on Addressing Climate Change between the Government of the Republic of India and the Government of the People's Republic of China'; see http://moef.nic.in/downloads/public-information/India-China%20Agreement%20on%20Climate%20Change.pdf (accessed on 8 November 2010).

23 Volume of carbon dioxide emitted with every additional unit of Gross Domestic Product (GDP) generated.

24 During the period 1994–2007, the emissions intensity of India's GDP reduced by more than 30 per cent. India is also devoting 2.6 per cent of its GDP annually to measures having strong adaptation content, such as cyclone warning systems, drought relief, flood control, etc. (MoF 2010).

25 'Manmohan Singh helps draft BASIC deal at Copenhagen'; 19 December 2009; www.domain-b.com/environment/20091218_manmohan_singh.html (accessed on 9 November 2010.

26 Commitments of US$30 billion during 2010–12 and US$100 billion per year by 2020 (UNFCCC 2009).

27 'UN climate chief supports Indian plan'; www.samachar.com/India-will-be-more-flexible-at-Cancun-climate-talks-says-Ramesh-kllcLahfggi.html (accessed on 11 November 2010).

28 Efforts to curb emissions might discourage extensive commercial farming for exports having significant implications for trade liberalisation measures. Furthermore, with the global transport sector accounting for 20–25 per cent of total GHG emissions, cross-border movement of goods will also be influenced (South Centre 2008).

29 This G20 is different from the G20 group on agriculture at the WTO, discussed earlier in the chapter.

30 The trade estimates include intra-EU trade; www.g20.org/about_what_is_g20.aspx (accessed on 10 November 2010).

31 The US and Turkey are Annex 1 non-ratifying parties.

32 China and India had US$2.5 trillion and US$300.2 billion foreign exchange reserves at the end of September and November 2010 respectively; http://en.wikipedia.org/wiki/List_of_countries_by_foreign_exchange_reserves (accessed on 15 November 2010). With 1054.1 tonnes and 557.1 tonnes at the end of September 2010, China and India were ranked sixth and eleventh in world gold rankings (World Gold Council 2010).

33 'Major foreign holders of Treasury securities (in billions of dollars)' Department of the Treasury/Federal Reserve Board, 28 February 2011; www.treasury.gov/resource-center/data-chart-center/tic/Documents/mfh.txt (accessed on 6 September 2011).

34 The FSF was subsequently replaced by the Financial Stability Board (FSB), which included all FSF members, G20 members, Spain and the European Commission.

35 In nominal terms China and India are the third and eleventh largest economies in the world, while in PPP terms they are the second and fourth largest. IMF (2010a).

36 'IMF's Executive Directors and Voting Powers', www.imf.org/external/np/sec/memdir/eds.htm (accessed on 20 November 2010).

6 The economics–politics dynamics, competition and collaboration

1 It would be inaccurate to describe Sino-Indian political ties as 'bad' since they are strictly not so, given the large numbers of high-level political visits, official exchanges, declared areas of mutual cooperation and partnering of each other at global forums. However, the not-too-distant history of political skirmish (the Sino-Indian War in 1962) and spats over border disputes make the relationship politically disturbed and volatile.

2 Computed from Trade Statistics, Bureau of Foreign Trade, Government of Taiwan. The figures are exclusive of re-exports and re-imports. Japan, the US, Hong Kong, Korea and Singapore have been the next largest trade partners of Taiwan with shares of 14.6 per cent, 13.1 per cent, 8.5 per cent, 4.9 per cent and 3.4 per cent respectively during 2002–10.

3 Both China and Taiwan arrived at a consensus in 1992 that, though both agreed to there being only 'one' China (including both the mainland and Taiwan), the interpretation of the term was left to them individually. Since then countries recognising the PRC accept it as representative of all China including Taiwan and do not recognise the latter separately. The reverse applies for countries recognising the ROC as representative of all China.

4 'Direct cross-strait links in place', *The China Post*, 15 December 2008, Taiwei; www.chinapost.com.tw/taiwan/china-taiwan-relations/2008/12/15/187643/Direct-across-strait.htm (accessed on 3 March 2011).

5 *Kimchi* is a traditional Korean dish of pungent raw pickled vegetables. It is popular in both China and Korea. South Korea reacted adversely to Chinese exports of *kimchi* in October 2005 on the grounds that they contained parasite eggs. The products were recalled and destroyed. China retaliated by banning several other Korean exports of foodstuffs and also began investigating Korean cosmetics. For more details on the dispute, see Zhou (2010) and 'Kimchi war between China–Korea is resolved', *Korea*

Joongang Daily, 11 January 2008; http://joongangdaily.joins.com/article/view.asp?aid=2884973 (accessed on 11 March 2011).

6 See 'Culture shock', *The Economist*, 8 July 2010; www.economist.com/node/16542339 (accessed on 11 March 2011).

7 The Yasukuni shrine is a memorial to Japanese soldiers who lost their lives during its war against China. The China–Japan friendship treaty signed during resumption of diplomatic ties, while exempting soldiers, criticised Japanese leaders for engineering war crimes. These leaders, executed by orders passed by the Tokyo Tribunal of War Criminals, have also now been enshrined at Yasukuni. For China, the shrine represents memories of atrocities suffered at the hands of Japanese forces and visits to the shrine by Japanese leaders is indicative of Japan overlooking its war responsibilities. For Japan, though, the shrine may have come to represent a symbol of nationalistic pride. For more details see 'Japan China relations at the crossroads (Part I: Why do Japanese nationalists hate China?' at 'Nakaoka's alternative viewpoints on Japan', www.redcruise.com/nakaoka/en/?p=5 (accessed on 11 March 2011).

8 'China, EU reach "important consensus" at economic, trade talks: vice premier', 21 December 2010; www.gov.cn/english/2010–12/21/content_1770544.htm (accessed on 11 March 2011).

9 The US trade figures for 2002 and 2008 are from the Direction of Trade Statistics (DOTS) database of the IMF with China as the reporting country. These are different from the US International Trade Commission DataWeb figures reported in Morrison (2011). As Morrison (2011) points out, US import data reflects the full value in terms of the cost of each unit of import from China. Much of the value, though, could have originated in other countries in the course of the supply chains involving US, Taiwanese, Chinese and other firms and their affiliates. Thus the US trade data might actually show a higher value of its imports from China.

10 'China takes US to WTO', *People's Daily Online*, 1 March 2011; http://english.peopledaily.com.cn/90001/90778/90861/7303709.html (accessed on 1 March 2011).

11 'System on foreign trade performance analysis', Department of Commerce, Ministry of Commerce and Industry, Government of India; http://commerce.nic.in/ftpa/default.asp.

12 Bilateral trade had reached US$47 billion in 2008–9. It declined to US$43.4 billion because of recessionary conditions.

13 See 'India/UAE: use visit to raise migrant worker issue', 22 November 2010; www.hrw.org/en/news/2010/11/22/indiauae-use-visit-raise-migrant-worker-issue (accessed on 13 March 2010).

14 See Swami (2001) for more details.

15 The DMIC is a 1,483 km dedicated freight corridor between Delhi and Mumbai. The corridor envisages high-speed connectivity for container trains and is equipped with a large number of infrastructure facilities. Passing through six northern and western states of India, the project also includes nine large industrial zones, a high-speed freight line, three ports, six airports, a six-lane intersection-free expressway, a mega power plant and several industrial clusters. The corridor envisages provision of backward and forward linkages of a variety of industrial and commercial activities around high quality infrastructure. The estimated cost of the project is US$90 billion, with financial and technical aid from Japan. For more details see http://delhimumbaiindustrialcorridor.com/ (accessed on 18 March 2011).

16 The Civil Liability for Nuclear Damage Bill introduced in the Indian Parliament in May 2010 tries to provide guarantees to nuclear material and equipment suppliers in the event of nuclear accidents in India.

17 'India's trade barriers hampering economic ties: EU'; daijiworld.com; 17 March 2011; www.daijiworld.com/news/news_disp.asp?n_id=97279&n_tit=India%27s+Trade+Barriers+Hampering+Economic+Ties%3A+EU (accessed on 19 March 2011).

18 Both the Indian and the German foreign ministers commented to the press after their meeting at Berlin in May 2007 that cooperation between the EU and India on climate protection and energy policy was difficult. See 'Differences remain between India and EU on climate change, energy', *earthtimes*, 31 May 2007; www.earthtimes.org/articles/news/67965.html (accessed on 20 March 2011).

19 'India: Country Strategy Paper 2007–2013', European External Action Service (EEAS), European Union; http://eeas.europa.eu/india/index_en.htm (accessed on 10 March 2011).

20 The H-1B visa is a non-immigrant visa allowing business professionals to live and work in the US for a specified period of time up to a maximum of six years. US companies use the visa for bringing in skilled professionals from countries like India. The annual quota is usually capped at 65,000 visas, though there are no upper ceilings for non-profit organisations and higher education institutions.

21 'US India aim to settle differences on trade issues', Rediff.com, 22 September 2010; http://business.rediff.com/slide-show/2010/sep/22/slide-show-1-us-india-seek-to-settle-differences-on-trade-issues.htm (accessed on 5 March 2011).

22 'India may contest Obama's move against outsourcing in WTO', *Hindustan Times*, 26 February 2009; www.hindustantimes.com/India-may-contest-Obama-s-move-against-outsourcing-in-WTO/H1-Article1–384083.aspx. (accessed on 5 March 2011).

23 During the period 2000–1 to 2008–9, India's trade with Bangladesh, Nepal, Pakistan and Sri Lanka increased from US$1.0 billion to US$2.8 billion, US$396 million to US$2 billion, US$251 million to US$1.8 billion and US$685 million to US$2.7 billion respectively. India's total trade during this period increased from US$95.1 billion to US$489 billion. The shares are the author's computations on the basis of statistics provided by the RBI.

7 Gazing into the crystal ball

1 NIIT has 183 cooperative education and training sites in more than 25 provinces in China. It has trained more than 100,000 students and has received several awards from the Chinese government. For more details see http://niit.com/newsandevents/Lists/NIIT%20News/disformCustomv3.aspx?List=a325a1cf-a064–4573-b17a-3ce893a0d178&ID=191 (accessed on 14 March 2011).

2 'Indian tech firms link with China to take on Western brands', physorg.com; 30 November 2010; see www.physorg.com/news/2010–11-indian-tech-firms-link-china.html (accessed on 14 March 2011).

3 'China to give Indian companies greater access to Domestic Market'; *2point6billion.com*; www.2point6billion.com/news/2010/08/30/china-to-give-indian-companies-greater-access-to-domestic-market-6893.html (accessed on 14 March 2011).

4 'India, China drug makers draft MoU', livemint.com; 16 December 2010; www.livemint.com/2010/12/16005756/IndiaChinadrugmakersdraft.html?atype=tp (accessed on 23 March 2011).

References

Abbott, P.C., Hurt, C. and Tyner, W.E. (2009) 'What's driving food prices? March 2009 update', *Farm Foundation, Issue Report* (FFIR), Oak Brook, IL; www.farmfoundation.org/news/articlefiles/1702-Farm%20-%203-10-09%20-%20Food%20Prices%20Update%20-%20Book%20for%20Posting.pdf (accessed on 7 August 2011).

ADB (2008) *Asian Development Outlook 2008 Update*, Manila, September; www.adb.org/Documents/Books/ADO/2008/Update/default.asp (accessed on 17 January 2011).

Ahmad, A. (2008) 'India and China: conflict, competition and cooperation in the age of globalization', *Share The World's Resources (STWR)*, 21 February; www.stwr.org/india-china-asia/india-and-china-conflict-competition-and-cooperation-in-the-age-of-globalization.html (accessed on 24 November 2010).

Aiyar, Pallavi (2008) 'Huawei's perfect marriage', *Asia Times Online*, 16 August; www.atimes.com/atimes/China_Business/JH16Cb01.html (accessed on 7 August 2011).

Ando, Mitsuyo (2006) 'Fragmentation and vertical intra-industry trade in East Asia', *North American Journal of Economics and Finance*, Vol. 17, No. 3 (December), pp. 257–81.

Arimah, B.C. (2010) 'The face of urban poverty: explaining the prevalence of slums in developing countries', United Nations University (UNU) – World Institute for Development Research (WIDER), Working Paper No. 2010/30, March; www.wider.unu.edu/stc/repec/pdfs/wp2010/wp2010–30.pdf (accessed on 9 January 2010).

Armstrong, Shiro (2010) 'Improving Japan–China relations and the global trading system', *East Asia Forum*, 10 January; www.eastasiaforum.org/2010/01/18/improving-japan-china-relations-and-the-global-trading-system/ (accessed on 11 March 2011).

Bagchi, I. (2010) 'China admits to Brahmaputra Project', *Economic Times*, 22 April; http://economictimes.indiatimes.com/news/politics/nation/China-admits-to-Brahmaputra-project/articleshow/5842624.cms (accessed on 8 December 2010).

Baldwin, R.E. (1993) *A Domino Theory of Regionalism*, Working Paper No. 4465, Cambridge, MA: National Bureau of Economic Research (NBER), September; www.nber.org/papers/w4465 (accessed on 3 September 2011).

Bardhan, P. (2010) *Awakening Giants, Feet of Clay*, Princeton, NJ: Princeton University Press.

Basu, Kaushik (2009), 'China and India: idiosyncratic paths to high growth', *Economic and Political Weekly*, Vol. 44, No. 38 (September), pp. 19–25.

Bawa, S.K., Lian, P.K., Tien, M.L., Jianguo, L., Ramakrishnan, P.S., Yu, D.W., Ya-ping, Z. and Raven, P.H. (2010) 'China, India and the environment', *Science*, Vol. 327, 19 March; www.csis.msu.edu/Publications/JLiu_March_2010.pdf (accessed on 30 January 2011).

Bown, Chad P. (2007) 'China's WTO entry: antidumping, safeguards and dispute settlement', *National Bureau of Economic Research* (NBER), Working Paper 13349 August; see www.nber.org/papers/w13349 (accessed on 22 October 2010).

Bown, Chad P. (2010a) 'Taking stock of antidumping, safeguards, and countervailing duties, 1990–2009', Policy Research Working Paper, WPS5436, World Bank, Development Research Group, Trade and Integration Team, September; http://www-wds.worldbank.org/external/default/WDSContentServer/IW3P/IB/2010/09/28/000158349_20100928091836/Rendered/PDF/WPS5436.pdf (accessed on 1 March 2011).

Bown, Chad P. (2010b) 'Global anti-dumping database', http://econ.worldbank.org/ttbd/gad/.

Bown, Chad P. (2010c) 'China-specific safeguards database', http://econ.worldbank.org/ttbd/csgd/.

BP (2010) *BP Statistical Review of World Energy June 2010*, London: BP; see www.bp.com/statisticalreview (accessed on 19 November 2010).

Bradsher, K. (2011a) 'The limits of an industrial juggernaut', *International Herald Tribune* (France), 13 January.

Bradsher, K. (2011b) 'Rising prices in China send ripples around globe', *International Herald Tribune* (France), 31 January.

Brooks, Douglas H. and Ferrarini, Benno (2010) 'Changing trade costs between People's Republic of China and India', ADB Economics Working Paper Series, Asian Development Bank, No. 203, May; www.adb.org/Documents/Working-Papers/2010/Economics-WP203.pdf (accessed on 27 February 2011).

Burke, Michael E., Cutshaw, Kenneth A. and Krishna, Rahul (2006) 'The legal systems in India–China: a comparative perspective', *Indian Journal of Economics & Business*, Special Issue China and India, pp. 1–28; http://www.icainstitute.org/ijeb/Michael%20E.%20Burke.pdf (accessed on 1 August 2011).

Bush, J. (2005) 'China and India: a rage for oil', *Business Week*, 5 September; www.businessweek.com/print/magazine/content/05_36/b3949086_mz015.htm?chan=gl (accessed on 24 November 2010).

Chanana, D. (2009) 'India as an emerging donor', *Economic and Political Weekly* (EPW), Vol. XLIV, No. 12 (21 March), pp. 11–14.

Cherian, John (2002) 'Zhu Rongji in India', *Frontline*, Volume 19, Issue 3 (2–15 February); www.hindu.com/fline/fl1903/19031220.htm (accessed on 25 March 2011).

Cheru, F. (2005) 'Globalization and uneven development in Africa: the limits to effective urban governance in the provision of basic services'; UCLA Globalization Research Center-Africa; www.international.ucla.edu/africa/grca/publications/article.asp?parentid=107324 (accessed on 8 September 2011).

Chien, S. (2007) 'The political economy of urban and regional development', in G. Wang and J. Wong (eds) *Interpreting China's Development*, Singapore: World Scientific Publishing.

Chithelen, I. (2005) 'New high for global crude oil prices', *Economic and Political Weekly* (EPW), 26 March, pp. 1321–2.

Chow, G.C. (2001) 'The impact of joining the WTO on China's economic, legal and political institutions', speech delivered at the International Conference on Greater China and the WTO organised by the City University of Hong Kong, 22–24 March; see www.princeton.edu/~gchow/WTO.pdf (accessed on 24 October 2010).

Dalliwall, S. and Clarke, R. (2008) 'Sino-Indian competition for Burmese oil and natural gas', *Harvard International Review*, 4 September; http://hir.harvard.edu/sino-indian-competition-for-burmese-oil-and-natural-gas?page=0,0 (accessed on 25 November 2010).

Devarakonda, R.K. (2007) 'Emerging G5 take counter-proposal to G8', Inter Press Service News Agency (IPS) 7 June; http://ipsnews.net/news.asp?idnews=38088 (accessed on 7 November 2010).

Dhar, A. (2009) 'Jairam Ramesh: 20–25 pc carbon emission intensity cut by 2020', *The Hindu*, 3 December; www.thehindu.com/news/national/article59592.ece?service=mobile (accessed on 8 November 2010).

Dinar, S. (2002) 'Water security, conflict and cooperation', *SAIS Review*, Vol. 22, No. 2 (Summer–Fall), p. 232.

Diwan, Shradha (2010) 'India–UAE partnership – an insight', Institute of International Trade; www.iitrade.ac.in/kmarticle.asp?id=359 (accessed on 13 March 2011).

Dreyer, Iana (2011) 'China is no white knight in Europe's debt crisis', *Bloomberg*, 26 January; www.bloomberg.com/news/2011–01–26/china-is-no-white-knight-in-europe-s-debt-crisis-iana-dreyer.html (accessed on 12 March 2011).

Economy, E. (2008) 'Asia's water security crisis: China, India and the United States', in J.A. Tellis, M. Kuo and A. Marble (eds) *Strategic Asia 2008–09: Challenges and Choices*, Washington, DC: National Bureau of Asian Research (NBR).

EIA (2010a) 'India energy data, statistics and analysis – oil, gas, electricity, coal', Energy Information Administration (EIA), Country Analysis Briefs, August; www.eia.doe.gov/emeu/cabs/India/pdf.pdf (accessed on 28 November 2010).

EIA (2010b) 'China energy data, statistics and analysis – oil, gas, electricity, coal', Energy Information Administration (EIA), Country Analysis Briefs, November; www.eia.doe.gov/emeu/cabs/China/pdf.pdf (accessed on 28 November 2010).

Eilperin, J. (2009) 'China sets target for emission cuts', *Washington Post*, 27 November; www.washingtonpost.com/wpdyn/content/article/2009/11/26/AR2009112600519.html?sid=ST2009112602519 (accessed on 8 November 2010).

Elliott, Lorraine (2011) 'Climate migration: why it is a human security issue', RSIS Commentaries No. 28/2011, S. Rajaratnam School of International Studies, Nanyang Technological University (NTU), Singapore, 25 February; www.rsis.edu.sg/publications/Perspective/RSIS0282011.pdf (accessed on 25 February 2011).

Exim Bank of India (2009a) 'Terms and conditions and procedure to be adopted in respect of Government of India (GOI) Supported Exim Bank Lines of Credit (LoCs)'; www.eximbankindia.com/goi-loc.pdf (accessed on 22 December 2010).

Exim Bank of India (2009b) 'Exim Bank's operative lines of credit', Exim Bank of India; http://eximbankindia.com (accessed on 22 December 2010).

FAO (2009) *FAO Statistical Yearbook 2009*, Volume 4, Rome: Food and Agriculture Organisation of the United Nations; www.fao.org/docrep/014/am079m/am079m00.htm (accessed on 23 April 2011).

Fox, John and Godement, François (2011) 'A power audit of EU–China relations', Policy Report, European Council on Foreign Relations (ECFR), London, April; http://ecfr.eu/page/-/documents/A_Power_Audit_of_EU_China_Relations.pdf (accessed on 12 March 2011).

G20 (2008a) *Communique*, Meeting of Ministers and Governors, Sao Paulo, Brazil, 8–9 November; www.g20.org/Documents/2008_communique_saopaulo_brazil.pdf (accessed on 16 November 2010).

G20 (2008b) 'Declaration summit on financial markets and the world economy', 15 November, Washington, DC; www.g20.org/Documents/g20_summit_declaration.pdf (accessed on 16 November 2010).

G20 (2009a) 'The global plan for recovery and reform', 2 April, London; www.g20.org/Documents/final-communique.pdf (accessed on 16 November 2010).

G20 (2009b) 'Leaders' statement: the Pittsburgh summit 24–25 September 2009', 25 September, Pittsburgh; www.g20.org/Documents/pittsburgh_summit_leaders_statement_250909.pdf (accessed on 16 November 2010).

G20 (2009c) 'Progress report on the economic and financial actions of the London, Washington and Pittsburgh G20 summits prepared by the UK chair of the G20', 7 November, St Andrews; www.g20.org/Documents/20091107_progress_report_standrews.pdf (accessed on 16 November 2010).

G20 (2010) 'The G20 Seoul summit leaders' declaration November 11–12, 2010', www.g20.org/Documents2010/11/seoulsummit_declaration.pdf (accessed on 19 November 2010).

Gao, H. (2009) 'China's strategy for free trade agreements: political battle in the name of trade'; www.networkideas.org/ideasact/dec09/pdf/Henry_Gao.pdf (accessed on 17 December 2010).

Gertler, J.L. (2002) 'What China's WTO accession is all about', World Bank; http://siteresources.worldbank.org/INTRANETTRADE/Resources/gertler_china.pdf (accessed on 22 October 2010).

Gomes, C. (2011) *Global Auto Report*, Scotiabank Group, Canada, 5 January; www.scotiacapital.com/English/bns_econ/bns_auto.pdf (accessed on 17 January 2011).

Government of India (2003) *Agriculture Framework Proposal* (submitted along with Argentina, Brazil, Bolivia, China, Chile, Colombia, Costa Rica, Cuba, Ecuador, El Salvador, Guatemala, Mexico, Pakistan, Paraguay, Peru, Philippines, South Africa, Thailand and Venezuela), JOB(03)/162/Rev.1 29 August; http://commerce.nic.in/trade/international_trade_papers_nextDetail.asp?id=4 (accessed on 20 October 2010).

Goyal, K. (2010) 'Subbarao's accelerated rate increases leave India inflation eroding income', *Bloomberg*, 28 July; www.bloomberg.com/news/2010–07–27/subbarao-s-accelerated-rate-increases-leave-india-inflation-eroding-income.html (accessed on 28 January 2011).

Greene, William (2006) 'US–China competition in the Indian market', Office of Economics Working Paper No. 2006–09-A, US International Trade Commission (USITC), Washington, DC, September; www.usite.gov/publications/332/working-papers/EC200609A.pdf (accessed on 3 September 2011).

Gries, Peter Hays (2005) 'The Koguryo controversy, national identity, and Sino-Korean relations today', *East Asia*, Vol. 22, No. 4 (Winter), pp. 3–17.

Gupta, Poonam and Palit, Amitendu (2010) 'State-owned enterprise reforms in the People's Republic of China', *Resurging Asian Giants*, Manila: Asian Development Bank.

Helleiner, E. and Pagliari, S. (2009) 'Towards a new Bretton Woods? The first G20 leaders summit and the regulation of global finance', *New Political Economy*, Vol. 14, No. 2, pp. 275–87.

Hodum, R. (2007) 'Conflict over the Brahmaputra River between China and India', The Inventory of Conflict and Environment (ICE) Case Studies No. 205, May; http://www1.american.edu/ted/ice/brahmaputra.htm (accessed on 6 December 2010).

IANS (India Abroad News Service) (2010) 'India under fire as climate talks deadlocked', 8 December; www.samachar.com/India-under-fire-as-climate-talks-deadlocked-kmixLRdjehg.html (accessed on 8 December 2010).

ICTSD (2010) 'Tianjin climate meeting delivers little, overshadowed by US–China spat', International Centre for Trade and Sustainable Development (ICTSD), *Bridges Weekly Trade News Digest* (Geneva), Vol. 14, No. 35 (13 October); http://ictsd.org/i/news/bridgesweekly/86988 (accessed on 4 November 2010).

IEA (2007) *World Energy Outlook 2007: China and India Insights*, Paris: OECD.

IEA (2010) *World Energy Outlook 2010: Executive Summary*, Paris: OECD; see www.worldenergyoutlook.org/docs/weo2010/WEO2010_ES_English.pdf (accessed on 20 November 2010).

IMF (2010a) 'IMF Executive Board approves major overhaul of quotas and governance', IMF Press Release No. 10/418, Washington, DC, 5 November; www.imf.org/external/np/sec/pr/2010/pr10418.htm (accessed on 20 November 2010).

IMF (2010b) *World Economic Outlook: Recovery, Risk and Balancing*, Washington DC: IMF; www.imf.org/external/pubs/ft/weo/2010/02/pdf/c1.pdf (accessed on 16 November 2010).

IMF (2010c) 'Illustration of proposed quota and voting shares by member'; www.imf.org/external/np/sec/pr/2010/pdfs/pr10418_table.pdf (accessed on 14 November 2010).

IMF (2011) *World Economic Outlook*, April; www.imf.org/external/pubs/ft/weo/2011/01/pdf/text.pdf (accessed on 1 May 2011).

Jiang, Liping (2011) 'How to combat water scarcity in China', *China Daily*, 3 March; www.chinadaily.com.cn/opinion/2011–03/03/content_12106871.htm (accessed on 3 March 2011).

Jianfu, Chen (2010) 'China, India and developing countries in the WTO: towards a pro-active strategy', in Sornarajah Muthucumaraswamy and Wang Jiangyu (eds) *China, India and the International Economic Order*, New York: Cambridge University Press.

Jiangyu, W. (2010) 'The role of China and India in Asian regionalism', in Sornarajah Muthucumaraswamy and Wang Jiangyu (eds) *China, India and the International Economic Order*, New York: Cambridge University Press.

Jonasse, R. (2008) 'The Doha collapse: time to get agriculture out of the WTO', Institute for Food and Development Policy, Policy Brief No. 15, August, Oakland; www.foodfirst.org/sites/www.foodfirst.org/files/pdf/PB_15_Doha_Collapse_Full.pdf (accessed on 2 November 2010).

Jotzo, F. (2004) 'Developing countries and the future of the Kyoto Protocol', Australian National University, Economics and Environment Network (EEN) Working Paper EEN0406, 15 October; http://een.anu.edu.au/download_files/een0406.pdf (accessed on 6 November 2010).

JSG (India–China Joint Study Group) (2005) *Report of the India–China Joint Study Group on Comprehensive Trade and Economic Cooperation*, 23 March. See http://commerce.nic.in/trade/international_ta_pipeline_details.asp for details of JSG and www.hindu.com/thehindu/nic/0041/report.pdf for the report (both accessed on 7 August 2011).

Kapila, Subhash (2010) 'Saudi Arabia – India diplomatic overtures: perspectives', South Asia Analysis Group (SAAG), Paper No. 3701, 4 March; www.southasiaanalysis.org/%5Cpapers38%5Cpaper3701.html (accessed on 13 March 2011).

Kawai, M. and Petri, P.A. (2010) 'Asia's role in the global economic architecture', ADB Institute (ADBI), ADBI Working Paper Series No. 235, Tokyo, August; www.adbi.org/working-paper/2010/08/04/4025.asia.role.global.financial.architecture/ (accessed on 15 November 2010).

Khanna, Tarun (2007) 'Billions of entrepreneurs: how China and India are reshaping their futures – and yours', *Harvard Business Press*, December.

Kilby, P. (2010) 'China's aid: a challenge for new aid paradigms', 16 November; http://devpolicy.org/chinas-aid/ (accessed on 19 December 2010).

Kragelund, P. (2010) 'India's African engagement (ARI)', Real Instituto Elcano ARI 10/2010, 19 January; www.realinstitutoelcano.org/wps/portal/rielcano_eng/Content?

WCM_GLOBAL_CONTEXT=/elcano/elcano_in/zonas_in/sub-saharan+africa/ arilo-2010 (accessed on 3 September 2011).

Kronstadt, K. Alan, Kerr, Paul K., Martin, Michael F. and Vaughn, Bruce (2010) 'India–US relations', Congressional Research Service (CRS) Report for Congress 7–5700, www.crs.gov, RL33529, 27 October; www.fas.org/sgp/crs/row/RL33529.pdf (accessed on 5 March 2011).

Kuhrt, Kate (2009) 'Opportunities to sell APIs from regulated markets into India and China', *Scrip*, World Pharmaceutical News, 1 May; http://thomsonreuters.com/content/science/pdf/ls/hub/api_asian_regulated_markets.pdf (accessed on 10 February 2011).

Lancaster, C (2007) 'The Chinese aid system', essay for Center for Global Development, June; www.cgdev.org (accessed on 10 November 2010).

Lawrence, R.Z. (2008) 'China and the multilateral trading system', in B. Eichengreen, Y.C. Park and C. Wyplosz (eds) *China, Asia and the New World Economy*, New York: Oxford University Press.

Lim, C.L. and Wang, J.Y. (2009) 'China and the Doha Development Agenda', working paper prepared for presentation at the World Trade Organisation Forum, Geneva, 28 September; www.nsi-ins.ca/english/pdf/China%20at%20Doha.pdf (accessed on 27 October 2010).

Lum, T., Fischer, H., Julissa, G.G. and Anne, L. (2009) 'China's foreign aid activities in Africa, Latin America and Southeast Asia', Congressional Research Service (CRS) Report for Congress, R40361, 25 February; www.fas.org/sgp/crs/row/R40361.pdf (accessed on 20 December 2010).

Lynch, Elizabeth M. (2010) 'Pencils, staplers and pens, oh my! China submits government procurement bid to WTO body', 2 August; http://chinalawandpolicy.com/tag/chinas-state-owned-enterprises/ (accessed on 30 April 2011).

Ma, Lydia (2010) 'Calls for safeguards surge as Taiwan enters post-ECFA era', 20 October; www.bilaterals.org/spip.php?article18326 (accessed on 3 March 2011).

Maddison, Angus (2007) *Contours of the World Economy 1–2030 AD*, New York: Oxford University Press.

Malawer, Stuart S (2007) 'United States–China trade litigation in the WTO', worldtradelaw.net, December; www.worldtradelaw.net/articles/malawerchinalitigation.pdf (accessed on 12 March 2011), pp. 28–31, 56, 57

Martin, Philippe, Mayer, Thierry and Thoenig, Mathias (2010) 'The geography of conflicts and regional trade agreements', CEPR Discussion Paper 7740, 4 January; www.cepr.org/pubs/dps/DP7740.asp (accessed on 5 March 2011).

Mattoo, Aditya and Subramanian, Arvind (2003) 'India and the multilateral trading system post-Doha: defensive or proactive?' in Aditya Mattoo and Robert M. Stern (eds) *India and the WTO*, Washington, DC: World Bank and Oxford: Oxford University Press, pp. 327–66.

Mills, E. (2009) 'Keep friends close but enemies closer', *Harvard International Review*, 10 July; http://hir.harvard.edu/keep-friends-close-but-enemies-closer (accessed on 19 January 2011).

MNP (2007) 'Greenhouse gas emissions of countries in 2005 and ranking of their per capita emissions'; http://en.wikipedia.org/wiki/Kyoto_Protocol#cite_note-21 (accessed on 6 November 2010).

MoF (Ministry of Finance) (2010) *Mid-Year Analysis 2010–2011*, Department of Economic Affairs, Economic Division, Government of India, December; www.finmin.nic.in/reports/MYR201011English.pdf (accessed on 8 December 2010).

Morgenthau, Hans J. (1967) *Politics Among Nations*, New York: Alfred A Knopf.

Morris, S. (2010) 'Issues in real estate and urban management – a note', Indian Institute of Management, Ahmadabad (IIM-A), Working Paper No. 2010–11–01, November.

Morrison, Wayne M. (2011) 'China–US trade issues', Congressional Research Service (CRS), 7–5700, www.crs.gov, RL33536, Washington, DC, 7 January; www.fas.org/sgp/crs/row/RL33536.pdf (accessed on 12 March 2011).

Moxley, M (2010) 'China moves from aid recipient to aid donor', 9 July; http://ipsnews.net/news.asp?idnews=52098 (accessed on 15 November 2010).

Mulgan, Aurelia George (2010) 'A sea of trouble in Sino-Japanese relations', *East Asia Forum*, 28 September; www.eastasiaforum.org/2010/09/28/a-sea-of-trouble-in-sino-japanese-relations/#more-14280 (accessed on 11 March 2011).

Nanda, T. (2011) 'India auto sales set to slow after record surge in 2010', 11 January; www.reuters.com/article/idUSSGE70907Z20110111 (accessed on 17 January 2010).

Narlikar, Amrita and Tussie, D. (2004) 'The G20 at the Cancun Ministerial: developing countries and their evolving coalitions in the WTO'; *World Economy*; Vol. 27, No. 7, pp. 947–66.

Nayyar, Dhiraj (2011) 'Trade wall of China', *India Today*, 3 January, Delhi; http://indiatoday.intoday.in/site/Story/124529/Economy/trade-wall-of-china.html (accessed on 5 March 2011).

OECD (2007) *OECD Environmental Performance Reviews: China*, Paris: OECD.

Okamoto, Y. (2010) 'ASEAN, China and India: are they more competitive or complementary to each other?'; www.eco.kindai.ac.jp/kansai48/paper2.3.pdf (accessed on 15 December 2010).

Palit, Amitendu (2009) 'India's economic engagement with Southeast Asia: progress and challenges', Working Paper No. 60, Institute of South Asian Studies (ISAS), National University of Singapore (NUS), Singapore, 4 June; www.isas.nus.edu.sg/Attachments/PublisherAttachment/ISAS_working%20paper_59_21102009182431.pdf (accessed on 17 December 2010).

Palit, Amitendu (2010a) 'Census problems for China and India', *China Daily*, 7 September; www.chinadaily.com.cn/opinion/2010–09/07/content_11265411.htm (accessed on 18 January 2011).

Palit, Amitendu (2010b) 'Does the IMF matter anymore?' *Financial Express*, Delhi, 19 November; www.financialexpress.com/news/column-does-the-imf-matter-any-more/713080/ (accessed on 19 November 2010).

Palit, Amitendu (2010c) 'High on octane, low on clean', *Financial Express*, Delhi, 27 November; http://financialexpress.com/news/column-high-on-octane-low-on-clean/716611/ (accessed on 27 November 2010).

Palit, Amitendu and Palit, Parama Sinha (2009) 'Hats off to the merchants', *Financial Express*, Delhi, 14 September.

Palit, Parama Sinha (2010) 'China's soft power in South Asia', Working Paper No. 200, S. Rajaratnam School of International Studies (RSIS), Singapore, 8 June; www.rsis.edu.sg/publications/WorkingPapers/WP200.pdf (accessed on 25 March 2011).

Panagariya, Arvind (2005) 'An India–China free trade area?' *The Economic Times*, (Delhi), 20 April; www.columbia.edu/ap2231/ET/et77_April20_05/htm (accessed on 3 September 2011).

Panagariya, Arvind (2007) 'India and China: past trade liberalization and future challenges', 4 February; www.nomurafoundation.or.jp/data/2006120607_Arvind_Panagariya.pdf (accessed on 27 February 2011).

Panagariya, Arvind (2008) 'India and China: trade and foreign investment'; www.usitc.gov/research_and_analysis/economics_seminars/2008/Panagriya.pdf (accessed on 27 February 2011).

Pandita, K.N. (2010) 'India–Saudi Arabia relations: an appraisal', *Geopolitical Analysis*, 4 March; http://geopolitics.world-citizenship.org/wp-archive/238 (accessed on 13 March 2011).

Pannu, S.P.S (2010) 'Chinese power imports may face govt levy', *India Today*, 30 November; http://indiatoday.intoday.in/site/Story/121667/chinese-pms-india-visit/chinese-power-imports-may-face-govt-levy.html (accessed on 15 February 2011).

Pant, Harsh V. (2010) *The China Syndrome*, New Delhi: HarperCollins India.

Pathak, P. and Mehta, D. (1995) 'Recent trend in urbanisation and rural–urban migration in India: some explanations and projections', *Urban India*, Vol. 15, No. 1, pp. 1–17.

Paul, S. and Bhattacharya, R.N. (2004) 'Causality between energy consumption and economic growth in India: a note on conflicting results', *Energy Economics*, Vol. 26, pp. 977–83.

Peiser, B. (2008) 'The G8's crafty climate-change strategy', *Financial Post*, 10 July; http://network.nationalpost.com/np/blogs/fpcomment/archive/2008/07/10/the-g8-s-crafty-climate-change-strategy.aspx (accessed on 7 November 2010).

Prasad, Eswar C. (2010) 'The US–China economic relationship: shifts and twists in the balance of power', US–China Economic and Security Review Commission Hearing on 'US Debt to China: Implications and Repercussions', 25 February (revised 25 March); www.brookings.edu/testimony/2010/0225_us_china_debt_prasad.aspx (accessed on 12 March 2011).

Prasad, G.C. (2010) 'India, China could join hands to check oil spike', *Financial Express*, 17 December; www.financialexpress.com/news/india-china-could-join-hands-to-check-oil-spike/725891/0 (accessed on 18 December 2010).

Press Information Bureau (PIB) (2010) *UN Millennium Development Goals for Slum Dwellers*, 5 August, Government of India; http://pib.nic.in/release/release.asp?relid=64187 (accessed on 11 January 2011).

Pucher, J., Zhong-Ren, P., Mittal, N., Yi, Z. and Korattyswaroopam, N. (2007) 'Urban transport trends and policies in China and India: impacts of rapid economic growth', *Transport Reviews*, Vol. 27, No. 4, pp. 379–410.

Qiang, H. (2009) 'The relationship between energy consumption growths and economic growth in China', *International Journal of Economics and Finance*, Vol. 1, No. 2 (August), pp. 232–7; www.ccsenet.org/journal.html (accessed on 19 January 2011).

Rajamohan, P.G., Rahut, Dil Bahadur and Jacob, Jabin T. (2008) 'Changing paradigm of Indo-Japan relations: opportunities and challenges', Indian Council for Research on International Economic Relations (ICRIER), Working Paper No. 212, April; www.icrier.org/pdf/Working_Paper_212.pdf (accessed on 3 September 2011).

Ramachandran, V. (2010) 'India emerges as an aid donor', 5 October; www.hufftington-post.com/vijaya-ramachandran/india-emerges-as-an-aid-d_b_751008.html (accessed on 20 December 2010).

Renfeng, Zhou (2007) 'Short report: China and India: a comparison of trade, investment and expansion strategies', Chatham House, UK, 1 June; www.chathamhouse.org.uk/files/9201_010607workshop.pdf (accessed on 15 February 2011).

Rosen, Daniel H. and Wang Zhi (2010) 'Deepening China–Taiwan relations through the economic cooperation framework agreement', Policy Brief No. PB10–16, Peterson Institute for International Economics (PIIE), Washington, DC, June; www.iie.com/publications/pb/pb10–16.pdf (accessed on 3 March 2011).

Rosenthal, E. (2010) 'West's push to limit coal doesn't cover Asia exports', *International Herald Tribune* (Paris), 23 November.

Sandhu, Joel (2009) 'EU India relations: from blind spot to strategic engagement', euobserver.com, 9 January; http://euobserver.com/9/27364 (accessed on 19 March 2011).

Savchuk, K., Echanove, M. and Srivastava, R. (2009) 'Lakhs of residents, billions of dollars', 24 February; http://dharavi.org/B._Introduction (accessed on 11 January 2011).

Sawyer, William C., Sprinkle, Richard L. and Tochkov, Kiril (2009) 'Patterns and determinants of intra-industry trade in Asia', *International Trade and Finance Association*, 19th International Conference Working Papers, Paper 13, Year 2009, Berkeley Electronic Press (bepress); http://services.bepress.com/cgi/viewcontent.cgi?article=1152&context=itfa (accessed on 26 February 2011).

Sen, Amiti (2008) 'India China FTA prospects appear bleak', *The Economic Times*, 15 January; http://economictimes.indiatimes.com/News/Economy/India_China_FTA_prospects_appear_bleak/articleshow/2700543.cms (accessed on 27 February 2011).

SFG (Strategic Foresight Group) (2010) 'The Himalayan challenge: water security in emerging Asia'; www.strategicforesight.com/Himalayan%20Challenge%20ES.pdf (accessed on 20 November 2010).

Sharma, Amol (2010) 'India rethinks reliance on China in power sector', *The Wall Street Journal*, 10 February; http://online.wsj.com/article/SB10001424052748703630404575053173929691614.html (accessed on 18 February 2011).

Sharma, Vijay Paul and Thaker, Rima (2009) 'Fertilizer subsidy in India: who are the beneficiaries?' Indian Institute of Management (IIM), Ahmedabad, Working Paper No. 2009, 1 July; www.iimahd.ernet.in/publications/data/2009–07–01Sharma.pdf (accessed on 27 March 2011).

Sheikh, F. (2009) 'India facing fierce competition in its search for oil and natural gas resources', Oilprice.com, 24 December; http://oilprice.com/Geo-Politics/Asia/India-Facing-Fierce-Competition-in-its-Search-for-Oil-and-Natural-Gas-Resources.html (accessed on 25 November 2010).

Snyder, Scott (2004) 'A turning point for China–Korea relations?'; http://csis.org/files/media/csis/pubs/0403qchina_korea.pdf (accessed on 11 March 2011).

Snyder, Scott (2007) 'Teenage angst: 15th anniversary of diplomatic relations?' *Comparative Connections*, CSIS, October; http://csis.org/files/media/csis/pubs/0703qchina_korea.pdf (accessed on 11 March 2011).

South Centre (2008) 'The WTO's July 2008 mini-Ministerial: agriculture, NAMA, process issues and the road ahead', analytical note SC/TDP/AN/MA/AG, October, Geneva; www.southcentre.org/index2.php?option=com_docman&task=doc_view&gid=1063&Itemid=69 (accessed on 5 November 2010).

Spencer, R. and Foster, P. (2007) 'China and India reject climate change deal', *Telegraph* (UK), 9 June; www.telegraph.co.uk/news/worldnews/1554055/China-and-India-reject-climate-change-deal.html (accessed on 3 November 2010).

Srinivasan, T.N. (2006) 'China, India and the world economy', Stanford Centre for International Development, Working Paper No. 286, Stanford University, July; www.stanford.edu/group/siepr/cgi-bin/siepr/?q=system/files/shared/pubs/papers/pdf/SCID286.pdf (accessed on 3 May 2011).

Su, Fubing (2008) 'Land market in China's modernization: regulations, challenges, and reforms', EAI (East Asia Institute) Background Brief No. 418, 11 December; www.eai.nus.edu.sg/BB418.pdf (accessed on 10 January 2011).

Swami, Praveen (2001) 'The great escape', *Frontline*, Vol. 18, No. 23 (10–23 November); www.frontlineonnet.com/fl1823/18230290.htm (accessed on 15 March 2011).

Tang J., Zhang Y., Wang C. and Feng L. (2010) *China's Social Development*, Beijing: China Intercontinental Press.

Times News Network (TNN) (2010) 'India joins $10bn gas pipeline project', *Sunday Times of India* (New Delhi), 12 October; http://articles.timesofindia.indiatimes.com/2010-12-12/india/28241790_1_gas-pipeline-pipeline-project-ashgabat (accessed on 3 September 2011).

Tiwari, Manish and Jacob, Jaynath (2010) 'Extradition treaty with Saudi soon', *Hindustan Times*, 27 January; www.hindustantimes.com/Extradition-treaty-with-Saudi-soon/Article1–502095.aspx (accessed on 18 March 2011).

Trivedi, Yashi (2009) 'China's role in India's power wector', 13 May; http://theviewspaper.net/china%E2%80%99s-role-in-india%E2%80%99s-power-sector/ (accessed on 19 February 2011).

Tsai, Kellee S. (2005) 'Persistence of informal finance', in Edward Friedman and Bruce Gilley (eds) *Asia's Giants*, New York: Palgrave Macmillan.

UN (2010) 'Carbon dioxide emissions (CO_2), thousand metric tonnes of CO_2', United Nations Statistics Division, Millennium Development Goals Indicators; http://mdgs.un.org/unsd/mdg/SeriesDetail.aspx?srid=749&crid= (accessed on 30 January 2011).

UN Habitat (2010) 'Urban trends: China, India in giant strides to improve slums', press release for 'State of the World's Cities 2010/11', 18 March.

UNDP (2010) *The Real Wealth of Nations: Pathways to Human Development*, *Human Development Report 2010*, Twentieth Anniversary Edition, New York: United Nations Development Programme.

UNFCCC (2009) 'Draft Decision-/CP.15 Copenhagen Accord', United Nations Framework Convention on Climate Change (UNFCCC), FCCC/CP/2009/L.7, Copenhagen, 18 December; http://unfccc.int/resource/docs/2009/cop15/eng/l07.pdf (accessed on 9 November 2010).

UNFPA (2007) *State of World Population 2007*, New York: United Nations Population Fund.

UNFPA (2010) *State of World Population 2007*, New York: United Nations Population Fund.

Verman, A.R. (2010) 'India promotes entrepreneurial skills in developing world', India Abroad News Service (IANS), 25 December; www.samachar.com/India-promotes-entrepreneurial-skills-in-developing-world-kmzoLTcabei.html?source=recommended_news (accessed on 25 December 2010).

Vignesh, P. (2010) 'Brahmaputra River – dispute between India and China', www.jeywin.com/blog/brahmaputra-river-%E2%80%93-dispute-between-india-and-china/ (accessed on 5 December 2010).

Villholth, Karen G. (2009) 'Towards better management of groundwater resources – lessons from an integrated capacity building project in the Indo-Gangetic and Yellow River basins', in Bharat R. Sharma, Karen G, Villholth, Aditi Mukherji and Wang Jinxia (eds) *Groundwater Governance in the Indo-Gangetic and Yellow River Basins: Realities and Challenges*, New York: CRC Press.

Vines, A., Wong, L., Weimer, M. and Campos, I. (2009) 'Thirst for African oil: Asian national oil companies in Nigeria and Angola', Chatham House, August; www.chathamhouse.org.uk/files/14524_r0809_africanoil.pdf (accessed on 29 November 2010).

Wang, Jingqiong (2011) 'Land seizures threaten to disrupt countryside calm', *China Daily*, 1 March; www.chinadaily.com.cn/china/2011–03/01/content_12092034.htm (accessed on 1 March 2011).

Wang, Z. and Lim, T.S. (2007) 'China's growing influence in Africa', in G. Wang and J. Wong (eds) *Interpreting China's Development*, Singapore: World Scientific Publishing.

Wang, Xixin (2011) 'Forced land seizure policy needs revision', *China Daily*; www.chinadaily.com.cn/cndy/2011–01/13/content_11841809.html (accessed on 13 January 2011).

Whalley, J. and Agarwal, M. (2010) 'China, the developing countries and the G20', Centre for International Governance Innovation (CIGI), G20 Web Commentary, 16 June; www.cigionline.ca/publications/2010/6/china-developing-countries-and-g20 (accessed on 9 November 2010).

Wong, John and Lye, Liang Fook (2011) 'China's National People's Congress endorses the 12th Five Year Plan: laying a stronger foundation for socio-economic progress', EAI Background Brief No. 608, East Asian Institute (EAI), National University of Singapore, Singapore, 15 March; www.eai.nus.edu.sg/BB608.pdf (accessed on 4 September 2011).

Workman, Daniel (2010) 'China's export advantages versus India in computers and modems', suite101.com, 18 October; www.suite101.com/content/chinas-export-advantages-versus-india-in-computers-and-modems-a298312 (accessed on 20 February 2011).

World Bank (2008) 'Development and climate change: a strategic framework for the World Bank Group', Background Report for the Development Committee Meeting on 12 October 2008 prepared by the World Bank Group, Washington, DC, 30 September; http://siteresources.worldbank.org/EXTCC/Resources/407863–1219339233881/DCCSFReporttoDevelopmentCommitteeOct122008.pdf (accessed on 5 November 2010).

World Bank (2010) *Development Committee Communique*, Washington, DC, 25 April; http://siteresources.worldbank.org/DEVCOMMINT/NewsAndEvents/22556084/FinalCommunique%28E%29042510.pdf (accessed on 19 November 2010).

World Gold Council (2010) 'World official gold holdings September 2010'; www.gold.org/assets/file/value/stats/statistics/archive/pdf/World_Official_Gold_Holdings_September_2010.pdf (accessed on 15 November 2010).

WRG (2030 Water Resources Group) (2009) *Charting our Water Future*, New York: McKinsey; www.mckinsey.com/App_Media/Reports/Water/Charting_Our_Water_Future_Full_Report_001.pdf (accessed on 20 November 2010).

WTO (2001) 'Accession of the People's Republic of China', World Trade Organisation Document No. WT/L/432, 23 November; www.wto.org/english/thewto_e/acc_e/completeacc_e.htm#chn (accessed on 22 October, 2010).

WTO (2003a) 'Statement by H.E. Mr Arun Jaitley, Minister of Commerce and Industry and Law and Justice, India', World Trade Organisation Document No. WT/MIN(03)/ST/7, 11 September; www.wto.org/english/thewto_e/countries_e/india_e.htm (accessed on 24 October 2010).

WTO (2003b) 'Statement by H.E. Mr Lu Fuyuan, Minister of Commerce, China', World Trade Organisation Document No. WT/MIN(03)/ST/12, 11 September; www.wto.org/english/thewto_e/countries_e/china_e.htm (accessed on 24 October 2010).

WTO (2005) 'Market access for non-agricultural products' (circulated along with Argentina, Bolivarian Republic of Venezuela, Brazil, China, Egypt, India, Indonesia, Namibia, Pakistan, Philippines and South Africa), Document No TN/MA/W/65; 8 November; http://commerce.nic.in/writereaddata/IndianSubmission/international_trade_non_agricultural_market_access_nama_5.pdf (accessed on 15 October 2010).

WTO (2008) 'Day 9: Talks collapse despite progress on a list of issues', WTO: 2008 News Items, 29 July; www.wto.org/english/news_e/news08_e/meet08_summary_29july_e.htm (accessed on 2 November 2010).

WTO (2010) 'China, India trade profiles', October; http://stat.wto.org/CountryProfile/WSDBCountryPFView.aspx?Language=E&Country=CN,IN (accessed on 10 December 2010).

Wu, Y. (2009) 'Comparing pollution by Asian giants: China vs India', East Asia Institute Background Brief No. 434, 5 March; www.eai.nus.edu.sg/BB434.pdf (accessed on 29 January 2011).

Xing, Yuqing (2008) 'Japan's unique economic relations with China: economic integration under political uncertainty', East Asia Institute Background Brief No. 410, 23 October; www.eai.nus.edu.sg/BB410.pdf (accessed on 11 March 2011).

Yan, J. (2011) 'Housing corruption put in crosshairs', *China Daily*, 12 January; www.chinadaily.com.cn/bizchina/2011–01/12/content_1183 (accessed on 13 January 2011).

Yang Yao (2008) 'The Chinese land tenure system: practice and perspectives', in Ashok Gulati and Fan Shenggen (eds) *The Dragon and the Elephant*, Delhi: Oxford University Press.

Yongnian, Zheng and Kong, Q. (2009) 'China in the WTO: from accession to the Doha failure', East Asia Institute, National University of Singapore Working Paper No. 147, 27 March; www.nus.edu.sg/NUSinfo/EAI/EWP147.pdf (accessed on 5 November 2010).

Zha, Daojiong (2010) 'Dangerous myths: making the case for water diplomacy', in Foresight, *Through a Billion Voices: India's Role in a Multi-polar World*, London: Foresight; http://clients.squareeye.com/uploads/foresight/documents/Foresight%20India%20-%20low%20res%20.pdf (accessed on 20 November 2010).

Zhao, Hong (2007) 'India and China: rivals or partners in Southeast Asia?' *Contemporary Southeast Asia*, Vol. 29, No. 1 (April), pp. 121–42.

Zhao, Hong (2009) 'An energy comparison of the Asian giants: China and India', *Asian Affairs*, Vol. XL, No. III (November), pp. 377–90.

Zheng, Yongnian and Kong, Qingjiang (2009) 'China in the WTO: accession to the Doha failure', EAI Working Paper 147, East Asian Institute (EAI), National University of Singapore, Singapore, 27 March; www.eai.nus.edu.sg/EWP147.pdf (accessed 4 September 2011).

Zhou, Shengqi (2010) 'Sino-South Korean trade relations: from boom to recession', East Asia Institute Background Brief No. 508, National University of Singapore, 3 March; www.eai.nus.edu.sg/BB508.pdf (accessed on 10 March 2011).

Index

www.ingramcontent.com/pod-product-compliance
Lightning Source LLC
LaVergne TN
LVHW021127300926
849160LV00010B/895
* 9 7 8 0 4 1 5 8 2 4 5 6 9 *